Theorizing Museums

Representing identity and diversity in a changing world

Edited by Sharon Macdonald and Gordon Fyfe

Blackwell Publishers/The Sociological Review

Copyright © The Editorial Board of the Sociological Review 1996

First published in 1996

Blackwell Publishers
108 Cowley Road, Oxford OX4 1JF, UK

and
238 Main Street,
Cambridge, MA 02142, USA

British Library Cataloguing in Publication Data

A CIP catalogue record for this book is available from the British Library

Library of Congress Cataloging-in-Publication Data applied for

This book is printed on acid-free paper.

ISBN 0 631 20151 3

Theorizing Museums

A selection of previous *Sociological Review* Monographs

Life and Work History Analyses[†]
ed. Shirley Dex

The Sociology of Monsters[†]
ed. John Law

Sport, Leisure and Social Relations[†]
eds John Horne, David Jary and Alan Tomlinson

Gender and Bureaucracy*
eds Mike Savage and Anne Witz

The Sociology of Death: theory, culture, practice*
ed. David Clark

The Cultures of Computing
ed. Susan Leigh Star

[†] Available from The Sociological Review Office, Keele University, Keele, Staffs ST5 5BG.
* Available from Marston Book Services, PO Box 270, Abingdon, Oxon OX14 4YW.

Contents

List of illustrations

Gaby Porter, seeing through solidity: feminist perspectives on museums

Gordon Fyfe and Max Ross, Decoding the visitor's gaze: rethinking museum visiting

Gordon Fyfe, A Trojan Horse at the Tate: theorizing the museum as agency and structure

Introduction

Sharon Macdonald

'The museum, instead of being circumscribed in a geometrical location, is now everywhere, like a dimension of itself' (Baudrillard, *Simulations*).

Museums occupy an intriguingly paradoxical place in global culture as we approach the new Millenium. Bound up with much that is heralded to be nearing its end – stability and permanence, authenticity, grand narratives, the nation-state, and even history itself – their numbers are growing at an unprecedented rate.[1]

Yet this increase does not indicate security. On the contrary, museums face an unremitting questioning about whom they are for and what their role should be. Falling visitor numbers, failure to attract minorities, massive expenditure on art works, storage and conservation problems of ever-expanding collections (many of which are never displayed), and competition from the electronic media and other leisure pursuits, all threaten the future of the museum.[2] Most of museums' long-held assumptions and functions have been challenged over the last decade or so; and at the same time the boundaries between museums and other institutions have become elided such that museum professionals can declare: 'The truth is, we do not know any more what a museum institution is' (Sola, 1992:106). While there is challenge to the traditional museum, however, there is also a new level of interest in museums, witnessed both in their increasingly frequent presence in the news and in the expanding academic literature on them. Not only is the number of museums increasing globally, museums are also diversifying in form and content. They are tackling controversial subjects, sometimes in controversial ways – eg the Holocaust Memorial Museum in Washington DC, the Museum of Famine, Ireland; exhibitions on colonialism (including museums' role in it, Riegel, below), on warfare (Zolberg, below), on gender and sexuality (Porter, below).[3] They are opening themselves up to use by diverse communities and are exhibiting collections which would previously not have been thought 'museum-worthy' (as in the Canadian *Fluffs and Feathers* exhibition discussed by Riegel, below; or *The People's Show* exhibitions at many provincial museums in Britain, to which local people were invited to bring and display their own collections – Smartie tops, teddy bears, beer mats). They are also being appropriated to other cultural idioms, as in the 'Culture Houses' developments in Zimbabwe, where the usual format of the museum has been partly reshaped through local notions of the past and of material culture (Ucko, 1994).[4] Museums are also employing new media, new techniques of interactivity, and new styles which have more in common with the funfair or theatre than the traditional museum (Hooper-Greenhill, 1995a). Many now employ actors to dramatize historical themes, sophisticated sound effects, video projections to bring models to life ('alive' being a keyword in contemporary museum promotional literature), museum fun-days and even sleepovers. Exhibitions are opening consisting only of reproductions or interactive exhibits (as in historical reconstructions such as *The Ulster American Folk Park* and hands-on science halls); and museum collections are being catalogued on CD ROM and the Internet (eg through the Virtual Library of Museums on the World Wide Web: *http://www. comlab.ox.ac. uk/archive/other/museums.html*) (see *Museums Journal* November 1994 and August 1995). It is now possible to visit museums such as the National Gallery, London, without leaving home and to dip in electronically to different collections around the world and effectively construct your own museum on screen. Alongside the insecurity, then, there is also a revitalization of the idea of the museum, a diffusion of the museum beyond its walls, a 'museumification' of ever more aspects of culture, and a claiming of the museum by ever more sectors of society.

The contradictory, ambivalent, position which museums are in makes them key cultural loci of our times. Through their displays and their day-to-day operations they inevitably raise questions about knowledge and power, about identity and difference, and about permanence and transience. Precisely because they have become global symbols through which status and community are expressed, they are subject to appropriation and the struggle for ownership. Yet despite the fact that museums clearly act as 'staging grounds' (Annis, 1986) for many questions which are also at the heart of debates in social and cultural studies, the social scientific study of the museum is still relatively under-developed by comparison with, say, that of the school or television. This volume is intended as a contribution towards changing that. It aims both to highlight the pertinence and rich theoretical potential of the museum as an analytical locus for anthropology, sociology and cultural studies; and to show how social and cultural theorizing can illuminate many contemporary museum issues. It is intended as a contribution towards establishing an anthropology and sociology of museums.

The volume brings together a range of theoretically informed studies which explore the changing contexts and nature of museums. It is concerned with 'theorizing museums' in two senses. First, it is concerned with museums as sites in which socially and culturally embedded theories are performed. The interest here is in the stories museums tell, the technologies they employ to tell their tales, and the relation these stories have to those of other sites, including those of social and cultural studies. Second, the volume is concerned to highlight ways in which museums may be theorized within social and cultural studies. What stories can we tell, and what devices can we employ, to make sense of museums?

Contributors to this book are anthropologists, sociologists and museum professionals. All are concerned with aspects of the changing nature and context of museums, particularly since the 1980s; and with the critical feedback between social theory and museum practice. All show how social and cultural theorizing can illuminate practice by asking awkward questions, suggesting connections and throwing the spotlight onto omissions and their significance. They also show how such theorizing can inform exhibition-making, leading to innovative and experimental museum procedures and displays. They show too how developments within museums can challenge accepted theoretical wisdoms, forcing us to rethink assumptions about, say, modernity, nationhood, social memory, consumption, structure and agency, and the nature of material forms, to mention just some of those addressed here.

Towards theorizing the museum

While a single volume clearly cannot hope to be comprehensive, the aim here has been to provide examples of some of the areas which seem to the editors to be particularly theoretically fertile: the anthropology and sociology of globalization, time, space, and consumption, feminism, psychoanalysis, experimental ethnography and literary theory. The aim has also been to present theorizing which tackles both broad questions of the changing nature of museums, as well as the specific content of museum displays or visitor narratives. Theoretical developments are needed on both fronts in moving towards a more adequate anthropology and sociology of museums.

While the intention in compiling this volume was theoretical range rather than unity, there is a good deal of theoretical overlap between the papers. Perhaps more than anything, all seem to share a conviction that much of the older theorizing of museums (and of social and cultural studies more generally) is too mono-dimensional and insufficiently nuanced to account for the specificity or the complexity of the museum. For example, to look at museums *only* as agencies of social control, is too simple; though such questions cannot be ignored. Likewise, to consider museums as sites for the definition of distinction and taste is important; though this surely does not exhaust their possible roles in consumption. All of the chapters here show that there are alternative possibilities and potentialities in the museum: *the* museum does not exist. At the same time they also show that, contestable though museum accounts may be, museums remain powerful and subtle authors and authorities whose cultural accounts are not easily dislodged. Museums are socially and historically located; and, as such, they inevitably bear the imprint of social relations beyond their walls and beyond the present. Yet museums are never *just* spaces for the playing out of wider social relationships: a museum is a process as well as a structure, it is a creative agency as well as a 'contested terrain' (Lavine and Karp, 1990:1). It is because museums have a formative as well as a reflective role in social relations that they are potentially of such influence.

Museums negotiate a nexus between cultural production and consumption, and between expert and lay knowledge. The nature of this relationship, which must be examined if the formative or constitutive role of museums is to be fully understood, is one which is still relatively undertheorized within the study of museums. As Gordon Fyfe describes below, too often it has been assumed that museums are unproblematic reflections of dominant ideological interests. This assumption has generally been coupled with a broadly semiotic approach which seeks to analyse the classifications, analogies and juxtapositions of museum displays in order to reveal the cultural assumptions and political motivations that they may contain. While this has undoubtedly led to some excellent studies,[5] the status of the interpretations provided is problematic. In many cases the analyst's 'reading' is not acknowledged as a particular and positioned act of interpretation (as, by contrast, it is in Gaby Porter's sophisticated reflexive account here) but is presented as consonant with both the *motives* of exhibitors and the *messages* picked up by visitors. While this may on occasion be the case, the model does not allow for the investigation of whether there is indeed such a neat fit between production, text and consumption. It supposes both too clear-cut a conscious manipulation by those involved in creating exhibitions and too passive and unitary a public; and it ignores the often competing agendas involved in exhibition-making, the 'messiness' of the process itself, and the interpretive agency of visitors. It also provides no account of the *dynamics* by which museum exhibitions are formed – including the routes by which 'dominant interests' or unconscious associations might come to make themselves felt, or of the contexts in which they may be challenged.

While museums clearly have much in common with other institutions and media, they are also distinctive – distinctive in the ways in which they objectify particular orders of knowledge and experience, and in the classificatory possibilities which they offer up to audiences. Likewise, while the analysis of museums as *texts* has been extremely important (and still underdeveloped) both for suggesting literary theoretical techniques for analysing exhibitions, and for raising questions of authorship and of readers, we also need to move towards further elaboration of ways in which museums are *unlike* texts. The contributions in this volume highlight some of the distinctive features of museums: especially, their authoritative and legitimizing status, their roles as symbols of community, their 'sitedness', the centrality of material culture, the durability and solidity of objects, the non-verbal nature of so many of their messages, and the fact that audiences literally enter and move within them. While museums may not be unusual with respect to each of these features alone, together they constitute a distinctive cultural complex. Each, however, entails both constraints and indeterminacies. Each is an act of classification, but one which may be challenged with greater or lesser ease. Moreover, like all classification, that of the museum inevitably contains contradictions (Fyfe, 1995:10), and the playing out, or attempted resolution, of these also forms part of the characteristic dynamic of museums.

The 'museum-ness' of museums, then, is a subject which needs to be addressed and theorized in its own right. In doing so, however, it is vital that we pay attention to the ways in which museums are and are not like other institutions, and to their historical and contemporary relationships with other institutions (see Bennett, 1995:5). The aim, as studies in this volume highlight, is to use the museum as a vantage point, not as the boundary of the study (as might be said to characterize museum studies by contrast); It is to problematize the museum rather than take it for granted. Such a problematization of the museum is particularly foregrounded by the inclusion here of Kevin Hetherington's chapter on Stonehenge, a site which, he argues, can be seen as a 'museum without walls.' Like other contributors, his aim is not to provide a categorical definition of 'museum' but a theorized account of its (changing) nature. Why a site might or might not count as a museum, or as museum-like, is, we contend, a question deserving cultural analysis rather than legislation.

Hetherington's account, which locates itself within the sociology of space, also raises, as do other chapters, the question of whether the museum is an appropriate theoretical topic for social and cultural studies. Clearly, there are many alternative categories of study into which museums might be partly or wholly subsumed: visual anthropology, the sociology of art, material culture studies, the sociology and anthropology of organizations, media studies, to name but a few. This volume argues, however, that museums are a fertile theoretical field precisely because they can be tackled from a range of theoretical perspectives which cross many of the established divisions of the disciplines (eg production and consumption, knowledge and practice, sacred and secular). They are like a kind of theoretical thoroughfare: a place where unexpected meetings and alignments may take place.

More specifically, however, museums hold a particular reflexive promise for social and cultural theorising because of their close historical associations with the development and concerns of the social sciences. Museums, which are often centres of research and training, provide a site – and perhaps one of academia's most public sites – for the representation and development of sociological, and more especially anthropological, theories of the day.[6] In exhibitions, social Darwinism or structural functionalism, say, can be not just spoken of, but physically manifest through the organization of artefacts into, respectively, sequential series or discrete, ordered, conflict-free and timeless cultures (Jones, 1992, Coombes, 1994). Racial differences or class relations can be encoded in the juxtaposition and style of exhibits, and in classifications such as that between 'art' and 'ethnography', and different types of museums. In this, museums have acted not simply as the embodiment of theoretical ideas, but also as part of the visualizing technology through which such ideas were formed.[7] Moreover, they also provide visitors with 'object lessons' and embodied experiences of, say, evolutionary progress, the individual as consumer, or the reflexivity of modern technology (Bennett, 1995; Macdonald, 1993; Harvey, 1996).

Like anthropology and sociology, museums are products of modernity and their development is deeply implicated in the formation of the modern nation-state. Like anthropology and sociology, museums are also technologies of classification, and, as such, they have historically played significant roles in the modernist and nationalist quest for order and mapped boundaries. In particular, like anthropology and sociology, museums have been supremely important in what Richard Handler refers to as 'cultural objectification' (1988:14): the construction of culture (and society) as 'a thing: a natural object or entity made up of objects and entities ("traits")' (1988:14), which gains its own reality and can be gazed at, learned from and fought for. Museums, which literally employ physical objects in their constitution of culture, are unusually capable among institutions of turning culture into an object: of *materializing* it. They have played a role not just in *displaying* the world, but in structuring a modern way of seeing and comprehending the world 'as if it were an exhibit' (Riegel, below; see also Prösler, below).

If museums, anthropology and sociology have collaborated in the formation of modernity and the nation-state, they have also all come to question many of modernity's 'totalizing paradigms' and to share many of the same insecurities about *how* to represent in the contemporary world (Harvey, 1996). Like anthropology and sociology, museums have been subject to extensive criticisms from outside and from within; and this critique has led to a new wave of critical, self-reflexive scrutiny – in particular over science-based models, colonialism and excluded 'voices' – and to new experimental modes of representing. Exhibitions, like monographs, have been given over to the representation of multiple perspectives, to voices of the previously 'spoken for' or ignored, to the acknowledgment of ambivalence, uncertainty and objectivity, to irony and the disruption of established form, and to self-reflection. Both have also found that their experiments are not always received as expected and some of the assumptions of those experiments have themselves, in turn, been questioned (see, especially Riegel, below). At the same time, museums and academia have been subject to similar, though not always identical, pressures and opportunities, with regard to new communication and information technologies, increasingly mobile and heterogeneous communities, and the demand that they demonstrate their use-value and 'relevance.' As such, museums offer a parallel (though not identical) context in which to explore questions about the enterprise of anthropology and sociology: they act as (sometimes distorting) mirrors in which to reflect upon the disciplines themselves (Macdonald, 1996; Herzfeld, 1987).

In different ways contributions to this volume all share a concern with the areas specified above: (a) museums and change; (b) the nature and specificity of museums; (c) the relationship between museums and social and cultural theorizing. The volume is divided into three interrelated parts, each dealing with distinct, though overlapping, themes: I Contexts – Spaces and Times; II Contests – Identities and Differences; III Contents – Classification and Practice. These relate to three dimensions of theorizing which are, we argue, essential to the 'radical re-examination of the rôle of museums' (Vergo, 1989: 3) which Peter Vergo has called for under the banner of 'the new museology.'[8] We need to be able to account for museums theoretically as contextualized and contextualizing; as contestable and contested; and as having a content not just to their displays, but also to their form and institutional practice.

Contexts – Spaces and Times

Museums not only exist within a particular time and space, they also help articulate particular temporal and spatial orders. It is in this respect that we can see them as not just existing within a context but also as themselves creating cultural contexts. Chapters in this first part of the volume deal with both these dimensions of museums by drawing respectively upon recent theorizing of space and of time. They are concerned with the particular, though changing, place and role of museums and in the social potency of the museum form.

Martin Prösler's chapter on 'Museums and Globalization' provides a broad account of the political historical development of museums worldwide to begin our volume. Drawing especially upon Robertson's theory of globalization, he emphasizes the significance of global processes (increased international connections) for museums and for our approaches to analysing museums (a point also developed by Zolberg). Arguing that museums have played and continue to play a significant constitutive role within the development of the nation-state and global relations, he illustrates his claim that 'Third World' museums are thoroughly part of the globalization process with a discussion of the National Museum of Sri Lanka.

Prösler shows well how museums are capable, through their strategies of display, of summoning up and collapsing together different places into a particular 'world-view.' They do likewise with time, and indeed Robert Lumley has referred to them as 'time-machines' for just this reason (1988). However, the nature of their mediation of time requires theoretical elaboration, and this is provided here by John Urry who draws upon developments in the sociology and anthropology of time and memory to explore museums as embodiments of temporal relations and social remembering. He considers the roles that museums may play in the social objectification of the past and the kinds of temporal orders with which they deal particularly well (especially 'glacial time'); and this leads him to reflect on the heritage debates, and in a different though related manner from Prösler's account, to suggest why it is that museums might be such significant and expanding cultural forms in the present time. Both Prösler and Urry show us why museums may be so implicated in the articulation of identity; and while Prösler looks particularly at their role in the formation of national consciousness, Urry, by emphasizing the ambiguous nature of heritage, shows us why museums are also being claimed for the articulation of many 'sub-national' identities.

Contests – Differences and Identities

The emphasis upon museums as projections of identity, together with the idea of museums as 'contested terrains,' has become increasingly salient over the past decade as museum orthodoxies have been challenged by, or on behalf of, many minorities which have previously been ignored or marginalized by museums. In this second part of the book, the chapters collectively provide more theoretical input to the analysis of this growing contest.

The increased representation of minority voices in museums – which has been matched in many other cultural spheres – has played a part in shifting the emphasis of social theoretical perspectives on museums from 'control' to 'contest.' This is part of a shift in theoretical emphasis in the social sciences from production to consumption – a shift which might also be argued to mirror shifts in social relations. While it is undoubtedly important to leave theoretical space for allowing for visions of the museum as non-controlling, production (in this case the production of museums and exhibitions) and social legitimacy are surely still in need of further understanding, and some of the chapters here would caution against moving towards an unqualified celebration of consumers and popular culture as seems to be the case in some areas of cultural studies (a move which would in any case seem to merely parallel certain capitalist cultural developments). The chapters in this part of the volume, then, would suggest that the idea of contest needs to be developed in the following ways to recognize (a) that contestable though exhibitions may be, they are not always contested – and that this itself is deserving of analysis (especially Porter); (b) that contest may come from all manner of groups – including the powerful – and that theory needs to account for the process and outcome of differentials in contests (especially Zolberg, Riegel); (c) that the *form* and poetics of exhibitions is a crucial aspect of their contestability and that this again needs further theoretical elaboration (especially Riegel and Porter); and (d) that contests may not necessarily be overt challenges but may be alternative readings by visitors – though again, we need further theoretical development of the ways in which such alternative readings may, nevertheless, be socially and culturally positioned (Fyfe and Ross).

Chapters in this part of the volume cover national identity, ethnicity, gender and class, and include discussion of various innovatory exhibitions. Vera Zolberg, like Urry, argues for the importance of developing the sociology of memory and sees museums as key sites of contests of social remembrance. She looks particularly at the recent controversy over the Smithsonian Institution display of the aircraft which dropped the atomic bomb on Hiroshima – a case which highlights not just contests *within* nation-states but also *between* them, and which effectively raises questions about the ways in which museums (and social theorists) conceptualize nations. The Enola Gay affair evokes forcefully the problem of how museums deal, or should deal, with controversial subjects. This is extended by Henrietta Riegel to a discussion of museums' own attempts to address through exhibitions the roles of museums in colonialism and the representation of otherness. Through an analysis of two such controversial exhibitions in Canada – one by an anthropologist about Africa, the other by Native Americans about the ways in which they perceive themselves to be represented – she provides an insightful account of the ways in which the detailed poetics of exhibitionary strategies may lead to visitor interpretations, and to political inflections, other than those intended by the exhibitors.

Gaby Porter's analysis, which draws on psychoanalytic and feminist theory, also addresses the question of the ways in which exhibitionary styles and strategies may suggest or repress certain kinds of readings, in this case in relation to gender. Also, like Riegel, she discusses examples of exhibitions which attempt to challenge traditional museum representation. These feminist exhibitions, in parallel fashion to feminist theory, move beyond just attempting to 'put women in' and draw upon women's experience to create exhibitions which incorporate the personal, the emotional and the bodily, and which portray these as intrinsic to, rather than separable from, the political and social.

How those who visit exhibitions respond to them is a subject to which a large and growing body of research – mainly carried out in relation to specific museums and exhibitions – has been dedicated in recent years.[9] Much of this research, however, perhaps because it is usually directed towards rather specific institutional questions and requirements, has been rather limited from a social scientific perspective. Broader questions of how people conceptualize museum visiting and how it articulates with their conceptions of their identity and locality have scarcely been broached. A methodology and theoretical framework for doing so, together with some much needed data, are introduced in the chapter by Gordon Fyfe and Max Ross. This highlights the rich variability of local appropriations of museums, showing clearly that visitors are very active in the ways in which they contextualize museums within their own lives. The analysis goes further, however, to argue that these variable appropriations are structured and may be understood as, among other things, expressions of class identity. Museums are one medium through which selves and others may be defined – through which the detailed identity contests of everyday life may be waged.

Contents – Classifications and Practice

Contest, then, this volume shows, must be understood as potentially occurring at any point of the museum process: from production through to consumption. We can view this process as one of attempts to establish and fix classifications (Fyfe, below). This, however, is always a tenuous business both because classifications often contain contradictions and ambivalence, and because, in the details of practice – the collision between classifications, objects, museum workers, visitors etc – classifications are liable to be recast. Both of these points are made strongly by the three chapters in this final section of the book which deals with the content not just of museum displays, but of the idea of the museum and its institutional practice.

Kevin Hetherington's analysis of Stonehenge takes up the issue of alternative readings of a site by its 'consumers' but in doing so is also concerned to provide an account of the kind of space – and ambiguous potentials – that such a 'museum without walls' might offer. In presenting the site as 'heterotopic,' and arguing through historical material that this is not just a late twentieth century development, he also challenges the notion that 'multivocality' is a 'postmodern' phenomenon. His analysis suggests rather that it has always been contained, though perhaps 'displaced' and sometimes denied, within modernity. In this way, Stonehenge – as a site thoroughly implicated in museal notions of past, heritage and identity – reveals ambiguities at the heart of the museum project.

Where Hetherington gives us a theorized account of a space in which multivocality could be played out, Gable and Fyfe both provide detailed instances of the ways in which museum classifications might shift in the details of practice. Gable's analysis of the representation of black history at Colonial Williamsburg illustrates well the different groups, interests, tensions and misunderstandings which may shape the outcome of a display; and, as in this case, how a museum 'even when . . . ostensibly run by revolutionaries [may] end up promoting a reactionary mindset' (below). His analysis is grounded in detailed ethnographic study, and this has theoretical as well as methodological implications for it allows Gable to show how unexpected details and cultural assumptions redefine the museum in process. This has implications not just for this particular exhibition but for the ways in which theorists (in this case primarily social historians) conceptualize the issues involved and attempt to turn theory into practice. The process of exhibition-making, then, is constitutive and may take many forms, including, as Gable shows, the very way in which notions such as 'the facts' are conceptualized. This may also be understood as the 'agency' of the museum, an idea theoretically developed here by Gordon Fyfe in his historically detailed analysis of the Chantrey Bequest at the Tate Gallery. Drawing particularly upon Bourdieu, Fyfe is concerned to move beyond the analysis of museums as simply outcomes of dominant class interests while at the same time providing a theoretically informed account of the 'complex interweaving of power relations' (below). The museum, he makes clear, is thoroughly part of its broader social context, it is deeply contested by different interests, and its own content – its institutional structures and contingencies – play a part in shaping its nature and effects. Theorizing needs to tackle all of these: context, contest and content.

Conclusion

Alongside the expansion and diversification of the museum, particularly since the 1980s, has come a massive increase in the amount of critical commentary upon museums. The end of the 1980s saw the publication of a number of academic collections whose aim was to bring together and develop the study of museums – museology (especially Lumley, 1988 and Vergo, 1989). These were produced in part out of a dialogue with a number of earlier studies of the massive extent and proliferation of heritage within Europe and especially Britain,[10] the developing art and social historical analysis of museums[11] and also the growing critique of museums' role in colonialism and their representation of minorities.[12] A good deal of the commentary emanated from countries such as Australia and Canada (which hosted the first World Heritage Congress in 1988) which faced particular problems over establishing ancient and homogeneous national identities and from the vantage point of which the European, and especially British, concern with being 'old' seemed culturally remarkable.[13] A conference on 'The Poetics and Politics of Representation' at the Smithsonian in 1988 led to the publication

13

of two notably extensive and important collections providing, in particular, examples both of critiques of the representation of minorities as well as many cases of new innovatory exhibitions which attempted to give those minorities voice (Karp and Lavine, 1990; Karp, Kreamer and Lavine, 1992). During the 1990s this expansion of critical literature on museums has continued apace with historical and cultural analysis,[14] including a number of important new histories of (mainly European) museums,[15] and a number of collections providing some much needed account of non-Western museums[16] and volumes dealing with particular museums and particular types of museums.[17]

This growth of interest in museums is indicative of the fact that the museum at the end of the twentieth century is a focus around which many of our global and local preoccupations can coalesce. Museums demand attention to questions of how identity and difference are performed, and to how senses of continuity might be intimated in the face of the apparent acceleration of transnational movement and global transformation. They are sites in which seductive totalizing mythologies of nation-state and Enlightenment rationality struggle against alternative classifications, and in which 'high culture' and 'popular culture' battle for legitimacy. Moreover, their cultural remit – to preserve and to create public displays – demands that they produce at least partial and temporary answers to these dilemmas. Any museum or exhibition is, in effect, a statement of position. It is a theory: a suggested way of seeing the world. And, like any theory, it may offer insight and illumination. At the same time, it contains certain assumptions, speaks to some matters and ignores others, and is intimately bound up with – and capable of affecting – broader social and cultural relations. For this reason, museums and exhibitions, like social and cultural theorizing, deserve careful and critical scrutiny.

The present volume is intended both to contribute to the growing literature on museums and to add its own distinctive voice to the current admirable 'cacophony' (cf. Dias, 1994 on innovatory museum practice). The hope of contributors here is that the collection will provide not merely more talk about museums but – in the spirit of critical reflexive feedback that has provided much of the developing vitality of this field of research – new ways of seeing and understanding museums. And even, perhaps, new ways of exhibiting and of 'museuming.'

Notes

1 It is difficult to be precise about the overall number of museums globally but from the regularly published *Museums of the World* (Munich: K.G. Sauer) rapid expansion clearly appears to be the case. For UK and several other 'western' countries see Feist and Hutchinson (1989 and 1990).

2 The excellent *Museums Journal* – the monthly publication of the Museums Association – provides regular reports and discussion on such matters.

3 For other examples see *Museums Journal*, and also, for example, Ames (1992), Karp and Lavine (1990), Karp, Kreamer and Lavine (1992), Pointon (1994), Glaser and Zenetou (1994).

4 Other examples of local appropriations include Clifford (1990) and Blancke and Cjigkitoonuppa J.P. Slow Turtle (1994) on Native Americans and Appadurai and Breckenridge (1992) on India. Several chapters in this book also give consideration to this: especially, Prösler, Urry, Riegel, and Fyfe and Ross.

5 For some good and more or less self-critical examples see Hodge and de Souza (1979), Duncan and Wallach (1980), and Pearce (1992).

6 For discussion of these interrelationships see, for example, Ames (1992), Coombes (1994), Jenkins (1994), Dias (n.d.).

7 These ideas are being developed in relation to various aspects of the visual (eg painting, science) in a number of areas of history and social and cultural studies at present. See, for example, Fyfe and Law (1988), Jordanova (1989), Rudwick (1992), Taylor (1994), Jenks (1995).

8 The phrase 'the new museology' was in use before this, eg in Canada in 1984, and Vergo's version has been contested (Walsh, 1992:161).

9 For a review of this work see the International Laboratory of Visitor Studies (ILVS), an enormous, annually updated, bibliography of visitor research, largely carried out by museums. For recent reviews of visitor research and its directions, see Lawrence (1991), Hooper-Greenhill (1995b), Falk and Dierkling (1992), Bicknell and Farmelo (1994) and the journal *Publics et Musées*).

10 See especially Horne (1984), Wright (1985), Lowenthal (1985), Hewison (1987).

11 Duncan and Wallach (1980), Crimp (1985).

12 Examples include Ames 1992 [orig. 1986], Haraway (1984–5), and Stocking (1985), the *Making Exhibitions of Ourselves* conference held at the British Museum in 1986 and the first Women, Heritage and Museums conference in 1984.

13 The contrast between Europe and countries such as Canada sparked off some commentators' interest in these matters: see Wright (1985:2); and Horne (1984:4) for some doubts.

14 Eg Pearce (1990), Sherman and Rogoff (1994).

15 Pomian (1990), Hooper-Greenhill (1992), Findlen (1994), Bennett (1995).

16 Kaplan (1994), and Stone and Molyneaux (1994).

17 Eg Coombes (1994), Pearce (1994), Macdonald (1995).

References

Ames, M., (1992, 2nd ed.) *Cannibal Tours and Glass Boxes: The Anthropology of Museums*, London: University College of London Press.

Annis, S., (1986), 'The museum as a staging ground for symbolic action,' *Museum* 151, pp. 168–71.

Appadurai, A. and Breckenridge, C.A., (1992), 'Museums are Good to Think: Heritage on View in India,' in I. Karp, C.M. Kreamer and S.D. Lavine (eds), *Museums and Communities. The Politics of Public Culture*, Washington: Smithsonian Institution, pp. 34–55.

Bennett, T., (1995), *The Birth of the Museum: History, Theory, Politics*, London: Routledge.

Blancke, S. and Cjigkitoonuppa J.P. Slow Turtle, (1994), 'Traditional American Indian education as a palliative to western education,' in P.G. Stone and B.L. Molyneaux (eds), *The Presented Past: Heritage, Museums and Education*, London: Routledge, pp. 438–52.

Clifford, J., (1990), 'Four Northwest Coast Museums: Travel Reflections,' in I. Karp and S.D. Lavine (eds), *Exhibiting Cultures: The Poetics and Politics of Museum Display*, Washington: Smithsonian Institution, pp. 212–54.

Coombes, A.E., (1994), *Reinventing Africa: Museums, Material Culture and Popular Imagination in Late Victorian and Edwardian England*, Yale University Press.

Crimp, D., (1985), 'On the museum's ruins,' in H. Foster (ed.), *The Anti-Aesthetic: Essays on Postmodern Culture*, Washington: Bay Press.

Dias, N., (n.d.) 'La visibilité de la différence' (unpublished manuscript).

Dias, N., (1994), 'Looking at objects: memory, knowledge in nineteenth century ethnographic displays,' in G. Robertson, M. Mash, L. Tickner, J. Bird, B. Curtis and T. Putnam (eds), *Travellers' Tales: Narratives of Home and Displacement*, London: Routledge, pp. 164–76.

Duncan, C. and Wallach, A., (1980), 'The universal survey museum,' *Art History*, vol. 3 no. 4, pp. 448–69.

Falk, J.H. and Dierkling, L.D., (1992), *The Museum Experience*, Washington: Whalesback Books.

Feist, A. and Hutchinson, R. (eds), (1989), *Cultural Trends 4: Museums, Visual Arts and Crafts*, London: Policy Studies Institute.

Feist, A. and Hutchinson, R. (eds), (1990), *Cultural Trends 5: Cultural Trends in the Eighties*, London: Policy Studies Institute.

Findlen, P., (1994), *Possessing Nature: Museums, Collecting and Scientific Culture in Early Modern Italy*, Berkeley: University of California Press.

Fyfe, G., (1995), 'The Chantrey Episode: Art Classification, Museums and the State, c1870–1920,' in S. Pearce (ed.) *Art in Museums*, London: Athlone, pp. 5–41.

Fyfe, G. and Law, J. (eds), *Picturing Power*, London: Routlege.

Glaser, J.R. and Zenetou, A.A., (1994), *Gender Perspectives: essays on women in museums*, Washington: Smithsonian Institution.

Handler, R., (1988), *Nationalism and the Politics of Culture in Quebec*, Madison: University of Wisconsin Press.

Haraway, D., (1984–5), 'Teddy Bear Patriarchy: Taxidermy in the Garden of Eden, New York City, 1908–36', *Social Text*, 11, pp. 19–64.

Harvey, P., (1996), *Hybrids of Modernity: Anthropology, the Nation-State and the Universal Exhibition*, London: Routledge.

Herzfeld, M., (1987), *Anthropology through the Looking Glass: Critical Ethnography in the Margins of Europe*, Cambridge: Cambridge University Press.

Hewison, R., (1987), *The Heritage Industry*, London: Methuen.

Hodge, R. and D'Souza, W., (1979), 'The museum as a communicator: a semiotic analysis of the Western Australia Museum Aboriginal Gallery, Perth,' *Museum*, vol. 31, no. 4, pp. 251–67.

Hooper-Greenhill, E., (1992), *Museums and the Shaping of Knowledge*, London: Routledge.

Hooper-Greenhill, E. (ed.), (1995a), *Museum, Media, Message*, London; Routledge.

Hooper-Greenhill, E., (1995b), Audiences – a curatorial dilemma,' in S. Pearce (ed.) *Art in Museums*, London: Athlone Press, pp. 143–63.

Horne, D., (1984), *The Great Museum: The Re-Presentation of History*, London: Pluto Press.

Jenkins, D., (1994), 'Object Lessons and Ethnographic Displays: Museum Exhibitions and the Making of American Anthropology,' *Comparative Studies in Society and History*, pp. 242–70.

Jencks, C. (ed.), (1995), *Visual Culture*, London: Routledge.

Jones, D., (1992), 'Dealing with the Past,' *Museums Journal* (January), pp. 24–7.

Jordanova, L., (1989), *Sexual Visions. Images of Gender in Science and Medicine between the Eighteenth and Twentieth Centuries*, Hemel Hempstead: Harvester.

Kaplan, F.E.S. (ed.), (1994), *Museums and the Making of 'Ourselves': The Role of Objects in National Identity*, London: Leicester University Press.

Karp, I., (1990), 'Culture and Representation,' in I. Karp and S.D. Lavine, (eds), *Exhibiting Cultures: The Poetics and Politics of Museum Display*, Washington: Smithsonian Institution, pp. 11–24.

Karp, I. and Lavine, S.D. (eds), (1990), *Exhibiting Cultures: The Poetics and Politics of Museum Display*, Washington: Smithsonian Institution.

Karp, I., Kreamer, C.M., and Lavine, S.D., (eds), (1992), *Museums and Communities. The Politics of Public Culture*, Washington: Smithsonian Institution.

Lavine, S.D. and Karp, I., (1990), 'Introduction: Museums and Multiculturalism,' in I. Karp and S.D. Lavine, (eds), *Exhibiting Cultures: The Poetics and Politics of Museum Display*, Washington: Smithsonian Institution.

Lawrence, G., (1991), 'Rats, street gangs and culture: evaluation in museums,' in G. Kavanagh, (ed.), *Museum Languages: Objects and Texts*, London: Leicester University Press, pp. 11–32.

Lowenthal, D., (1985), *The Past is a Foreign Country*, Cambridge: Cambridge University Press.

Lumley, R. (ed.), (1988), *The Museum Time-Machine: Putting Cultures on Display*, London: Routledge/Comedia.

Macdonald, S.J., (1993), 'Un nouveau "corps des visiteurs": musées et changements culturels,' *Publics et Musées*, No. 3, pp. 13–27.

Macdonald, S.J. (ed.), (1995), *Science on Display*, special issue of *Science as Culture*, Vol. 5, part 2, no. 22.

Macdonald, S.J., (1996), 'The Museum as Mirror,' in A. James, J. Hockey and A. Dawson (eds), *Anthropology and Representation*, London: Routledge.

Merriman, N., (1991), *Beyond the Glass Case: The Past, The Heritage and The Public*, London: Leicester University Press.

Pearce, S. (ed.), (1990), *Objects of Knowledge*, London: Athlone.

Pearce, S., (1992), *Museum Objects and Collections: A Cultural Study*, London: Leicester University Press.

Pearce, S. (ed.), (1994), *Museums and the Appropriation of Culture*, London: Athlone.

Pointon, M. (ed.), (1994), *Art Apart: Museums in North America and Britain Since 1800*, Manchester: Manchester University Press.

Pomian, K., (1990), *Collectors and Curiosities: Paris and Venice, 1500–1800*, Cambridge: Polity.

Rudwick, M. (1992) *Scenes from Deep Time*, Chicago: University of Chicago Press.

Sherman, D. and Rogoff, I. (eds), (1994), *Museum Culture: Histories, Discourses, Spectacles*, London: Routledge.

Sola, T., (1992), 'Museum professionals – the endangered species,' in P. Boylan (ed.) *Museums 2000*, London: Routledge, pp. 101–13.

Stocking, G.W. (ed.), (1985), *Objects and Others: Essays on Museums and Material Culture*, Madison: Wisconsin University Press.

Stone, P.G. and Molyneaux, B.L. (eds), (1994), *The Presented Past: Heritage, Museums and Education*, London: Routledge.

Taylor, L. (ed), (1994), *Visualizing Theory. Selected Essays from V.A.R., 1990–1994*, London: Routledge.

Ucko, P.J., (1994), 'Museums and sites: cultures of the past within education – Zimbabwe, some ten years on,' in P.G. Stone and B.L. Molyneaux (eds), *The Presented Past: Heritage, Museums and Education*, London: Routledge, pp. 237–82.

Vergo, P. (ed.), (1989) *The New Museology*, London: Reaktion Books.

Walsh, K., (1992), *The Representation of the Past. Museums and Heritage in the post-modern world*, London: Routledge.

Wright, P., (1985), *On Living in an Old Country: The National Past in Contemporary Britain*, London: Verso.

Part I
Contexts: Spaces and Times

Museums and Globalization

Martin Prösler

Abstract

The chapter explores the diffusion of museums around the globe. It draws upon world systems and globalization theory to argue that we can understand this as the diffusion of an institutionalized form which seeks to realize the world in its organization. This is explored particularly in relation to cosmological models of order in early museums and the role of museums in the process of nation building; and the argument is illustrated through contemporary examples from the National Museum of Sri Lanka.

Ever-increasing global flows of trade, the migration of peoples and individuals, together with perpetual streams of information, images and knowledge generate relations of intensified exchange on a world-wide scale. In this process the world is connected up through institutions of the most diverse kind: e.g. non-governmental organizations, religious communities, criminal syndicates. These and other institutions operate according to their own interpretative model of the world. One part of this global network is formed by the 35,000 museums around the world (Gilette, 1990), together with international museum organizations and the discipline of museology itself.

This insight has hitherto played no great part in museology besides some inter-'national' comparisons. Nonetheless, there is constant indirect reference to the phenomenon. For example there are discussions of the importance for museums of the increasing reach of the information super-highway and the electronic digitalization of museum objects. In museological literature the general issue of 'globalization' is primarily reflected in references to the importance of conservation in the face of rapid, world-wide cultural change (e.g. Bettenhausen, 1990: 1). Another reflex of

© The Editorial Board of The Sociological Review 1996. Published by Blackwell Publishers, 108 Cowley Road, Oxford OX4 1JF, UK and 238 Main Street, Cambridge, MA 02142, USA.

'global' consciousness is represented by proposals to create a 'Musée planetaire' (Nicolas, 1988:198), or a global 'Ecomuseum . . . that would integrate in all their possible forms men, space and time' (Barblan, 1988:51). This is not a new idea, of course – it was put forward right at the beginning of the museum movement in the fifteenth and sixteenth centuries, and these suggestions are merely the most recent manifestations of this basic idea.

In contrast to museology's mainly indirect treatment of the world as a 'unity of spaces' the social sciences have systematically subjected this approach to critical scrutiny since the mid-1960s (Moore, 1966). This marked the beginning of world-systems and globalization theory, today most closely associated with the names of Wallerstein and Robertson. The latter succinctly outlines globalization as 'the actual form of recent and contemporary moves in the direction of global interdependence and global consciousness' (1990a:22), or as 'the form in terms of which the world becomes "united," but by no means integrated in naive functionalist mode' (1990a:18).

The unsystematic way in which museological discourse treats the relation between museums, on the one hand, and globalization, on the other, seems to originate in a misconception which sees museums as merely following world developments and reflecting globalization. In fact, the world-wide diffusion of museums was tied in with European colonialism and imperialism. Their expansion, then, occurred in close connection with those political factors in globalization which have provided the contemporary *world order* with its basic structure. Moreover, the museum was, and remains, epistemologically a space in which the *world is ordered*, in which, with the assistance of material objects, the 'world' is realized, understood and mediated. This role, matured over a period of five hundred years, lends a high degree of consistency to the basic structures manifest in contemporary museums. In this way museums form a significant part of the global diffusion of ideas and images.

The central roles and functions of 'Third World' cultural-historical museums can also be viewed in this fashion. According to the International Council of Museums (ICOM), which is the most important forum for 'Third World' museology, their role is to strengthen cultural identity and consciousness in the face of rapid and world-wide cultural change; to strengthen national identity within an internationalized system of states; and to make use of the educational potential of museums in the context of development.[1] These functional definitions touch directly upon questions of the world political order.

The indirect manner in which the relationship between museums and global change is broached is matched by a lack of studies of the history of institutional diffusion. As Lewis wrote in 1986: 'The story of the development of museums is still largely unwritten' (1986:5). A later article from the same author provided relatively extensive data on foundations, together with contextual information, for the period up to the end of the nineteenth century. However, neither Lewis nor other commentators such as Varine-Bohan deal with the ambiguities of those museums founded in the 'Third World' during the colonial period, relying instead upon the current paradigmatic distinction between developed and developing countries. Pomain is right to argue that there has so far been no detailed political history of museums, just some broad outlines; nor has there been any real attempt to deal with the museum as an institution from the sociological perspective (1990:54).

The 'Third World' has to be taken thoroughly into account if one is to gain a truly global perspective, but it is here that the conceptual limitations referred to above are most in evidence. This can be seen from the majority of the museum 'histories' published in the periodical *Museum*, the largest forum for such publication, or in other publications associated with UNESCO and ICOM. The specific situation of institutions in the 'Third World' is barely touched on by more general treatments of the socio-cultural context of museums. For example, both Vergo's *New Museology*, which specifically addresses fundamental questions, and Ames' *Cannibal Tours and Glass Boxes: An Anthropology of Museums*, restrict their attention to the First World. Even Karp and Lavine's *Exhibiting Cultures: The Poetics and Politics of Museum Display* and Karp, Kreamer and Lavine's *Museums and Communities: The Politics of Public Culture*, which pay a good deal of necessary attention to minorities, contain few examples from 'Third World' countries.

Many contributions to global museological discourse betray an unreflective Eurocentrism, together with a set of implicit developmental assumptions with respect to tradition and modernity, cultural identity and national culture, and so on. The 1982 ICOM study by de la Torre and Monreal, *Museums: An Investment for Development*, stands four-square in this tradition of writing. Here we find the relationship between the number of museums and Gross Domestic Product proposed as an indicator of social development, positioning each society within an international hierarchy. A similar approach is to be found in Hudson and Nicholls' 'Foreword' to their *Directory*, likewise making a direct link to GDP:

> . . . developing countries will make great sacrifices in order to have museums, which are needed both to reinforce and confirm a sense of national identity and to give status within the world community. To have no museums, in today's circumstances, is to admit that one is below the minimum level of civilization required of a modern state. (Hudson and Nicholls, 1985: x).

Macrosociological perspectives

Wallerstein's vision of the wave-like diffusion of 'historical capitalism' and the incorporation of ever further-flung regions into such a world system can be applied, with little difficulty, to the diffusion of museums around the world.

The first institutions were founded during the fifteenth and sixteenth centuries in the European capitals of the time – Florence, Madrid, Paris and London – being followed in the late eighteenth and early nineteenth centuries by diffusion of museums to 'peripheral Europe', a process that occurred in parallel with the first wave of global diffusion. The first of these non-European museums were in the white settler colonies: the first North American museum was opened in Charleston in 1773, the first Australian museum in Sydney in 1821, the first Latin American museum in Rio de Janeiro in 1815 and the first African museum in Cape Town in 1825 (see Lewis, 1992). During this period the only relevant foundations outside white settler colonies were in Batavia (1778) and in Calcutta (1796/1814). In the white settler colonies, once the first museums had been founded the development continued without interruption; whereas in Africa and Latin America, by contrast, the initial foundations remained the only ones for around fifty years. This hiatus was also true of Asia, where new foundations were limited to British colonial territory: Madras (1851), Lucknow (1863), Lahore (1864), Bangalore (1865), Mathura (1874) and Colombo (1877).

It was not until the 1870s that a worldwide museum boom began to fill in the blank spaces in the museum map. Outside India and the Dutch East Indies the first Asian museums were opened in Bangkok (1874), Japan (1871, 1877), China (1905), Korea (1908), East Bengal (1913), Phnom Penh (1917), Ulan Bator (1921) and Kabul (1922). In Africa the second museum in the entire continent was created in Egypt during the building of the Suez Canal in 1863. Subsequent museums were established in Oran (1884), Tunis (1889), Madagascar (1897), Rhodesia (1901), Uganda (1908), Kenya (1909) and Mozambique (1913). In Latin America museums were established in Cuba (1870 and 1899), Costa Rica (1887), Panama (1903), and in Argentina (1888, 1889, 1895). As early as 1889 the first plans for a museum in Papua New Guinea were drawn up but they were not realized for almost another one hundred years (Smidt, 1977). After the 1870s a series of provincial museums was rapidly established as, for example, in Latin America.

The foundation of the museum in Ceylon highlights the colonial situation. The Royal Society had during the 1840s supported the establishment of a museum. The plan, however, was only realized three decades later. During a period in which the plantation economy flourished, in which railway lines were constructed and the harbour extended after the opening of the Suez Canal, the then Governor, Sir William Gregory, wrote in his autobiography:

> The flourishing condition of the Exchequer enabled me to begin in good earnest on the northern roads, and to construct two buildings greatly wanted; the one, a new Custom House, the other a Museum. They were both designed by the Government architect, Mr. Smither, a man of great taste and refinement, and they are both an honour to the colony. (Gregory, 1894:314).

The development of the museum thus reflects the inclusion of ever more extensive regions in the world system. Here Robertson's works on globalization provide insights into the cultural dimension of this process which can be extended to museums. He seeks to incorporate 'hard' political factors, while at the same time emphasizing 'that it is directly necessary to adopt a cultural focus to what is often called world politics' (Robertson, 1992: 4ff., see also 50ff.). By contrast with world systems approaches, Robertson lays emphasis upon the action-oriented ideas of any actors in the world, rendering them a central aspect of his treatment of the globalization process: ' "world images" play a crucial role in framing the directions in which [ideal as well as material interests] are pursued.' 'Images of global order' are one type of 'world image' (Robertson, 1992:75). In this manner he converges, from the macrosociological perspective, with the 'poetics and politics' of the debate on representation – two theoretical approaches which are not readily combined (see King, 1991a, 1991b; Wolff 1991).

Individual institutions such as museums do not of course play a central role in Robertson's writings. He focuses upon four aspects of the globalization process which have on the one hand a direct significance for the political world order, and on the other are just as important to the formation of ideas of the 'world' and hence for the identity of individuals and social groups across the world (Robertson, 1989; 1990a; 1990b; 1992).

Beginning with the global diffusion of the concept of a national society – as a specific form of institutionalized social association – he concentrates on the mutually-connected aspects of 'national societies', 'the world system of societies', 'individuals, or selves', and 'humankind'. (Robertson, 1992:27; cf. Lechner, 1989) These four aspects are connected historically: the formation of the concept of the (sovereign) 'nation' and of the nation state as a special form of social association went together with the creation of a specific conception of the human being, of the individual as citizen. The relatively autonomous individual faces the nation state, with specific rights and duties. In the ideal case those social relations arising from local or other allegiance (such as ethnicity or clan) gave way to a higher loyalty to the nation, or to the state. This could be seen most clearly in the case of military obligations, as well as in the recognition and propagation of equal legal norms throughout the state territory (Robertson, 1992:56; 1990b:49; 1989:19; and in general the writings of Hobsbawm).

Referring to Anderson, Robertson reduces these to a succinct formula: 'The homogenous nation state – homogenous here in the sense of a culturally homogenized, administered citizenry – is a construction of a particular form of life' (Robertson, 1992:58; Anderson, 1983). The diffusion of the nation state and the establishment of the international system as an aspect of the process of globalization was associated with the idea of the human being as citizen as well as a specific notion of 'humanity', as expressed for instance in the Geneva or Hague Conventions. Robertson understands his four aspects of globalization to be key points of reference with respect to the differing ideas that humans can, or could, form of the world. These points of reference are shared (even if this is sometimes through their rejection) while at the same time they are perceived and constructed variously by individuals. Such 'conjunctions' represent a space of increasing global exchange in the conduct of thought and action.

The formation and diffusion of the concept of nation and of the nation state is understood by Robertson as *one* aspect of the globalization process which cannot be reduced to homogenization or westernization. With respect of the diffusion and moulding of the nation state the process appears as the *universalisation of a particular form which is always reconfigured locally*. Robertson's notion of 'conjunctions' captures this openness to basic difference, especially at the level of cultural consciousness. In globalization, according to Robertson, particular forms from all parts of the world, of quite varying range and meaning, are generalized and then once more particularized.[2] The 'First World' doubtless plays a major role in the asymmetric process of the universalization of specific forms; but this process is often reduced to one of world-wide homogenization, simply because from the standpoint of the First World it is this 'original element' which can be repeatedly recognized and registered (cf. Hannerz, 1989; 1991; Handler and Segal, 1992).

These theoretical considerations are my point of departure for reflections in the history of the museum as an institution through which the 'world' can be understood and ordered. Two aspects of the creation of museums will now be dealt with in greater detail to illustrate my argument: conceptions of order in the original establishment of museums; and the relationship between museums and nation-building.

Museum Conceptions of order in early modernity

Museums and the knowledge they display are culture-bound and formed in relation with one another. The history of museums in the early modern period testifies to the manner in which the 'global perspective' is rooted within an institutional structure – not just geographically, but above all in the way that the sense of an ordered world is acquired. During the European Middle Ages collections of material objects were chiefly established in courts and churches, for most part without system. Material objects and their deliberate investigation with the aim of acquiring knowledge of the world meant little during the Scholastic era; knowledge was primarily drawn from a *studium literarum*. It was only in the fourteenth century that collecting became more systematic, a consequence of the rise of early Humanism; and it was first in the fifteenth century that rooms were set aside specifically for collections established for the education and cultivation of their owner, breaking with the conventions of the treasure-house (Scheicher, 1979:36f.). *Kabinette, Estudes* and *Studiolos* were created in the Courts and in some cases by rich non-aristocratic families.

The geographical discoveries of the late fifteenth and sixteenth centuries extended the European horizon, just as in the same way did technical inventions such as the telescope, and the ever more rapid distribution of books. In this phase of fundamental change a 'culture of curiosity' developed,[3] in which the cabinet became the focus for everything new, unknown or unseen that needed to be integrated into the existing perception of the world. The catholicity with which such collecting activity was pursued made such cabinets material corollaries of other modes (eg travel books) through which the *homo universalis* apprehended the world.

One of the most fascinating endeavours in the organization of knowledge during this early phase is Camillo's 'memory theatre' of the first half of the sixteenth century (Yates, 1966:166–72; Bernheimer, 1956). Camillo's theatre attempted an encyclopedic summation of contemporary knowledge. The ordering principle was provided by a cosmological scheme which classified all textual knowledge; and this scheme served at the same time as a memory aid, rendering comprehensive knowledge accessible. One decisive innovation shaping Camillo's enterprise was the notion of the spatial disposition of objects of knowledge. This idea was derived from the writings of Cicero on rhetoric, who had proposed, as a way of assisting memory and organizing knowledge that we conceive our ideas as organized as though within rooms, within houses, within a city. Each object of knowledge, then, could be thought of as though it had a specific spatial location.

Camillo's 'Theatre of Memory' was a *theatrum mundi*: a space in which all the creations of the universe would have their place. The number seven served here as an ordering principle: in the seven rows of the theatre, beginning with the seven planets, there were the simple elements, compound elements, the productions of humankind, the unity of body and soul, human activity in nature, and finally the arts. In the middle of the first row there stood a pyramid symbolising God, but which could also be interpreted as King Francis I of France, the *Rex Christianissimus*. The stage was reserved for the visitor to the theatre; from there the universe could be viewed. Painted images and inscriptions on caskets and small boxes helped in orientation and clarification.[4]

This conception of the microcosm as principle of order is encountered in other collections of the sixteenth century, one example being the *studiolo* of Francesco di Medici in the Palazzo Vecchio. This was created by Georgio Vasari and painted according to a programme conceived by V. Borghini in 1570, and is among the most conspicuous examples of the contemporary spirit informing such collection. The decoration of the room conveys allegorically the contents of the object-filled cabinets, ordering them hierarchically in the cosmos after a scheme which can be traced back to Isidor de Sevilla. Borghini described in his letters how the cosmological system of images also served quite pragmatically as an inventory, enabling the numerous pieces to be located (Scheicher, 1979:42f.).

Not all collections of this period were so well planned, nor (especially among the less influential collectors) did the actual contents of a collection fulfil their encyclopedic claim. Nevertheless, collecting was extensive. In sixteenth century Italy, for instance, there were 250 private collections of natural objects (Lewis, 1992), some of which were considerable and provided the basis for the descriptive works of scholars such as Ulisse Aldrovandi (1522–1605), Conrad Gesner (1516–65) and Felix Plattner (1536–1614).

The later sixteenth century saw the basic institutionalization of the cabinet and the employment of the first curators. The first writings on the principles of collecting were published, for example, by von Quiccheberg in 1565 and by Kaldemarckt in 1587. A little later the first catalogues appeared. Objects were acquired by agents working to the orders of rich collectors. The ideal of a close relationship between a collection of objects organized along encyclopedic lines and the acquisition and transmission of knowledge took shape and became consolidated.

Of great significance at this time as an organizing principle of knowledge was the resemblance of the macrocosm with the microcosm. Foucault's *Order of Things* is of great interest in this context, for, as he argues, the fundamental experience of knowledge in the sixteenth century – the form and content of knowing – rested upon a complex series of similitudes and resemblances, linking all elements of the cosmos. Things as well as words were God's creation, bearing his signature at a 'deeper level'. These signs were laid down at the moment of the Creation, so that ultimately man might reveal its secrets. The form of knowing therefore corresponded to an *interpretation of signs* and of the resemblances that arose among them. Just as words and things meshed together seamlessly, so in the description of natural phenomena no distinction was made between observation, document and fable. The task of a historian like Aldrovandi, writing a natural history based upon his collection, was to represent this complex system – to draw together all that was known about an animal or a plant and to present it in terms of the semantic relationships that connected it into the world.

In the transition from the sixteenth to the seventeenth century a fundamental change in the order of knowledge occurred: thought ceased to work in terms of a system of resemblances. Francis Bacon and others rejected the system of resemblances as a means of gaining knowledge, and along with Descartes replaced it with a more 'pure' form of *comparison* (Foucault, 1970:52). This took only two forms: the comparison of measurement and of order ('mathesis' and 'taxonomia'). Henceforth, no longer did one search for signs of covert resemblance and affinity, but rather, through *observation*, isolated those characteristics whose comparison betrayed the identity, or diversity, of cosmic creations.

The loss of connecting elements at the level of the sign system meant that a transition occurred, from the older tripartite logical form to a binary one, based on a relationship between a signifier and a signified. This had fundamental consequences for the way in which humans thought, and, for the basis and form of representation of the museum cabinet. The earlier form of natural history rested primarily upon the interpretation of signs as a system of resemblances; its documents were an archive of words and texts. The new natural history was by contrast located in the ordered collections of natural objects, and in natural gardens. Here things were placed alongside each other, devoid of commentary and any linguistic context. It was this dialogue with natural history that shaped the new way of looking (Fabian, 1983).

Natural history became the new legitimate form for existing cosmological ideas. The words of Francis Bacon, referring to the garden, the library and the cabinet, mark the beginnings of this new development: 'And so you may have in small compass *a model of the universal nature made private*' F. Bacon, *Gesta Grayorum* (1594); cited as in Impey and MacGregor, 1985:1 (my emphasis M.P.).

From *theatrum mundi* to *theatrum nationis*

Nations are not 'as old as history', as Bagehot maintained some one hundred years ago. The 'Nation' is scarcely older than the eighteenth century, when in Europe the concept began to assume its modern shape (Anderson, 1983; Gellner, 1983; Hobsbawm, 1990; etc.). The fundamental social changes of the time are also reflected in the manner in which collections were assembled. What had in the sixteenth century begun as an encyclopedic venture was now developed within the framework of new phenomena, the 'territorial state' and the 'nation'. In England the Royal Society, founded in 1660, established in 1666 a collection, which it called the 'repository'. The development of the repository through private gifts had something of an arbitrary character, and soon voices were raised demanding a systematic approach to the collection more in tune with Bacon's ideas. The Royal Society accordingly recruited a botanist in 1669, whose task was to traverse the British Isles searching for those natural objects which the collection lacked. The idea, according to the 1681 foreword to the collection's catalogue, was to create an 'Inventory of Nature' limited to British territory. This ambition remained for the most part at the level of an idea, as was self-critically acknowledged in the Society's catalogue (Hunter, 1985:166).

It is about this time that we first encounter the nation being used as a point of reference for collecting activity. In England, where the concept of nation in its political sense first emerges, we find John Tradescent (1608–1662) writing during 1656 in the introduction to the catalogue of his celebrated collection that 'the enumeration of these Rarities . . . would be an honour for *our Nation*' (cited in MacGregor, 1985:151, my emphasis M.P.) This idea of the nation had, Tradescent wrote, been introduced to him by Elias Ashmole (1617–1692). Ashmole was a founding member of the Royal Society and, as one of the best-known collectors of his time, founded in 1683 the Oxford Ashmolean Museum.

It was, however, only in the second half of the eighteenth

century that nation and state territory became significant structuring elements in the organization of collections. For example, the first American museum was established in Charleston in 1773 with the purpose of assembling a natural inventory of South Carolina (Hudson, 1975:31f.). The idea of creating an American national museum can be dated no later than 1792, when Peale, a well-known collector, made a public appeal to this effect (Hudson, 1975:35). In France the notion that a collection could honour the nation was expressed in 1765, in the entry on museums in the *Encyclopédie*. The enterprise of 'inventarizing' the nation increasingly became a key dimension of cultural historical collection. The Musée des Monuments Francais was founded in 1795 in Paris with the objective of inventarizing national monuments, and provided a model for subsequent European institutions.

Just what the nation might be was still very unclear in the eighteenth century, leading to varying constructions on the part of different social strata. The concept of the 'nation' belonged primarily to a bourgeoisie struggling for its political rights within the society of estates. The design for a future national museum included in the 1765 *Encyclopédie* article was in this respect a political provocation. As early as the first half of the eighteenth century the demand was raised for free access for all citizens to those collections owned by the higher estates, until in 1750 Louis XV placed one hundred paintings on display in the Palais Luxembourg for a year. It was not, however, until 1793 that a museum, freely open to the public, was established, the king's collection being 'nationalized' and placed on display in the Grande Galerie of the Louvre. It was in this political context that the Hermitage in St. Petersburg opened (1764), then the Nationalmuseet in Stockholm (1772), the Museo Pio-Clementino in Italy (1772), then the Belvedere in Vienna (1784), and in which plans were developed for a Polish national museum in 1775, and a Spanish national museum in 1787 (Lewis, 1992; von Plessen, 1992).

But it was the nineteenth century which saw the real development of nations and nation states. At the beginning of the century the idea of the 'nation' was a novelty, based neither on personal experience nor on any other familiar mode of social association. The museum was one of the spaces within which the nation could present itself as an 'imagined community' (Anderson, 1983) in all possible aspects. The stages of development of the nation and of nationalism have been traced by Hcbsbawm in his *Nations and Nationalism since 1780*, and these stages are also apparent in the collections made at this time.

During the first half of the nineteenth century nationalist movements concerned themselves primarily with literature and folklore, without having necessarily a strong political dimension. Jacob Grimm for instance engaged in a wide-ranging collection of German historical material, from which he published his *History of the German Language* and *German Imperial Antiquities*. Applying the methods of the Historical School to folklore, he edited the *German Sagas* and *German Mythology*, and also drew up plans for the publication of a comprehensive book on German customs as well as the creation of a collection of antiquities (Bausinger, 1987:40f.). Many historical collections were formed under the influence of this nationalistic folklorism; for example the Museum for Nordic Antiquities in Copenhagen (1807), the National Gallery in Budapest (1802) and the National Museum in Prague (1818).

After 1840, however, nationalist movements entered a new phase. National associations were formed all over Europe, together with newspapers and educational and cultural institutions which promoted the 'national idea'. It was in this context for example that the Germanisches Nationalmuseum was founded in 1853 in Nuremberg, as an expression of the liberal bourgeoisie. Discussions among the founders of this museum clearly expose the political ambiguities of this early phase of national unification – for in the absence of a national state, the territory from which this new museum should draw its material was not obvious. The decision to site the museum in Nuremberg was determined by the current fashion for medieval romanticism, for a connection could be made in this way with the glory and importance of the first German Empire (Bott, 1992). Two years after the foundation of the Germanisches Nationalmuseum Maximilian II founded the Bavarian National Museum in Munich, as a kind of monarchic riposte. His object was to convey the importance of the Wittelsbach line for Bavaria at a time when the family was under increasing political pressure (Glaser 1992). The National Museum in Warsaw followed a little later in 1862, although in the absence of a Polish state the collection had partly to be located in Switzerland (Stölzl, 1992:15). The National Museum in Turin, founded in 1878, followed Italian unification, rather than preceded it as in the German case.

Step by step the Europe of nation states took shape: Italy, Germany and Romania were founded, Hungary achieved partial autonomy, and fundamental changes took place in other countries. This is the time of 'the making of nations', as Walter Bagehot put it. But in Italy at the time of unification less than 2.5% of the population used Italian as their first language, the vast majority employing a wide range of dialects. This accounts for Massimo d'Azeglio's call at the time of Unification: 'We have made Italy, now we have to make Italians!' (Hobsbawm, 1975:89). State-financed educational institutions, among them museums, were of great importance in this work of construction. Museums played a part in defining the nature of the nation; it was a space in which national culture and history were constructed, expressing the difference between one nation and all the others, a distinction all the more necessary since their state structures were broadly similar. In the form of a 'national museum' a museum could embody 'common' culture and history, symbolising at a political level the unity of the nation. In parallel to this the creation of ethnological museums based on the cultures of 'non-civilized' peoples, and the introduction of colonial pavilions at world exhibitions, served to chart a difference between peoples and hence reinforce a national consciousness during the phase of the definition of a 'standard of civilisation'.

Nationalist movements entered a new phase at the end of the nineteenth century – they became mass movements. Museums and exhibitions flourished at an unprecedented rate and assumed a broader appeal. Even trade fairs exhibiting agricultural, craft and industrial products found an audience among the lower classes. Following the contemporary educational trend, such fairs frequently displayed paintings and other *objets d'art* which the visiting peasants, workers and servants had never seen in their lives before. These fairs and exhibitions, especially the world fairs, are the very first mass spectacles in the history of the museum, made possible by new forms of communication such as the railway. From the 1880s museums began to be integrated into the state schooling system. The Liverpool Museum for example made some of its holdings available to schools, and panoramic displays began to be used so that exhibitions might be more educational.

The arguments of Hobsbawm and Ranger (1983) and Mosse (1993) can be extended to show how with the extension of state structures and the onset of mass nationalism, many museums became symbols of the state, and not only of the nation.

Museums of the post and telegraph appeared; school museums; police museums; and army museums, museums dedicated to the memory of a prominent founder of the state, or even the transformation of a founder's home into an exhibit. During this period the number of museums rose dramatically, and this in turn prompted the formation of the first national museum organizations – the Museums Association in England (1899); the American Association of Museums (1906); the German Museum Association (1917); and the Russian Museum Conference (1919).

Anderson has argued that the nation is well fitted for dealing with cosmological questions of life and death that had previously been dealt with primarily by religion. Nationalism's emphasis on mortality, expressed for instance in memorials and graves dedicated to the unknown soldier, is a manifestation of this. Nations, like religions, are concerned with the 'transformation of fatality into continuity, contingency into meaning' (Anderson, 1983:19). Moreover,

> If nation-states are widely conceded to be 'new' and 'historical', the nations to which they give political expression
> always loom out of an immemorial past, and, still more
> important, glide into a limitless future (1983:19).

In this context the cosmological tradition of the museum has meaning for the nation state, and is at the same time one of its richest symbols.

The museum takes on the form of a complete microcosmic representation of the sovereign nation state. The collected objects in the museum document a human community extending in time and space: the nation. They also document by their (territorial) origins the state's spheres of political influence. The building contains representatively everything in the state territory – and in this way becomes itself a symbol of a power relationship. The museum embodies the nation state while at the same time providing it with a place in the general order of things. 'A national heritage is a nation's umbilical cord' – a metaphor employed by Assogba of Benin. The task of the museum is to preserve this national heritage within the course of time, handing it down to the succeeding generation. Its significance lies in 'educating and forming the young' (Assogba, 1976: 218).

Within this perspective the national museum assumes a quite particular symbolism and meaning for the nation and the national state. This transcendental quality, embodying the order of things and embedding the nation within it, is peculiar to the museum – it is a quality not shared by the artistic productions of the national theatre or the daily politics of the national parliament.

The globalization of the *Theatrum Nationis*

This 'national' conception of museums is one which has become widely diffused through the development of a global discursive system focused on museums. The first international museum organization, the International Museums Office, was formed in 1922, associated with the Committee of Intellectual Co-operation of the League of Nations. ICOM was founded in November 1946 within UNESCO, sharing its political obligations and objectives. ICOM has since become the largest and most important international museum organization, with some 10,000 members and regional offices in ninety states. In this way a global discursive system turning upon museum affairs has been created.

This discursive system has promulgated the idea of the museum as a space for locating individual as well as national identity: the museum 'should give everybody the opportunity to find themselves not only in time but also in space ' (Decarolis et al., 1988: 126). An international colloquium in Bogota came to a similar conclusion: 'the museum should be an instrument enabling the individual to become aware of his present reality and human condition' (Mutal, 1978:127). The idea of museums as symbols of national identity and the manifestation of national coherence is widely found. For example, the Zambian national museum claims that the purpose of its ethnographic department is 'to represent the nation of Zambia as a whole' (Chellah, 1983:128). The national museum itself becomes perceived as a symbol of national unity and identity, and placed in the context of the country's development:

> The government's present social and economic development
> policy is based on the concept of 'One Zambia, One Nation'.
> Zambians have to be aware of their common history so they
> may work together towards building a strong and united
> modern nation (Chellah, 1983: 130).

The African museologist Aithnard argues that a museum, in presenting the cultural and natural history of a country, is 'practically a reproduction in miniature of the whole country, the country "in a nutshell".' It is a 'symbol of national cohesion, . . . the living profile of a people's history and culture' (Aithnard, 1976:193, 194).

The National Museum in Colombo: A local reinterpretation in global categories

The argument that the museum is a symbol of national cohesion has been made of Sri Lanka's National Museum in Colombo:

> The exhibits in a national museum present . . . a concentrated image of the history and culture of a nation. They form a systematic historical statement showing the path the nation has traversed, its many-sided experience, the wealth of its physical and mental labours, its great material resources and its cultural resourcefulness (Bandaranayake, 1977:141).

However, this is only one perspective, for what we can also see in the details of the museum's displays is a hierarchical ordering of knowledge – and, in effect, of peoples and practices within Sri Lanka.

The main building of the National Museum contains a natural and cultural historical section which for the most part presents an inventory of the island. The relatively large ethnological section of the museum illustrates a well known aspect of the island's culture: over one hundred masks with their associated paraphernalia are displayed. Prominence is given to a series of masks belonging to Sanni Yakuma, an elaborate ritual of healing. Sanni Yakka are reputed to be beings who are able to make ill any humans who are out of balance. This state of affairs can be brought about through eating the wrong foods, social blunders, bad thoughts and so forth. A specialist in ritual then has the task of making a diagnosis and restoring the patient to equilibrium. In recent years this ritual has been seen less and less. It is an elaborate and expensive ritual which can be afforded by a dwindling number of people; on top of which the traditional analytical framework of health and sickness has fallen into widespread disrepute. Nonetheless, healing rituals retain a firm place within the island's medical system; patients alternate between doctors practising Western medicine and the healing methods of the ritual specialists (Amarasingham, 1980).

Healing rituals are part of the larger sphere of spirit religion in Sri Lanka, all of which maintain a complex and in part complementary relationship to Buddhism. The adherents of spirit religion come chiefly from the poorer classes, while the middle classes tend to favour a 'Protestant' form of Buddhism. At present both of these religious forms are undergoing great changes specific to their respective class basis (Gombrich and Obeyesekere, 1988).

The following text accompanies the presentation of the masks from Sanni Yakuma rituals in the museum:

Dahata Sanniya
Different ailments were known by 'Sanni' in the traditional society. Although it was believed that there were 18 diseases and hence 18 Sanni masks there are more than 18 varieties of Sanni masks. It was believed that different extra-terrestrial forces (Demons) were responsible for those diseases. In this healing system those responsible forces are brought on stage and made to vow to leave the sick and thereby cure the ailment. This is therefore a psychosomatic treatment. Leader of the Sanni demons is called Maha Kola Sanni Yaka.

This text ascribes the masks on display to the so-called 'traditional society' of the island, noting right at the beginning apparent inconsistencies within the traditional healing procedures. The grammatical form of the statements about 'traditional society' is that of the continuous preterite tense. Characteristic of this form is the phrase 'it was believed', a construction which places the topic firmly in the domain of the past and of credence. The text continues to its conclusion with the statement 'This is therefore a psychosomatic treatment', constructed in the present, connoting the realm of fact rather than of belief.

Discourse of this type which counters 'traditionalism' with 'modernism' represents contemporary social groups as remnants of a past epoch. The chronological relationships implicit in the museum texts reflect a hierarchical relationship between the Sri Lankan urban middle-class strata on the one hand, and the agricultural workers and fishermen of the rural areas, together with the urban poor, on the other. 'Traditional' society is construed with concepts such as 'psychosomatic', invoking conceptions of sickness and health which have virtually nothing to do with the cultural system from which the masks come.

The largest display of masks is that of the Kolam, a highly elaborated kind of village theatre. The presentation of the *Maru Raksha* mask is especially remarkable here. In earlier times it was thought potentially dangerous to catch sight of this mask, and especially so for pregnant women and unborn babies. To protect others from chance sightings it was possible on the southwest coast, even quite recently, to see the mask in reversed position, 'standing on its head'. In the museum the mask is shown upright among all the other objects of the 'material' culture. The 'mythical' order of things is counterposed to the museum order; and this effects a kind of disavowal of the place of the mythical in today's society. In this way the museum display with its accompanying texts becomes a representation of the representation:

Maru Raksha. Demon of Death. He is the most fearful demon. Since he *symbolises* death, even his sight could be sufficient to drive fear into the people.

An undue emphasis on the theatrical elements also implies that the Kolam should be regarded as representations rather than an integral part of life:

the *entertainment* oriented Kolam dramatisations . . . . . . the royal couple is given a prominent place on the stage . . . . . . ferocious- looking Rakshasa were *brought on to the stage* in Kolam dancing *to depict very frightening situations* . . . . . . *another folk drama* from Sri Lanka using masks is Sokari.

The mythic is also distanced from contemporary life by being defined as 'folklore' – a concept whose origin is in the European Romantic tradition:

Gurula Raksha. It is a mythical bird referred to in folklore. In Kolam dance it is depicted as a dreadful Raksha.

The masks, cleansed of their original context, then become art objects; and a visit to the exhibition becomes (as a guide to a special display of the masks in 1988 enthused) 'an opportunity which the art lover, whether local or foreign, should not miss'.

Martin Prösler

Beyond nations and nationalism

The museum, then, reinterprets the products of the nation and of the state's territory – plants, animals, human communities, demons and gods – within the universalized categories of a globalization process – psychotherapy, folklore, theatre, art. To the indigenous visitor from the 'Third World' these constructions upon her life world are presented in a complex and largely coherent system. The museum provides such a visitor with a permanent linkage between the local and the global and proposes an order for the things in her world. In this way diverse cultural interpretive systems are brought into relationship with one another and a mediation of meaning takes place (cf. Giddens 1976).

This does not mean, however, that the different visitors accept the interpretations offered to them in the museum, or understand museum terms, such as 'art', in the same way. What is on offer is conjunctions, points of reference, and these are open to quite varied interpretation. For example, religious offerings are sometimes placed at display cabinets containing sacrificial objects in First as well as 'Third World' ethnographic museums.

Culture-specific reinterpretations may occur also for the institutions themselves. For example, in the Singhalese language a museum is called *kautu kagare*, which can be translated as 'a place in which very old things are kept.' Colloquially museums are known as *kautu ge* – houses of bones. This pithy name probably originated in the fact that, during the first decades of the Colombo museum, only a British biologist, his assistant, and a taxidermist worked there. The museum, then, is partially perceived through local categories drawn from a specific local experience.

A museological discourse which is overly concerned with the presentation of national coherence cannot adequately confront such differences. As we have seen in the case of Sri Lanka, as long as analysis of museums is oriented towards a developmental paradigm it will not be able to recognize culture-specific responses, and will not, therefore, be able to comprehend their real significances for processes of identity formation. Museums, realizing the 'world' in their modes of ordering, are actively involved in globalization. They are implicitly bound up with conceptions of individuality and humanity, of national society and with the international system of societies – bound up within the global scope of political and cultural categories.

(Translated by Keith Tribe)

Notes

1 These functional definitions are derived from the UNESCO/ICOM periodical *Museum* for the period 1972–92, on the ICOFOM Study series of the Museological Committee of ICOFOM within ICOM, and on various others studies and publications connected with ICOM – for example K. Hudson's foreword to the international *Directory of Museums and Living Displays* of 1985; the contribution of museums by the former director of ICOM, H. de Varine-Bohan, to the 1985 *Encyclopedia Britannica*; and de la Torre and Monreal (1982).

2 Consider in this context the historical diffusion of Buddhism and associated variations, and then its later role in the context of emergent Singhalese nationalism at the end of the nineteenth century.

3 'Curiosity' derives from the Latin *curiosus*, meaning full of care, full of interest, careful, inquisitive, 'greedy for novelty'. It was in the course of the seventeenth century that the meaning began to shift from an implication of worthwhile knowledge to the modern usage, which has a negative connotation (Kluge, 1967).

4 The cabinet was made from wood and substantially supported financially by Francis I of France.

References

Ajona, M., (1977), 'History Museums and Collections in Cuba', *Museum* 2, 3.

Ames, M., (1992), *Cannibal Tours and Glass Boxes. An Anthropology of Museums*, London: University College London Press.

Aithnard, M.K., (1976), 'Museums and Socio-Economic Development in Africa', *Museum*. 4.

Amarasingham, L.R., (1980), 'Movement among Healers in Sri Lanka: A Case Study of a Singhalese Patient', *Culture, Medicine and Psychiatry* 4, 1.

Anderson, B., (1983), *Imagined Communities: Reflections on the Origin and Spread of Nationalism*, London: Verso.

Assogba, R.-P., (1976), 'Revolution and the Conservation of a National Heritage', *Museum* 4.

Bandaranayake, S., (1977), 'On the Role of the Museum in the Preservation of our Cultural Heritage', in de Silva (ed.) *1877–1977. Colombo Museum Centenary Souvenir*, Colombo.

Barblan, M., (1988), 'Identity, Museology and Development', ICOFOM Study Series 14, Stockholm.

Bausinger, H., (1987), *Volkskunde*, Tübingen: Tübinger Vereinigung für Volkskunde.

Bettenhaussen, P., (1990), 'Museums and Development – A Call for Action', paper presented at ICME Meeting, Copenhagen.

Bernheimer, R., (1956), 'Theatrum mundi', *Art Bulletin* 28 pp. 225–31.

Bott, G., (1992) 'Das germanische Nationalmuseum in Nürnberg – ein nationales Museum?' in von Plessen (1992).

Burnee, J., (1977), 'National Museum of Mongolia', *Museum* 2, 3.

Chellah, M., (1983), 'The national Museum of Zambia, Liningstone', *Museum*.

Costa, A., (1989), 'Making Museums a Permanent Source of Learning and Teaching', *Museums* 1.

De Varine-Bohan, H., (1985), 'Museums', *Encyclopaedia Britannica* 24.

De la Torre, M., Monreal, L., (1982), *Museums: An Investment for Development*, Paris, ICOM.

Decarolis, N., de Garro, D., Astesiano, M., (1988), No title, ICOFORM Study Series 14, Stockholm.

Fabian, J., (1983), *Time and the Other*, New York: Columbia University Press.

Foucault, M., (1970), *The Order of Things*, London: Routledge.

Gellner, E. (1983), *Nations and Nationalism*, Oxford: Blackwell.

Giddens, A., (1976), *New Rules of Sociological Method*, London: Hutchinson.

Gilette, A., (1990), 'One World, Not Enough Voices', *Museum* 3.

Glaser, H., (1992), 'ein Bayerisch historisches Museum im weitesten Sinne des Wortes', in von Plessen (1992).

Gombrich, R., Obeyesekere, G., (1988), *Buddhism Transformed*, Delhi: Motilal Banarsidass Publishers PVT Ltd.

Gregory, A. (ed.), (1894), *Sir William Gregory, K.C.M.G. An Autobiography*, London.

Guzman, R.G., (1973), 'Panama', *Museum* 3.

Hague, E., (1975), 'The Future of Museums in Bangladesh', *Museum* 1.

Hall, S., (1991), 'Old and New Identities, Old and New Ethnicities', in King (1991a).

Handler, R., Segal, D., (1992), 'How European is Nationalism?', *Social Analysis* 32.

Hannerz, U., (1989a), 'Culture between Center and Periphery: Towards a Macroanthropology', *Ethnos* 54 III–IV.

Hannerz, U., (1989b), 'Notes on the Global Ecumene', *Public Culture* 1,2.

Hannerz, U., (1991), 'Scenarios for Peripheral Cultures', in King (1991a).

Hobsbawm, E.J., (1975), *The Age of Capital*, London: Weidenfeld and Nicholson.

Hobsbawm, E.J., (1977), *The Age of Revolution*, London: Sphere.

Hobsbawm, E.J., (1987), *The Age of Empire*, London: Weidenfeld & Nicolson.

Hobsbawm, E.J., (1991), *Nations and Nationalism since 1780*, Cambridge: Cambridge University Press.

Hobsbawm, E.J., Ranger, T. (eds.), (1983), *The Invention of Tradition*, Cambridge: Cambridge University Press.

Hudson, K., (1975), *A Social History of Museums*, London: Macmillan.

Hudson, K., Nicholls, A., (eds.), (1985), *Directory of Museums and Living Displays*, London: Macmillan.

Hunter, M. (1985), 'The Cabinet Institutionalized: The Royal Society's 'Repository' and its Background', in Impey and MacGregor (1985).

ICOFOM (1986), *Museology and Identity*, ICOFOM Study Series Vols. 10 and 11, Stockholm.

ICOFOM (1988), *Museology and the Developing Countries – Help or Manipulation?*, ICOFOM Study Series Vols. 14 and 15, Stockholm.

Impey, O., MacGregor, A. (eds.), (1985), *The Origin of Museums*, Oxford: Clarendon Press.

Karp, I., Lavine, S.D. (eds.), (1991), *Exhibiting Cultures. The Poetics and Politics of Museum Display*, Washington: Smithsonian Institution.

King, A.D. (ed.), (1991a), *Culture, Globalization and the World System. Contemporary Conditions for the Representation of Identity*, Houndmills: Macmillan.

King, A.D., (1991b), 'Preface', to King (1991a).

Kluge, A.D., (1967), *Etymologisches Wörterbuch der deutschen Sprache*, Berlin: De Gruyter.

Lechner, F., (1989), 'Cultural Aspects of the Modern World-System', in W.H. Swatos (ed.) *Religious Politics in Global and Comparative Perspective*, New York: Greenwood Press.

Lewis, G.D., (1986), 'Introduction' in J.M.A. Thompson (ed.) *Manual of Curatorship: A Guide to Museum Practice*, London: Butterworth-Heinemann.

Lewis, G.D., (1992), 'Museums and their Precursors: A Brief World Survey' in J.M.A. Thompson (ed.), *Manual of Curatorship: A Guide to Museum Practice*, London: Butterworth-Heinemann.

MacGregor, A., (1985), 'The Cabinet of Curiosities in Seventeenth Century Britain', in Impey and MacGregor (1985).

Moore, W.E., (1966), 'Global Sociology: The World as a Singular System', *American Journal of Sociology*, 71.

Mosse, G.L., (1975), *The Nationalization of the Masses*, New York: Howard Ferty.

Museums of the World, (1992), *Handbook of International Documentation and Information*, Vol. 16.

Museum Department of the State Administrative Bureau of Museums and Archaeological Data, (1980), 'Museums in China Today', *Museum 4*.

Mutal, S., (1978), 'Museums and Cultural Heritage', *Museum 2*.

Nan-Young, L., (1986), 'Museums in the Republic of Korea', *Museum 1*.

Nicolas, N., (1988), 'Quelques bonnes vieilles idées . . .', ICOFOM Study Series 14, Stockholm.

Pomian, K., (1990), 'Museum und kulturelles Erbe', in G. Korff, M. Roth (eds.) *Das historische Museum*, Frankfurt: Campus.

Robertson, R., (1989), 'Globalization, Politics, and Religion', in J.A. Beckford, T. Luckmann (eds.), *The Changing Face of Religion*, London: Sage.

Robertson, R., (1990a), 'Mapping the Global Condition: Globalization as the Central Concept', in M. Featherstone (ed.) *Global Culture*, London: Sage.

Robertson, R., (1990b), 'After Nostalgia? Wilful Nostalgia and the Phases of Globalization', in B.S. Turner (ed.), *Theories of Modernity and Postmodernity*, London: Sage.

Robertson, R., (1992), *Globalization. Social Theory and Global Culture*, London: Sage.

Robertson, R., Chirico, J., (1985), 'Humanity, Globalization and Worldwide Religious Resurgence: A Theoretical Exploration', *Sociological Analysis* 46.

Robertson, R., Lechner, F., (1985), 'Modernization, Globalization and the Problem of Culture in World-Systems Theory', *Theory, Culture and Society* 2, 3.

Robertson, R., Nettle, P., (1968), *International Systems and the Modernization of Societies*, London: Faber and Faber.

Scheicher, E., (1979), *Die Kunst- und Wunderkammer der Habsburger*, Vienna: Mot den Edition.

Smidt, D., (1977), 'The national Museum and Art Gallery of Papua New Guinea in Port Moresby', *Museum 4*.

Smith, A.D., (1991), *National Identity*, London: Penguin.

Stölzl, C., (1992), 'Statt eines Vorwortes: Museumsgedanken', in von Plessen (1992).

van Mensch, P., (1988), 'What Contributions has Museology to Offer to the Developing World? Some Remarks', ICOFOM Study Series 14, Stockholm.

Vergo, P., (1989), *New Museology*, London: Reaktion Books.

von Plessen, M.-L. (ed.), (1992), *Die nation und ihre Museen*, Frankfurt: Campus.

Wallerstein, I., (1974), *The Modern World System*, New York: Academic Press.

Wolff, J., (1991), 'The Global and the Specific: Reconciling Conflicting Theories of Culture', in King (1991a).

Yates, F., (1966), *The Art of Memory*, Chicago: Chicago University Press.

How societies remember the past

John Urry

Abstract

It is argued that how societies remember the past should be a key element of social theory. The social sciences should direct attention to time, tradition, and memory. Some implications of developing such notions for heritage are examined. In particular, it is suggested that the implications of heritage are ambiguous and contradictory, especially in the light of arguments about 'travelling cultures' and 'detraditionalization.' The social practices involved in 'reminiscence' are briefly elaborated.

Introduction

Why is the past of any interest to us? Why do we look back? Since we can do nothing about everything that occurred before the present why is the past of any relevance? Why do societies not simply look to the 'future' and attempt to influence that in socially benign ways?

These are challenging questions about which the social sciences have typically not given very good answers. This is mainly because the question as to how societies collectively remember has typically not been central to social science concerns. And yet there is something strange about this. Much sociological theorizing has been concerned with the problem of order; and this is so in both the functionalist-consensus and Marxist-conflict models of society. Both models presuppose a process of reproducing social relations from the past to the present and on to the future; and both attempt to detail some of the processes by which historic norms and values persist and effect order/hegemony in the present.

© The Editorial Board of The Sociological Review 1996. Published by Blackwell Publishers, 108 Cowley Road, Oxford OX4 1JF, UK and 238 Main Street, Cambridge, MA 02142, USA.

However, what is lacking in such accounts is a clear and coherent account of just how societies do in fact 'remember' the past. There is little analysis of the precise mechanisms by which societies remember and incorporate the past into the present. How do such mechanisms actually work and what are the contradictions inherent in that process? What are the different mechanisms by which this remembering occurs in different kinds of society? How do these remembering processes within different societies do their work, not just at the level of ideas but of bodies, not just of ideologies but of practices, not just of images but of interpellated 'temporal' subjects?

And how are these processes of collective remembering changing in the contemporary world – a world in which the borders by which societies were kept apart are increasingly criss-crossed by ever-speeding flows of images, information, ideas and people (Lash and Urry, 1994; Rojek, 1995)? Such flows carry collective memories and cultures and consume the memories of other societies. These flows generate new hybrid cultures which are largely unremembered within existing institutional representations of the past. And what does all this do to those institutions which in western societies have been given the particular tasks of representing that past, such as galleries, museums, books, the law and so on? There may still be buildings carrying the name 'museum' but do they remain the same kind of entity? As societies appear now to be collectively remembering in quite different ways so the apparently same institutions are being transformed; as various chapters in this collection interestingly detail.

In this chapter I will stand back from such specific changes in museums and galleries and reflect more generally on how we should analyse those mechanisms by which societies remember the past. In particular I will argue that the failure to address this issue in any depth stems from the inadequacy of most attempts to theorize time, tradition and memory in the social sciences. I shall briefly outline the 'temporal turn' in the social sciences (see Adam, 1995). Following Mead I shall argue that how societies remember the past particularly reflects transformations in and of the present; that there is a need to develop a 'philosophy of the present' (1959). If we turn then to the present in those contemporary 'western' societies characterized by increasing rates of mobility of people, ideas and information, then we can see a clear shift in the construction of the past, from an auratic history to a commodified heritage, but the implications of such 'heritage' are ambiguous and contradictory, especially when what is turned into heritage originates from locations outside the 'centre' of a given society. As Samuel argues there are in any society different 'theatres of memory' (1994). More generally, it will be shown that global flows across national boundaries endlessly produce new centres and new peripheries, and these undermine apparently timeless and absolute traditions (Lash and Urry, 1994; Heelas, Lash, Morris, 1995). Finally, I examine some of the implications of travelling cultures for existing museums and galleries (see Clifford, 1992). There are a number of putative processes of 'de-traditionalization' which disrupt the transformation of tradition into a museum or gallery collection. Such institutions are caught in a double movement. On the one hand, they are becoming an integral part of the leisure and travel 'industry', which itself increasingly generates globalized mobility across borders. And on the other, that very industry is itself becoming 'decentred', transformed from a specific set of economic and social practices into a de-differentiated element of post-culture. There is a 'decentring' of tourism and leisure at the very moment that museums and galleries become part of that very 'industry', and indeed that the industry is itself becoming institutionalized within the academy (see Rojek, 1995, on the decentring of leisure more generally).

There are complex issues raised here and my treatment of many of them will be necessarily brief. The chapter is organized into three further sections: time; heritage and memory; and a brief conclusion.

Time

First then, in recent years there has been a (long awaited) temporal turn in the social sciences. The following are some of the key features of this discovery of 'time'. There are now said to be various senses of time and not just the objective matrix of clock time. Thus time is not to be viewed simply as a neutral and objective medium which permits comparison and equivalent movement across space. Moreover, clock time itself is seen as a human construction and is not inherent in or essential to nature. But that clock time is a human construction is not something which the social sciences have themselves sufficiently recognized. They have failed to appreciate that the 'times of nature', just like those of human society, are in fact characterized by movement, quality and direction, not just by reversibility and stability. Simultaneously though it has been shown by various studies that over the past two centuries clock time has been a crucial element in the very subjugation of 'nature' by human societies. Overall the new studies of time show that there is no common denominator or measure of time which is neutral, original and privileged. There needs to be a deconstruction of the very idea of 'historical time' and notions of linear causation, and its replacement by a multiplicity of locally specific and contingent 'ph(r)ase times' (Ermath, 1995; Adam, 1990, 1995; Lash and Urry, 1994; Rifkin, 1987; Nowotny, 1994).

Part moreover of what is involved in this temporal turn has been the rediscovery of early key authors and texts which elaborated more phenomenological approaches to the understanding of time (or durée), approaches which until recently were not really incorporated into the social sciences. These approaches did not presume that objective clock or historical time exhausted our understanding of the nature of time. Especially important here was Heidegger's ontology of being in which time was seen as expressing the very nature of human subjectivity (1962; see Giddens, 1981). More specifically Bergson argued that time should not be conceived spatially and that memory is to be viewed as itself temporal, as the piling up of the past on the past which has the effect that no element is simply 'present' but is changed as new elements are accumulated from the past (1910; Game, 1995).

Rather similarly Mead argued that time is embedded within actions, events and roles and is not to be viewed as an abstract framework (1959; see Adam, 1990). Mead regarded the abstract time of clocks and calendars as nothing more than a manner of speaking. What is real for Mead is the 'present'; what is thus the past is constructed in the paramount reality of the present. Each moment of the past is constructed anew. So there is no past out there or back there. There is only the present, in the context of which the past is being continually re-created. It is emergence which transforms the past and gives sense to the future. Such emergence stems from the interactions between people and the environment, humans being seen by Mead as indissolubly part of nature (see Macnaghten and Urry, 1995). Thus while the present is viewed as real, the past and future are ideational or what we would now say representational. The past is endlessly constructed in and through the present. And we thus add in parenthesis, that all representations of the past involve remaking in and through the present; and this is not true only of the so-called 'heritage industry'.

It was further argued by Bergson that time is inextricably bound up with the body. People do not therefore think time in some abstract way but experience it sensuously, qualitatively. Memories are embodied and involve an array of different senses. This was captured by Proust when he talks of our arms and legs being full of torpid memories (cited Lowenthal, 1985:203; and see Clifford, 1992).

However, there are few if any efforts to explore the implications of this for the social sciences. A noteworthy effort is Connerton's *How Societies Remember* (1989). He distinguishes between incorporating and inscribing practices and considers how memory is sedimented in even the bodily postures of those living in particular societies. Incorporating practices are messages which are imparted by means of people's current bodily activity, the transmission only occurring when their bodies are co-present. By contrast inscribing practices are the modern devices for storing and retrieving information, such as photographs, print, alphabets, indexes, tapes, date bases and so on. Such practices trap and store information long after the human organism has stopped informing. He argues that the transition from an oral to a literate culture involves a transition from incorporating practices to inscribing practices and this in turn depends upon various novel kinds of literacy. But his main point is to emphasize that part of what is passed on, and part of what does the passing on, is a set of bodily procedures, techniques and gestures (and see Bourdieu, 1990:66–79, here). The past gets passed on to us not merely in what we think or do but literally in how we do it: how we sit when we write, how we stand, how we eat, how we travel and so on. There are ways of sitting and standing, looking and lounging, ruminating and recollecting, that are passed on through either incorporating or inscribing practices.

The main difficulty with this formulation is that he overly concentrates upon how societies in general pass on bodily memories. Although this effectively brings out certain aspects of the nature of memory, there are many other aspects of the social nature of memory which this ignores. It remains at too general a level of analysis. There are various more localized processes to note (Middleton and Edwards, 1990). First, it seems that people remember together as much as they remember individually. Thus memories of a shared memory of an event, place or person involves cooperative work often in quite localised settings. There are complex rhetorics involved in the discourses surrounding memory-work. At the same time there are forms of institutional commemoration in societies which can silence alternative memories of the past (especially those of women, of the working class, of the young, of subordinate ethnicities and so on). Indeed forgetting is as socially structured as is the process of remembering.

Memories moreover are often organized around diverse artefacts such as rooms, buildings, furniture, objects, patina, photographs and so on. These often provoke memories, often in forms which are unpredictable and disruptive. Radley summarizes these kinds of artefactual memory and suggests that:

> remembering is something which occurs in a world of things,
> as well as words, and that artefacts play a central role in the
> memories of cultures and individuals . . . In the very variabil-
> ity of objects, in the ordinariness of their consumption and in
> the sensory richness of relationships people enjoy through
> them, they are fitted to be later re-framed as material images
> for reflection and recall (1990:57–8).

Artefacts are sensed through our bodies but how this sensing occurs and the impact that it has results from complex, historically changing processes of social production, communication and signification. Samuel delightfully brings out some recent characteristics of how objects are found attractive in his analysis of 'retrochic'; the objective being 'to age or "distress" what would otherwise appear brand new' (1994:83). He also particularly brings out the extraordinary attraction of the 'return to brick' in the past two or so decades; how the mellow brick symbolises the rejection of the vulgar modernisms of the 1950s and 1960s and a nostalgic return to the supposedly warm communities which existed before planning and modernization (signified by concrete) took their toll.

The complex significance of objects and buildings for our memories of place and identity raise many issues, which can be best approached via Benjamin's analysis of reading the city (1979; Buck-Morss, 1989). This is for him not a matter of intellectual or positivistic observation. Rather it involves fantasy, wish processes and dreams. The city is the repository of people's memories and of the past; and is a receptacle of cultural symbols. Such memories are embedded in buildings – but they can acquire meanings different from those intended by the architect. They can reveal collective myths which need to be unlocked and undermined. Conflicting elements can be brought together. Even derelict buildings may leave traces of such myths and reveal memories, dreams and myths of previous periods (see Wright, 1992, on a Benjaminesque 'journey through [English] ruins').

Benjamin particularly brings out the similarities between artistic perception and the reading of the urban text. He suggests that buildings are normally appreciated in passing, in a state of 'distraction', as people are moving on elsewhere. This is by contrast with people's 'concentrated' absorption of paintings in a gallery. This distracted perception helps to disrupt conservative cultural traditions. The flâneur (and not the flâneuse) wanders around the city sampling life in a distracted and unpremeditated fashion (see Wolff, 1990, chap. 3). The voyeuristic and distracted nature of the encounter with the urban means that memories of the past can be ignited by current events; with such distracted perception that there can be a chance linking of past and present events and hence the undermining of past traditions. There are moreover new places, such as the expositions in Paris, which Benjamin saw as transforming visitors to the level of the commodity, as they entered a phantasmagorical world.

Heritage and memory

Benjamin's brilliant analysis of the 'dialectic of seeing' raises a host of pertinent issues which can be formulated as follows. How much are memories in a society hegemonic and how much are they contested; to what degree are memories visual or are other senses involved; to what degree are memories provoked by artefacts and if so how does this form of memory work; and what role in collective remembering is played by non-hegemonic collective enthusiasms? In this section I shall briefly consider these points in relationship to the ways in which societies organize their collective memories of their particular 'histories'. I shall deal with British debates and examples.

The key texts in the recent rich debates in Britain include Wright's excavation of the nature of oldness in an old country (1985); Lowenthal's magisterial analysis of how societies regard their pasts (1985); Hewison's tirade against the heritage-isation of

Britain (1987); Samuel's robust attack on the heritage baiters through delineating a different geneaology of 'resurrectionism' (1994); and the dissection by McCrone, Morris and Kiely of the ambiguous significance within Britain of Scottish rather than English heritage (1995).

Lowenthal summarizes what is seen as widespread in Britain, namely a pervasive sense of nostalgia:

> Once the menace of a small elite, nostalgia now attracts or afflicts most levels of society. Ancestor-hunters search archives for their roots; millions throng to historic houses; antiques engross the middle class; souvenirs food consumer markets . . . 'A growing rebellion against the present, and an increased longing for the past', are said to exemplify the post-war mood (1985:11).

There are a number of aspects here which have been identified elsewhere in the heritage literature: the loss of trust of the future as it is undermined by what I would term 'instantaneous time' and the proliferation of incalculable risks; the view that contemporary social life is deeply disappointing and that there really was a golden age in the past; the increased aesthetic sensibility to signs or the patina of oldness, to old places, crafts, houses, countryside and so on; the attractive representation of the past through a heritage-look suitable for visual consumption; the interpretation of that past through an artefactual history which partly obscures the social relations and struggles which underlay that past; the belief that the past is to be understood through pastiched images and stereotypes which convert that past into simple narratives and spectacles; the belief that history is turned into heritage and made safe, sterile and shorn of danger, subversion and seduction; and the overall loss of belief in a historical subject which in seeking its own redemption will bring about a universal redemption of humankind (see sources above as well as Vergo, 1989; Fowler, 1992; Urry, 1990; Corner and Harvey, 1991; Roth, 1992).

McCrone, Morris and Kiely suggest that these various arguments can be reconceptualized into four main themes (1995:17). First, within rapidly expanding sites of rural and industrial heritage there is the commodification of history, the loss of authority of the past and its auratic quality, and the replacement of scholarly history by a visual artefactual heritage (Hewison, 1987). Second, there is the tendency for such sites to be disproportionately consumed by the service class, or more generally by the middle classes, whose habituses are remaking both urban and rural places (see Urry, 1995b; Urry, 1995a). Third, there are presumed political effects of heritage which in reinforcing a certain view of the past are necessarily conservative and deflect attention from the possibilities of change in the future (Wright, 1985). And fourth, heritage is said to function as ideology in which heritage sites are merely one of a number of simulated environments which are hyper-real, a depthless copy where there is no real or authentic referent (Eco, 1987; Baudrillard, 1988).

Although it is important to separate out these different themes there are some general points to be made about 'heritage' which will hopefully bring out the parallels between the heritage industry and more general cultural developments. The first point is that we are not well-informed as to how people's popular memories, of a place, industry, or social institution, are stimulated, enthused, and then organized into a potential documentation of remembrance. Of what media is that documentation comprised and what relationship do those 'documents' have to the places or events or activities that supposedly took place 'in the past'? How is the initial enthusiasm turned into a social practice? And how is such documentation converted into a commodified site, a site which captures a share of a particular market, because it represents some national, or regional or local achievement? More generally then, we can ask what are the conditions of existence of particular discourses and practices of heritage? One of the few such studies is Macdonald's account of the establishment of the heritage centre of Aros on the Isle of Skye (1996). She describes the nature of Gaelic revivalism and how this is seen by young upwardly mobile Gaelic-speakers as compatible with commercial enterprise. Setting up such a heritage centre is viewed by revivialists as a way of strengthening and not diluting Gaelic language and culture. The concept of 'cultural tourism' is employed to indicate tourism 'for the people' of Skye. And the account presented is an alternative to the romantic heritage account of Scottish history. So Aros partly develops out of Gaelic enthusiasm and of the desire to tell a different story of the Highlands, but one which is at the same time commercially profitable.

There are therefore various readings possible of the same heritage. Extreme versions of the heritage-critique presuppose a somewhat condescending, uniform and one-dimensional reading of such sites (see Bagguley, Mark Lawson, Shapiro, Urry, Walby,

Warde 1990: chap. 5; Urry, 1995a, on examples from the north west of England). These interpretations rest upon too simple a contrast between real history and false heritage, implying that those people who do not visit heritage sites acquire historical understanding through the reading and understanding of significant historical texts. This is obviously false and overstates the textual basis of people's memory practices.

Indeed it can be presumed that even the most apparently unambiguous of museums or heritage centres will be 'read' in different ways by different visitors. There is no evidence that sites are uniformly read and passively accepted by visitors. Macdonald shows in the case of an exhibition at the Science Museum that visitors frame and interpret the visit in ways not expected or planned by its designers (1995:21). They connect together exhibits not intended to be linked, they read the exhibits as prescriptive when they are not intended to be, and they mostly do not describe the exhibition in ways that the designers had intended.

Nevertheless in general we know relatively little about just how people do use and respond to heritage sites (although see Loomis, 1987, for an exception). One small piece of research was conducted at the Albert Dock in Liverpool. Mellor argued on the basis of this qualitative study that people actively use such sites as bases for reminiscence: 'as the point of departure for their own memories of a way of life in which economic hardship and exploited labour were offset by a sense of community, neighbourliness and mutuality' (1991:100). In the following I shall suggest that 'reminiscence' is indeed a major 'practice' at such sites, and that in order to comprehend how societies do indeed remember, we should develop a theory of reminiscence. Performances and heritage can clearly develop a multi-vocality.

Kershaw argues that reminiscence is not the same as nostalgia and indeed may offer considerable insight into recent history (1993). He talks of it allowing a kind of collective democratization of history memory. There is a 'reminiscence peak' in the more elderly who enjoy enhanced longer term memory. And with the 'greying' of the population this kind of reminiscence becomes more widespread and socially influential. But his most significant claim is that reminiscing involves performance – both by those 'real' performers who are there to stimulate memories, and by visitors who have to work often cooperatively with others in order to produce memories. Kershaw thus emphasizes the performativity of reminiscence which is by no means an apparently passive process of consumption. In some ways it is similar to the variety of other spatial practices which take place at tourist sites; these include walking, talking, sitting, photographing and so on (see Edensor, 1995). What then are the characteristic features of reminiscence as a spatial practice?

First, it involves a concentrated and not a distracted viewing of all kinds of objects and performances. There is a clear understanding that actors are performing; or that the objects on view have been placed in a simulated environment or are copies or fragments of the historical record. Just like an audience at a play visitors are reflexively aware that what they see has been 'staged'. One effect of such reminiscing is the reawakening of dreams. And these can be personal (what one might have done, if only . . .); or focused around the neighbourhood or locality where one was born or grew up; or focused on a broader collective interest, such as class, gender, generation, ethnic grouping. Seeing certain scenes or artefacts functions to reawaken repressed desires and thereby to connect past and present. It is also to remember how some collective dreams have failed or have faded from memory – while others have at least been partly realized (material abundance, educational qualifications, the opportunity to travel and so on). To reminisce is to open up possibilities of what might have been, of how events or relationships or careers, could have turned out differently. So while visiting museums and heritage sites is to experience an essentially artefactual history, it is not one which is necessarily received passively. To reminisce is collectively to effect a performance. There is no single or simple history conveyed through the performances of heritage.

It thus follows from this that the so-called heritage industry entails processes of memorizing and reminiscence that are not so different from those routinely involved in how cultures 'proper' remember the past in order to interpret the future. There are a number of points to note about this. First, cultures do not exist in a pure state, hermetically sealed from each other and possessing a clear and distinct essence. Indeed the culture which gets produced and consumed by visitors to a heritage site may be no less 'authentic' than any other cultural experience. The wide-ranging work on post-colonial cultures suggests that all cultures are in a sense inauthentic and contrived. They all get remade as a result of the flows of people and images across national borders, whether such flows result from colonial administrations, work-induced migrations, individual travel or mass tourism. Post-colonial societies are necessarily 'impure', resulting from both the particular sets of indigenous peoples the colonizer chose to administer as a single colonial territory; as well as from the flows of colonizers who passed through that society over the colonial period (Gilroy, 1993; Bhabha, 1990).

Further, cultural participants do not simply, straightforwardly and unambiguously adopt a culture as such. Knowing a culture involves work, of memory, interpretation and reconstruction. And most significantly for the argument here it almost always involves travel. Edensor brings out the exceptional levels of mobility in 'traditional India', such mobility being central to the maintenance of the diverse cultures of that 'society' (1995). Such travel will occur to the culture's sacred sites (in the case of 'English culture', to Buckingham Palace, Anfield, Albert Hall); to the location of central written or visual texts (Westminster Abbey, the Lake District and the Lake Poets, Stratford-upon-Avon); to places where key events took place (Hastings, the Blitz, War of the Roses); to see particularly noteworthy individuals or their documentary record (the monarch, 'Shakespeare', the Beatles); and to view other cultures so as to reinforce one's own cultural attachments (rest of 'Europe', former colonies which demonstrate the benign effects of Empire; see Urry, 1995a, for examples of most of these).

And in the case of many cultures, even that of well-established ones such as the 'English', the travel involved will entail the crossing of national frontiers. Indeed for some cultures the sacred places that have to be visited will be located in many different 'societies' and thus there will be even more work involved in reconstructing the sense of that culture. The importance of such patterns of mobility across borders are most marked in the case of diasporic cultures which entail the reconceptualization of the very sense of what is a social group's 'heritage' (Hall, 1990). Such cultures cannot persist without a great deal of travel; Clifford suggests these involve 'discrepant cosmopolitanisms' (1992:108). Modes of institutional commemoration across societal borders are crucial in attracting members from elsewhere and representing such a culture's often precarious achievements.

These points thus all demonstrate that travel is integral to the understanding of cultural process. Travel is symptomatic of an increasingly mobile society and should not be viewed as a marginal or peripheral activity. It is central to contemporary culture rather than something on its margins, as somehow less important than fixity. Apparently distinct cultures travel, people travel and, says Clifford, theories also result from travel (1992).

Moreover, within cultural analysis, metaphors of travel, or narratives of home and displacement, of borders and crossings, have become exceptionally widespread (see Wolff 1993). Deleuze employs the metaphor of the nomadic subject (1977); others of cultures being 'on the road' (a kind of 'Easy Rider' view of culture). Clifford invokes the hotel lobby as a site of travel encounters. He argues for that chronotype, a setting of time and space in a particular form, in preference to those which imply the stasis of particular fixed points, such as the home or dwelling (1992:101). However, he also notes that this chronotype of the hotel is itself rather nostalgic and he goes onto recommend Morris's chronotype of the motel (1988). The motel has no real lobby, it is tied into the network of highways, it functions to relay people rather than to provide settings for coherent human subjects, and it demolishes the sense of place and locale.

Nevertheless all of these chronotypes involve some distortion of the nature of travel. Wolff criticises the masculinist character of many of these travel metaphors (1993); while Clifford struggles unsuccessfully 'to free the related term "travel" from a history of European, literary, male, bourgeois, scientific, heroic, recreational, meanings and practices' (1992:106). This point leads us back to the issue of heritage but from a rather different direction. I have so far mainly talked of 'societies' remembering – but of course societies are composed of diverse social groups. It is clear that the 'heritage' that mostly gets remembered is that of élites or ruling classes. It is their houses and estates that have been 'saved for the nation' by the National Trust and other preservationist organizations (see Wright 1985; this is less the case in Scotland, Wales and northern Ireland). This produces a one-sided history which under-represents the poor, those who lived in the north, women, slaves, the disabled, the middle classes, convicts, industrial workers, in-migrants, Scottish, Welsh and people living in northern Ireland; and it conceals the social relationships of domination by which that ruling class exerted power.

However, the recent mushrooming of heritage has in necessarily uneven ways done something to redress this imbalance. There has been the identification of a large array of hidden histories and the assertion that all heritages have some merit (this causes difficulties in Germany with regard to Nazi heritage; see Huyssen, 1995). The post-modern undermining of grand narratives has authorized diverse histories and in the British case has begun to de-legitimate the anglocentric masculinist, home counties vision of Britain and British history. Hence, when John Major waxes lyrical about how in fifty years time:

> Britain will still be the country of long shadows on county grounds [male sport played in England], warm beer [male drink], invincible green suburbs [home counties housing type], dog lovers [??], and old maids bicycling to holy communion' [a patronising term for women who lack a 'man'],

he appears unaware of the diverse cultural currents which travel through any contemporary society, even one with such an apparent sense of tradition as Britain/England. His statement might be seen as a valiant, yet misguided, attempt to stem post-modernity, de-traditionalization and the cross-border flows of culture that Thatcherite Conservatism did much to enhance. He goes on bravely (if foolishly) to assert that 'Britain will survive unamendable in all essentials' (cited in McCrone, Morris, Kiely, 1995:23–4).

So part of what has generated a much more diverse set of heritages has been various post-modern cultural shifts which have been well-summarized by Rojek, most strikingly in his account of 'necro-fever' (1995). But there have been four other sources of new forms of heritage. First, there has been the extraordinarily rapid restructuring of the economy which has generated derelict areas and buildings which have nevertheless occupied a distinct place in the history of a given place or industry. Such empty buildings often possessed what is viewed as the attractive patina of age. Second, a number of companies have developed the capital, skills and expertise to re-represent buildings, areas and places and their often hidden histories. Third, many local authorities have developed a tourism (rather than a leisure) strategy in order to find sources of new employment; and heritage has been a relatively uncontroversial area to expand (partly because local people also may appear to benefit from such developments). And fourth, there has been a proliferation of social groups who have sought through their enthusiasm to preserve aspects of 'their' history (see Urry 1990, 1995a, for more detail). It is the last of these processes, the popular sources of heritage, that I will now consider in a little more detail (see particularly, Samuel, 1994).

A further aspect of what has been termed 'de-traditionalization' is how it 'forces' individuals and groups to seek to establish their 'own' institutions which are relatively separate from the wider society. It establishes 'new sociations' (see Hetherington, 1990). These new sociations are not like those of traditional communities since they are joined out of choice and people are free to leave. They are akin to Maffesoli's neo-tribes – flexible, elastic, semi-detached collectivities which cluster in intense bursts to develop or consume some enthusiasm (1990). People remain members of such loose-knit groupings because of the emotional satisfaction that they derive from the pursuit of common goals or experiences. Membership is from choice and many people will enter and exit from such sociations with considerable rapidity. Such sociations provide important sites through which new kinds of identity can be experimented with. They may empower people, they provide relatively safe sites for identity-testing, and they can provide a context for the learning of new skills.

Such sociations can be classified along a number of dimensions: the degree of decentralization of power from the centre; the degree of formal specification of the organizational structure; the level and forms of participation at the local level; the types of appropriate action that the membership may engage in; and the degree to which the membership is reflexive about whether the organization is appropriate for the realization of its ends (see Urry, 1995a:221). A particular realm of such sociations is concerned with heritage and the environment. Examples include conservation groups, steam preservation societies, bird watching organizations, amenity societies, enthusiasts for particular technologies, countryside protection societies, campaigns to save particular buildings and so on.

These groups have also been conceptualized by Hoggett and Bishop as 'collective enthusiasms' (1986; Moorhouse, 1991; Abercrombie, 1994:53–5). They have a number of characteristics: there is a great deal of 'work' involved although it is normally done in people's formal 'leisure' time; the members work for each other through a complex system of mutual aid; they are self-organized and are particularly resentful of outside experts instructing them how to act; they produce a large array of outputs many of which are consumed by the membership itself; their activity is not passive and individualistic but involves communication and emotional satisfaction; there is strong resistance to commodification; and much emphasis is placed upon acquiring arcane forms of knowledge and skill.

John Urry

Elsewhere I have suggested that many of these groups operate with a 'glacial' sense of time, to favour the very long term of many generations, as opposed to the 'instantaneous time' of an increasingly marketized post-modern economy and culture (1994). These groups of 'collective enthusiasts' will thus often view their preservation/conservation activities as part of a much larger struggle to challenge a notion of time in which change and transformation are far too short term and results in an over-rapid destruction of buildings, traditions, landscapes, street layouts, technologies, patterns of work and so on.

Useful accounts of the popular bases of conservation and heritage are found elsewhere (Wright, 1985; Hewison, 1987; Walsh, 1992; Samuel, 1994). These sources demonstrate that much of the early conservation movement in Britain was plebian in character, concerned to preserve railway engines, industrial archaeology sites, steam traction engines and so on. This plebian character has partly continued with the attempts to preserve derelict coalmines in Wales; this resulted from pressure from local groups of miners and families who sought to hold onto aspects of 'their' history. There has even been a campaign in Lancashire to conserve a slag heap from an extinct coal mine.

One of the first campaigns more directed to the built environment and resulting from a wider social base was that in 1962 to conserve the arch at Euston station. This was followed by many other conservation conflicts, particular in smaller towns and cities and of course in the countryside. Interestingly, of the conservation groups now operating in Britain, over half have been formed since 1970. By the early 1990s it is calculated that one in ten people are members of an environmental/conservation organization; nearly a quarter are active greens; and at least one-third of letters to MPs relate to such issues (Urry, 1995a:223). And of course the largest mass organization in Britain is the National Trust with over 2 million members, many of whom are particularly concerned with campaigns to preserve what they view as 'local' heritage. Samuel interestingly discusses 'do-it-yourself' curating and the proliferation of mini-museums (1994:27).

The significance of heritage is given a particular inflection in Scotland where its 'branding' has been recently examined by McCrone, Morris and Kiely (1995). They researched the life membership of the National Trust for Scotland and conclude that Scottish heritage is in fact a significant element in the development of cultural nationalism. They argue that heritage is seen by their respondents as involving a strong sense of lineage and inheritance, demonstrating what I termed above a glacial sense of time (Urry, 1994). Heritage has thus an identity-conferring status. Moreover, most of the membership of the organization are politically Conservative and anti-nationalist; and yet they overwhelmingly see themselves as Scots who strongly distinguish between English and Scottish heritage. For most of them conserving Scottish heritage is a centrally important enthusiasm. McCrone, Morris, Kiely thus write of the membership of the National Trust of Scotland:

> There is a rich network of local activity groups, travel outings, and active participation in heritage conservation through voluntary labour. What is available to life members is a coordinated lifestyle achieved through association . . . 'a timeless organisation upholding traditional values' (1995:155).

They conclude by arguing that heritage carries particularly strong resonance in Scotland because it is a nation without a state. Heritage in Scotland is a powerful source of cultural nationalism, even amongst those who on the face of it are most committed to maintaining the Union with England. Heritage thus in the Scottish context occupies a different role to the one characterized by many of the heritage-critics who are concerned with the English context. The key then for the post-modern cultural performer is to offer strategies of resistance and to emphasize traces of non-dominant cultures which fit awkwardly with nationally dominant cultures.

Conclusion

I have thus argued that how societies remember the past is of great importance to social theory, especially to any theory which embraces the temporal turn. In developing a theory of 'remembering', attention should be directed to the particular mechanisms by which it occurs in different societies and the changing hierarchy of such social modes of social remembering. I have also suggested that with the increasing flows of images, ideas, information and people across borders, so the processes of social remembering become even more disjointed, speeded up, hybridized and fractured. In the context of a critique of time, I argue that heritage is of ambiguous significance. My main point is to demonstrate the significance of travel for cultures and cultures for travel, to elaborate the concept of 'travelling cultures' in the context of some British debates about heritage.

Particularly important in affecting the role of museums in such a society are three processes. First, there is the undermining of many auratic and authoritative traditions such that there is no remaining single, autonomous essence to 'British' culture; there are many 'cultures' operating in Britain. Second, there is the proliferation of many new heritage sites, which are often started and run by enthusiasts who contest once-dominant traditions, enthusiasts who in a sense are helping to remake civil society (as Macdonald, 1996, shows in the case of Gaelicness). And third, all such museum/heritage sites are subject to the homogenizing power of the market and concerned to position themselves in an increasingly global and rapidly changing market-place. Great national collections and local collections developed by enthusiasts compete as elements of a putative global leisure industry – where what is in fashion is subject to enormously rapid changes. The global market-place and post-modern culture serve to dissolve the distinctiveness of both 'culture' and 'leisure' (see Rojek, 1995, on the 'decentring of leisure').

Samuel usefully brings out some of the implications of these processes for history and memory (1994). History he argues has never been simply the prerogative of the historian. Popular memories entail collecting various kinds of evidence. Key participants in this historically have been a huge array of different kinds of people: collectors, bibliographers, librarians, aesthetes, illustrators, antiquarians, musicologists, educators and so on. And in the current documentation of the past he argues that 'television ought to have pride of place' (1994:13). He details the exceptional significance of images of the past in current television programming. This can present a world of 'golden ages' but also a world of phenomenally rapid social change (through what I term instantaneous time; Urry, 1994). Television also presents a world of legends as well as 'real' history – both are equally relevant to identifying how societies remember their past. He summarizes the way in which a currently dominant 'theatre of memory' functions:

> Memory-keeping is a function increasingly assigned to the electronic media, while a new awareness of the artifice of representation casts a cloud of suspicion over the documentation of the past (Samuel, 1994:25).

This 'electronification' of memory provides another twist in understanding how societies do indeed remember their past within an extraordinarily changing present. Huyssen indeed argues that the 'current obsession with memory' is a general sign of the crisis of temporality (1995:7). He talks of the collapsing belief in possible futures with the frenetic pace of capitalist culture, the television politics of quick oblivion and the dissolution of public space in ever more channels of instant entertainment. The effect of the collapsing future results in a kind of collective amnesia, at the very same time that we are obsessed with memory. He suggests that the latter is no longer a vital and energizing antidote to the 'iron cage' but is rather 'an attempt to slow down information processing, to resist the dissolution of time . . . to claim some anchoring space in a world of puzzling and often threatening heterogeneity, non-synchronicity and information overload' (1995:7). Museums then, as he says, represent a chance to 'escape from amnesia', to develop what elsewhere I refer to as 'glacial time' (Urry, 1994).

Acknowledgments

I am very grateful for the comments and advice of Dede Boden, Baz Kershaw, Celia Lury, Caroline Schwaller, and Nigel Thrift.

Bibliography

Abercrombie, N., (1994), 'Authority and consumer society', in R. Keat, N. Whiteley, N. Abercrombie (eds), *Enterprise Culture*, London: Routledge.

Adam, B., (1990), *Time and Social Theory*, Cambridge: Polity.

Adam, B., (1995), *Timewatch*, Cambridge: Polity.

Bagguley, P., Mark Lawson, J., Shapiro, D., Urry, J., Walby, S., Warde, A., (1990), *Restructuring: Place, Class and Gender*, London: Sage.

Baudrillard, J., (1988), *America*, London: Verso.

Bergson, H., (1910), *Time and Free Will*, London: Swan Sonnenschein.

Bhabha, H. (ed.), (1990), *Nation and Narration*, London: Routledge.

Bourdieu, P., (1990), *The Logic of Practice*, Cambridge: Polity.

Buck-Morss, C., (1989), *The Dialectic of Seeing: Walter Benjamin and the Arcades Project*, Cambridge, Mass.: MIT Press.

Clifford, J., (1992), 'Travelling cultures', in L. Grossberg, G. Nelson, P. Teichler (eds), *Cultural Studies*, London: Routledge.

Connerton, P., (1989), *How Societies Remember*, Cambridge: Cambridge University Press.

Corner, J. and Harvey, S. (eds), (1991), *Enterprise and Heritage*, London: Routledge.

Deleuze, G., (1977), 'Nomad thought', in D. Allison (ed.), *The New Nietzsche*, New York: Delta.

Eco, U., (1987), *Travels in Hyperreality*, London: Picador.

Edensor, T., (1995), *Tourism and the Taj Mahal*, PhD, Lancaster University (in preparation).

Ermath, E.D., (1995), 'Ph(r)ase time: chaos theory and postmodern reports on knowledge', *Time and Society*, 1:91–110.

Fowler, P. J., (1992), *The Past in Contemporary Society: then, now*, London: Routledge.

Game, A., (1995), 'Time, space, memory, with reference to Bachelard', in M. Featherstone, S. Lash and R. Robertson (eds), *Global Modernities*, London: Sage.

Giddens, A., (1981), *A Contemporary Critique of Historical Materialism*, London: Macmillan.

Gilroy, P., (1993), *The Black Atlantic: modernity and double consciousness*, London: Verso.

Hall, S., (1990), 'Cultural identity and diaspora', in J. Rutherford (ed.), *Identity, Community, Culture, Difference*, London: Lawrence and Wishart.

Heelas, P., Lash, S., Morris, P. (eds), (1995), *De-traditionalisation*, London: Sage.

Heidegger, M., (1962), *Being and Time*, Oxford: Blackwell.

Hetherington, K., (1994), 'The contemporary significance of Schmalenbach's concept of the Bund', *The Sociological Review*, 42:1–25.

Hewison, R., (1987), *The Heritage Industry*, London: Methuen.

Hoggett, P. and Bishop, J., (1986), *Organizing around enthusiasms: patterns of mutual aid in leisure*, London: Comedia.

Huyssen, A., (1995), *Twilight Memories*, London: Routledge.

Kershaw, B., (1993), 'Reminiscing history: memory, performance, empowerment', paper given to De-traditionalisation Conference, Lancaster University.

Lash, S. and Urry, J., (1994), *Economies of Signs and Space*, London: Sage.

Loomis, R., (1987), *Museum Visitor Evaluation*, Nashville, Tenn.: American Association for State and Local History.

Lowenthal, D., (1985), *The Past is a Foreign Country*, Cambridge: Cambridge University Press.

Macdonald, S., (1995), 'Consuming science: public knowledge and the dispersed politics of reception among museum visitors', *Media, Culture and Society*, 17:13–29.

Macdonald, S., (1996), 'A people's story: heritage, identity and authenticity', in C. Rojek and J. Urry (eds), *Touring Cultures*, London: Routledge.

Macnaghten, P. and Urry, J., (1995), 'Towards a sociology of nature', *Sociology*, 29: 203–20.

Maffesoli, M., (1990), 'Post-modern sociality', *Telos*, 85: 89–92.

McCrone, D., Morris, A., Kiely, R., (1995), *Scotland – the Brand*, Edinburgh: Edinburgh University Press.

Mead, G.H., (1959), *The Philosophy of the Present*, La Salle, Ill.: Open Court.

Mellor, A., (1991), 'Enterprise and heritage in the Dock', in J. Corner and S. Harvey (eds), *Enterprise and Heritage*, London: Routledge.

Middleton, D. and Edwards, D. (eds), (1990), *Collective Remembering*, London: Sage.

Moorhouse, B., (1991), *Driving Ambitions*, Manchester: Manchester University Press.

Morris, M., (1988), 'At Henry Parkes Motel', *Cultural Studies*, 2:1–47.

Nowotny, H., (1994), *Time*, Cambridge: Polity.

Radley, A., (1990), 'Artefacts, memory and a sense of the past', in D. Middleton and D. Edwards (eds), *Collective Remembering*, London: Sage.

Rifkin, J., (1987), *Time Wars*, New York: Henry Holt.

Rojek, C., (1995), *Decentring Leisure*, London: Sage.

Roth, M., (1992), 'The time of nostalgia: medicine, history and normality in 19th century France', *Time and Society*, 2: 271–86.

Samuel, R., (1994), *Theatres of Memory*, London: Verso.

Urry, J., (1990), *The Tourist Gaze*, London: Sage.

Urry, J., (1994), 'Time, leisure and social identity', *Time and Society*, 3:131–50.

Urry, J., (1995a), *Consuming Places*, London: Routledge.

Urry, J., (1995b), 'A middle class countryside?', in T. Butler and M. Savage (eds), *Social Change and the Middle Classes*, London: UCL Press.

Vergo, P., (1989), *The New Museology*, London: Reaktion Books.

Walsh, K., (1992), *The Representation of the Past*, London: Routledge.

Wolff, J., (1990), *Feminine Sentences*, Cambridge: Polity.

Wolff, J., (1993), 'On the road again. Metaphors of travel in cultural criticism', unpublished.

Wright, P., (1985), *On Living in an Old Country*, London: Verso.

Wright, P., (1992), *A Journey Through Ruins*, London: Paladin.

Part II
Contests: Differences and Identities

Museums as contested sites of remembrance: the Enola Gay affair

Vera L. Zolberg

Abstract

In recent years, controversies concerning the construction of displays of historical events have turned attention to the role of these public sitings. Although virtually any location to which access is relatively unrestricted may give rise to disputes, museums in particular have become foci of these debates. Their prominence is not surprising, since they are institutions in which a nation's qualities are 'written' or 'shown.' In this chapter I turn my attention to an important polemic in which two nations are involved: the United States and Japan. The subject is how the atomic bombing of Hiroshima and Nagasaki was to be represented by a museum of the Smithsonian Institution in Washington. It allows me to examine more deeply the interactions of groups representing divergent interests within the United States, in the context of global relations with a relative equal, rather than a dominated subject. In the process, I analyze the role of the museum as an institution involved in the construction of national narratives in two countries, the political controversies unveiled, and the lost opportunities for innovation in the museum's relationship to its public as politicians intrude upon professions.

Introduction

In recent years controversies sparked by displays that commemorate historical events have turned scholarly attention to questions about how national histories are constructed. For this purpose, documentary evidence in the form of official writings has for a long time been a means of storing such remembering. In addition, particularly vivid sources of information about the past are found in public monuments and civic rituals of recollection. In fact, virtually any locale to which access is relatively unrestricted may serve this purpose. But commemoration in public places means that their very availability may provide the structural basis in which latent controversies may find lodgings. We are already acquainted with this phenomenon – the Vietnam Veterans' Memorial in Washington, DC, among others – even advertising posters, provided that they are publicly displayed.

Museums, too, are sites in which history, directly or unobtrusively, may be represented. Like other locations, museums have become prominent as scenes of contention. This may seem surprising, since as cultural institutions they aspire to a universalistic project of enshrining transcendant values, whether in art, science, or history. But it should not be forgotten that they also purport to serve as a storehouse of their nations' qualities. No less than other media, their displays create and reinforce a version of the past that constitutes a part of collective memory.[1] By studying them we should be helped to understand the cultural structures of meaning that direct – or misdirect – thinking about the past.

Memory is usually taken to be individual or personal in nature. For the psychologically oriented, memory is basically idiosyncratic, embodying the experiences of a particular individual, albeit according to ubiquitous processes. Whereas psychologists have usually viewed memory as autobiographical in nature – that is, based on past experiences statically present or hidden in the mind – more recent research suggests that individual memory consists in reshaping or 'refashioning' in light of new information received, and of ongoing or new emotional states. In this light, individual memory has two aspects: on the one hand as archivist, and on the other as shaper of the personal myth.

Myth does not necessarily entail falsehood, but emphasizes a 'truth' incorporating symbolic and metaphorical reconstructions.[2] This is not to suggest that a formulation based on the individual level is directly analogous to the social. In fact, it would seem that these trends in psychology are following thinking among historians and sociologists. The difference is that any *social* construction of memory is attentive to a different class of content and processes. Rather than emphasizing individual experiences and their impact on a person's subsequent character, from a sociological standpoint, memories based on *shared* experiences are central. Social scientists are less concerned with the individual level, attending, rather, to the construction of shared histories or myths, and often with social, political, or economic consequences.

This orientation is not entirely new, but has gained salience after a long hiatus. Collective or social memory, a field adumbrated by Maurice Halbwachs, an important follower of Emile Durkheim, has been re-emerging as a vital concern in the past decade and a half. Halbwachs tried to grasp the relationship between the past and the social concomitants of its reconstruction. Recent writings by sociologists such as Suzanne Vromen, Iwona Irwin-Zarecka, as well as many other scholars – sociologists, historians, political scientists, anthropologists – give proof of this revival of interest, not only with respect to particular topics, such as the Historians' War in Germany, but in terms of a more general inquiry into the intersection of history and sociology.[3] This trend represents a return to the sociological project as originally formulated by Durkheim in the founding of the sociological discipline in French academia in the last *fin-de-siecle*.[4]

Whereas Durkheim and most of his followers tended to look at societies as enclosed, self contained entities, I wish to enlarge their scope by focusing on a clearly *trans*national, *trans*societal case. The importance of extending historical and social scientific study beyond the boundaries of specific units such as single societies or nations is sustained by the fact that scarcely any important topics in which scholars may be interested exist within a closed arena. These include studies of the Holocaust, of the wartime behaviour of participants, combatants, occupiers, and occupied, and the conduct of imperialist or colonialist powers.

The present analysis deals with the construction of a national narrative that deals with the end of World War II as depicted in the National Air and Space Museum, Washington, DC. Although the dispute which surrounds it has been interpreted largely in terms of competing political groups within the United States, I argue that it should be placed within the context of divergent political interests within both of the nations involved. After presenting the events, still ongoing, I will discuss the role of the museum as an institution and site of collective memory, its relationship to national history, and outline some of the implications of focusing on transsocietal units.

Rashomon reenacted: how World War II ended

In the classic film by Kurosawa, *Rashomon* (1951), the director presents four different versions of the same double crime – the rape of a woman and the murder of her husband. Aside from the fact that this is a film by a major filmmaker, his approach seems particularly well adapted to the narration of the events which follow.

On August 14, almost immediately after the first atomic bomb had been dropped on Hiroshima (August 6), followed by a second bomb on the city of Nagasaki three days later, Japan surrendered unconditionally.[5] These three facts are practically the only ones on which all sides to the museum exhibit dispute agree. The how, the why, at what cost, for whom, and to whose benefit are all in contention. Whereas anti-Vietnam War activists reject the implied glorification of militarism and the A-Bomb that a museum exhibition provides, Veterans' groups and military officers take offence at the original scenario for the exhibit because it underscored the sufferings of Japanese civilians. In so doing, as they see it, the exhibition neglected the suffering that Japan had brought on its neighbours, on American POW's and, especially, on the United States, whose naval base at Pearl Harbour it had attacked, thereby bringing Americans into a global war.

Neglect cuts two ways: critics of the view sympathetic to Japanese civilians do not refer to the treatment accorded to Japanese immigrants in the United States for three quarters of a century or more before the outbreak of the war, nor the unjust internment of all Japanese, immigrants and American born, during the war. As the accounts that follow indicate, each faction prefers to see events wearing blinkers that exclude the sight of others.

The Curators' Version(s)

The National Air and Space Museum, a part of the Smithsonian Institution, has been planning since before 1993 to commemorate the fiftieth anniversary of the Second World War's ending.[6] Appropriately for an establishment representing all aspects of air and space technology, the exhibit was to feature the Enola Gay, as its pilots called the B-29 'Superfortress' that had carried the first atom bomb to its target. The idea had been popular with American veterans because they saw it as a tribute to the bravery of their comrades. However, instead of an accolade to the extraordinary losses of American troops in the Pacific campaign, the script for the exhibit, written by Michael Neufeld, the 43-year old curator in February 1993, had emphasized questions of the 'significance, necessity and morality' of the decision to drop atomic bombs on cities of large civilian populations.

Actually, the Veterans would probably have been even more infuriated by the script's original incarnation. Entitled *The Crossroads: The End of World War II, the Atomic Bomb and the Onset of the Cold War*,' its perspective was perceived as one-sided by the then Smithsonian Secretary, Robert McC. Adams. He cautioned that it could be interpreted as an unbalanced account and would put the Smithsonian 'unacceptably at risk.' Expressing his unease that the script focused on the horrors of the bombing, but omitted the horrors experienced by the Americans in the bloody island-hopping campaign of the Pacific, he urged that the exhibit instead commemorate the conclusion of the war. Without that, he argued, the exhibition would lack context and be open to controversy.[7]

The curators' first version, in which appeared statements such as 'For most Japanese it was a war to defend their unique culture against Western imperialism,' suggested that the atomic bomb was not really necessary for quick victory, but served other ends: to frighten the Soviet Union, justify its costs, and satisfy political pressures at home. It raised questions as to whether anti-Japanese racism may have played a role in the decision, but made no reference to the decades of Japan's brutal conquests in Asia and the Pacific, terror bombings of China, mistreatment of allied Prisoners of War, and the seeming obduracy of Japan's leadership to calls for its surrender, even in the face of certain defeat.

But it is a mistake to imagine that the Smithsonian Institution staff was of one mind. Indeed, opinions ranged widely between that of a former curator of science and technology, now a civilian historian for the Air Force, to the diametrically contrary position by another advisory board member, who opposed any display of the Enola Gay as an obscenity, 'because it would amount to a celebration of the bombing.'[8]

Although it is not clear how it happened, the internal dispute soon reached public attention. It would, of course, be in keeping with established 'inside the beltway' Washington practices for bureaucratic factions to use press 'leaks' in fighting things out. Each of the internal factions sought the support of forces external to the museum: historians for or against curators' version; the press, veterans, including the pilot of the Enola Gay, now a retired brigadier general, and their organization; peace and anti-nuclear groups; and, perhaps inevitably, elected officials and politicians. The most vociferous attack came from forces opposing what they termed 'historical revisionism at its worst' and 'political correctness.'[9]

The Veterans' Version(s)

Veterans' associations included the American Legion and the Air Force Association. Led by the Smithsonian's new Secretary, I. Michael Heyman (former Vice Chancellor of the University of California, Berkeley), the exhibit's organizers met with their representatives for several hours on more than one occasion, both in Washington and in Indianapolis. They agreed to exclude many of the artifacts and photographs of the blast and its aftermath from the section entitled 'Ground Zero.'

No sooner had Veterans' groups declared their satisfaction with the direction in which concessions were going, however, than peace organizations and anti-war activists, including a Jesuit priest, associated with Pax Christi, declared their intention of holding sidewalk demonstrations to denounce them, and of lobbying Congress members.[10]

But the Veterans' mollification was undone when they were made aware of still another change in the exhibit. Whereas the Veterans had insisted that between 250,000 to one million American casualties would have been taken had the bombs not been dropped (an estimate far removed from the figures in the original script – as low as 31,000), the new estimates cited by the museum's director, Martin O. Harwit were still only 63,000. This provoked an immediate demand by eighty conservative members of the House of Representatives (mostly Republican, but some Democrats as well) for Harwit's resignation because of what they termed 'his continuing defiance and disregard for needed improvements to the exhibit.' Elected officials pressured the Smithsonian's Secretary to cancel the exhibit or scale it back severely, and to fire the museum's director.[11]

The Japanese Version(s)

'An American problem, an American issue.' (Press Secretary of the Japanese Embassy)[12]

This phrase from an official Japanese source is more obscure than it seems. It might indicate that the Japanese truly consider this an internal problem for the United States and do not wish to intervene. But at the same time, another conflict was being waged by Japanese officials against the United States Postal Service about a similar matter. In that case, the Japanese government did not treat the matter as 'An American problem.'

The United States Postal Service had planned to issue a commemorative stamp depicting the atomic bombing of Hiroshima and Nagasaki in which was prominently displayed an image of the mushroom cloud. The accompanying caption was to have read, 'Atomic bombs hasten the war's end, August 1945.' The Japanese Foreign Minister, the Japanese Ambassador, the Mayor of Nagasaki, representatives of Japanese anti-nuclear and peace groups all protested against such 'heartlessness.'

US Post Office officials responded that the stamp was part of an issue of ten new stamps about the year 1945, culminating a series under this rubric for the previous four years that showed the main events of World War II.[13] Acknowledging that the imagery may have been overly strong, and that the Postal Service could have found a better way to commemorate the war's end, the writer for the *Chicago Tribune* evoked the Enola Gay affair. As she put it, these two events served as a warning that it was a 'serious mistake *to keep letting the Japanese impose their self-serving perversions of history on this country*' (my emphasis).[14]

A few days later, the White House announced that the stamp's design would be changed. Instead of the mushroom cloud, it would show President Harry Truman preparing to announce the end of the war. In acknowledgement, a Japanese Embassy spokesman thanked the officials for their 'deference to Japanese sensitivities, and the consideration of the importance of US–Japanese relations that this decision reflects.' He is later said to have revised his statement, omitting the phrase 'deference to Japanese sensitivities.'[15]

The Official (US) Version

The tumult caused by this controversy led to considerable damage control by Smithsonian officials. It is not the first time that they have been criticised as overly liberal, too willing to revise history (on the mistreatment of Native Americans by Anglo-Americans, for example), but their problems were compounded by the victory of conservative Republicans in Congress. The Smithsonian Institution is a Congressional establishment, not under Presidential authority. The bulk of its budget (some 75 percent) is provided by Congress from taxes, but in the case of this exhibit, the organizers foreseeing the problems that the exhibit might create had raised some $300,000 of the $1,600,000 budget from private bequests. In this way they hoped to avoid the reproach of 'misusing the taxpayers' money.' Even so, they were unable to defuse the attacks.[16]

The Smithsonian's Board of Regents, chaired by the Chief Justice of the Supreme Court, with the Vice President of the United States, three members of the House and three of Senators, along with nine citizens (not holders of public office), voted to scale back the exhibit to its bare bones. Part of the fuselage of the Enola Gay, accompanied by a plaque and video interviews with its flight crew are all that remain. Gone will be any evidence of the 600-page script (even revised); no museum catalogue; no discussions of the issues influencing President Truman's decision; no arguments over the morality of using atomic weapons; no testimony from survivors; no photos of the victims, and nothing about the beginnings of the Cold War.

Discussion: the museum as a site of remembrance

Museums as we know them are institutions closely intertwined with the collective memory of the nations in which they were created. Like censuses and maps, the formation of museums came to represent the social memory constituting the 'imagined communities', rich in symbolic meanings, of which Benedict Anderson has eloquently written. Placing them in the context of educational systems, literature, public monuments, symbols, ritual performances and other visual representations, Anderson astutely attributes to museums a role in constructing the narrative of the nation.[17]

On the surface, it is to museums of history that the tasks of narration and illustration of the nation state have been most clearly assigned. This objective is taken to be so important that even in the United States, where most museums had depended upon private donors for their primary support, history museums were among the few that were likely to obtain direct tax support from the national state, or from state governments. In a sense, museums of natural history or ethnology play an even more fundamental part in creating the cultural matrix on which the symbolic community is founded. After all, it is they that define the categories of the 'human' as opposed to the 'nonhuman.' In this way they reinforce conceptual categories as to *who* are to be the included, and who the excluded from the national body.[18]

Whereas history and natural history museums seem directly

embedded in the nation, art museums fall into another class. Aside from the long held view in American political life that the fine arts should be treated as a private pleasure of the rich, art works tend to be created by individuals trained, to a great extent, in what has come to be seen as a *universal* aesthetic tradition. They have entered museum collections from many different sources, and are not necessarily made by artists who might be defined as 'natives.' Although for these reasons it seems counter-intuitive, there is, nevertheless, a widespread belief in most countries that art works, even those that are merely acquired from abroad, *do* embody a nation's identity as well. Thus although art works are treated as market goods, once they are permitted entry into museums they rarely leave for the ordinary material world. Instead, institutionalization sacralizes them.

To what extent can we encompass artistic creation within the arena of conflicting national interests? The display of post-World War II Japanese art in the Guggenheim-Soho in 1994 highlights the interactions of groups representing divergent interests in Japan, revealing the diversity of interests in that country. This is important to bear in mind when the polemic surrounding commemoration of the atom bomb is considered. Even though it is a smaller country than the United States, and is often represented (and presents itself) as if the consensus among the Japanese is total, there is no reason to believe that this is literally the case.

But the Air and Space Museum is not exactly like these others. Fundamentally a technology museum, it was the brainchild of a United States Air Force general. The museum was enabled by Congress as early as 1946, its scope expanded later to include space, and was officially opened for the American Bicentennial in July 1976. Replacing a small air museum located near the Smithsonian's 'Castle', it became an immediate success, with about ten million visitors, largely families, during certain years. Later, in response to popular demand, the exhibiting of the Enola Gay was given high priority by its current director – now, ex-director.

Contested meanings of nationhood

But what about the nation itself? It is not immediately evident how the 'nation' is to be conceptualized. Is it a unitary construct based on some single 'essence' related to the Romantic ideas of European *literati,* or a more cosmopolitan and/or changing one? The mono-cultural notion of identity which is being challenged by new claims to diverse cultural identities today has a history. Whereas national identity has usually been ascribed to a population co-extensive with the geographic boundaries of a nation state, this has almost always been, at best, an approximation. The fact is that populations tend to spill over into adjacent areas, or to emigrate, establishing enclaves in other localities. This was the case of Japanese immigrants to the United States, along with many more from European nations, who, despite limitations under the longlasting quota system, were not debarred from entering. The fact that by the beginning of the Second World War a large proportion of Japanese had been born in, and were, therefore, citizens of the United States, did not preserve them from being incarcerated, regardless of age or status. This violation of their civil rights remained unpardoned for decades, long after it was known that they had been blameless for their former nation's policies.

This ambiguity of national identity emerges in the many controversies that surround the erection of national (or local) public monuments. The commemoration of the Vietnam War is a case in point. Although it is not strictly speaking a museum, when the Vietnam Veterans' Memorial was being planned for Washington DC, a group of citizens, led by the millionaire (and later, on and off candidate to the Presidency), Ross Perot, raised objections to it, partly on aesthetic grounds. They considered the abstract, black marble, minimalist monument, designed by a then young student of Asian origin, as too depressing and uninviting. There is little doubt, however, that the central issues in the debates were less aesthetic than political.[19]

More directly inside the world of the art museum, the American Flag controversy at the School of the Art Institute of Chicago illuminated the political cleavages of the 1980s. At the annual exhibition of students' work, one of the students produced a conceptual display consisting of an American flag placed on the floor, in the path of a book open to a blank page in which visitors were invited to write their opinions of how to display the flag. In order to reach the book, however, the visitors would have to step on the American flag. When this work became known to the public, several war veterans' groups protested. Since the display was not removed, a number of veterans took turns standing at attention in witness before it until the exhibition closed.

What we see from these cases is the extent of the area of inter-section of art and political or national symbolism. Museums reveal their importance as bearers of national identity through their direct association with national political issues, often ones that bring out cleavages in American political life. In a sense, this is an unanticipated consequence of the 'exhibitionary complex' that emanated, as Tony Bennett argues, from one of the layers of Foucault's conception of the carceral society. For Foucault, dis-plays are used to support the state's hegemony.[20]

Concluding comments

It has become a commonplace that historical monuments and texts were understood in terms of the particular present within which the past represented is framed. Historians differ among themselves as to whether there is a concrete basis for this past (these pasts?), or if it is (they are?) assembled out of whole cloth. Thus Halbwachs argued that the present constructs the past. Barry Schwartz, however, maintains that the foundation of the past sets limits on how it is constructed in the present. In a simi-lar mode, Lewis Coser, paraphrasing Marx, notes that the present generation rewrites history, but it does not write it on a blank page. What is certain, as analysis of the Hiroshima exhibition suggests, is that the problem of knowing what 'really' happened becomes more complex the more we know, the more viewpoints expressed, the thicker the description.[21]

Indeed, a nation's 'official history' conventionally highlights its glories. But this idea is increasingly being subjected to 'readers' who wish to know what *really* happened. How can we transfer our understanding of contention within a nation – competing groups (supporters of patriotism *v.* intellectual humanist cos-mopolitans) – into the international relations among competing states? Internal dissension is not confined to avowedly diverse nations, such as the United States. Nor are official Japanese responses necessarily more representative of opinion than are either representatives of certain Veterans' organizations or the many different schools of historians in the United States. In her *Chicago Tribune* article, Joan Beck observes that when the Japanese writer, Kenzaburo Oe accepted his Nobel Prize for Literature, he reproached his countrymen, saying that 'the Japanese still do not admit responsibility for their role in World

War II and for the long list of atrocities they committed . . .' Oe is far from being the only Japanese citizen who rejects an unapologetic official version. It is important to avoid the tendency to stereotype the 'other' – a proclivity exacerbated by the history of warfare between the two countries.

Perhaps the Enola Gay controversy is more important within the United States political arena, but I claim that it may have as much significance at an international level as recent furious negotiations in which the two nations are engaged concerning trade. What is important is that these interactions – economic or symbolic – take place in the context of global relations of relative equals. Beyond the bounds of a single nation, friction may pervade the subsequent relations of wartime enemies more or less permanently, or at least durably and recurrently. Discord is exacerbated when rivalries are based on a past history in which alternations in dominance among the nations in question are part of the configuration. The present circumstances of the Hiroshima-centred exhibit are profoundly unlike what they might have been in the immediate post-World War II aftermath, when the field of national actors consisted of formidable conqueror and abject vanquished. After the decline in American economic dominance – the end of the American Century – and the rise of Japanese fortunes, the context in which the exhibition was being planned was bound to take on more portentous significance and arouse deeper sensitivities.

This inquiry suggests that social memory is not reducible either to a semiotic reading of surfaces or to a simple analysis of dominance relations that are confined to a single society. Rather, in an increasingly global world, the localisms of national factions or interest groups may have unexpected consequences.

Are there lessons for museums to learn and to apply to their relation to their publics? This particular dispute may have contrary outcomes. It may lead museums to redouble their efforts to avoid controversy; or – more courageously – to construct their programs with an unaccustomed degree of transparency. To be sure, they then run the risk of creating or contributing to public outcry or scandal. On the other hand, there is a chance that they may promote a level of participation that negates the idea that the 'public' is reducible to being no more than the passive recipient of constructed memory. The safe approach takes us to the Museum as Disneyland; in which the past is sanitized, made unthreatening, albeit rather entertaining. It would be far more audacious if museums chose to create an intellectual experience for competing publics and even national states. They might end up engaging in open discussion and debate about important issues. Whether this fearless path is likely to be followed by the increasingly bureaucratized and money-conscious institutions that museums have become, however, is most doubtful.

Notes

1 The Vietnam Memorial has been analysed by Robin Wagner-Pacifici and Barry Schwarts, in 'The Vietnam Veterans Memorial: Commemorating a Difficult Past', *American Journal of Sociology*, 97, 1991: pp. 375–421. Maruska Svasek of the Netherlands presented her paper, 'Rites and Sights of Recollection: Hranice's Liberation in Monumental Art', at the World Congress of Sociology held at Bielefeld, Germany in July 1995. The more general phenomenon of public culture as sites of contention is developed by Arjun Appadurai and Carol Breckenridge in the journal they co-edit, *Public Culture*.
2 Some of this research is summarized by John Kotre in *White Gloves: How We Create Ourselves Through Memory*, New York: Free Press, 1995.
3 Suzanne Vromen, 'The Sociology of Maurice Halbwachs' (Ph.D. diss., New York University, 1975); Iwona Irwin-Zarecka, *Frames of Remembrance: The Dynamics of Collective Memory*, New Brunswick, NJ: Transaction Publishers, 1994; Pierre Nora, ed. *Les lieux de mémoire*, 3 volumes, Paris: Gallimard, 1982–86. Lewis A. Coser has edited, translated, and written the introduction to many of Halbwachs's writings in *Maurice Halbwachs: On Collective Memory*, Chicago and London: The University of Chicago Press, 1992.
4 As I recently pointed out in my paper, 'Contested Remembrance: The Hiroshima Exhibit Controversy,' presented at the conference, Interpreting Historical Change at the End of the Twentieth Century, at the University of California, Davis, 21–26 February 1995, Durkheim envisioned sociology and history as allies whose union would redound to scholarly advances by enhancing our understanding of social processes, *L'Annee Sociologique*, 1896–97; 1897–98.
5 The formal surrender on the battleship Missouri in Tokyo harbour was signed on September 2, *Columbia Encyclopedia*, sv. 'Japan' p. 1399.
6 According to one account, planning had begun as long as six years ago (Ken Ringle, 'At Ground Zero: 2 Views of History Collide over Smithsonian A-Bomb Exhibit' in *The Washington Post* September 26, 1994: p. A1.
7 This account was reported by Ringle in the *Washington Post*. The part that Adams had played was confirmed in an interview with Adams himself. Adams had announced his intention to resign as early as September, 1993, according to Irvin Molotsky, 'Head of Smithsonian Institution is quitting After 10 years at Helm' in *The New York Times* September 14, 1993: p. 209.
8 According to the Director of the Air and Space Museum's division of aeronautics, this was the only real objection from a Board member, who was a historian at Dartmouth University. Cited in Ringle (note 7).
9 The historians who supported the curators were Guy A. Perowitz, Barton J. Bernstein of Stanford University; those opposed were Robert Cowley, editor of

Military History Quarterly, Peter Maslowski of the University of Nebraska. More neutral were Robert McCullough, who had recently published a biography of President Harry S. Truman. The Congressmen were led by Massachusetts Representative Peter Blute, according to Jeff Jacoby, a staff writer, in his Op-Ed, 'Smithsonian Drops a Bomb in World War II Exhibit' in *The Boston Globe* August 16, 1994: p. 15.

10 Eugene L. Meyer, 'No Peace for Enola Gay: Exhibit Now Has Anti-War Groups Up in Arms' in *The Washington Post* October 21, 1994 [Style Section]: p. C2.

11 Eric Schmitt, '80 Lawmakers Demand Ouster of Director of Air Museum' in *The New York Times* January 26, 1995: p. A12.

12 Taukasa Uemura is cited by Eugene L. Meyer (see Note 10).

13 Andrew Pollack, 'Japan Protests U.S. Stamp on A-Bombs' in *The New York Times* December 4, 1994: p. 25.

14 Joan Beck, 'Japan Should Quit Trying to Distort WWII History: A Prototype of the Stamp Commemorating the Atomic Bombing of Japan,' December 8, 1994: p. 31.

15 Todd S. Purdom, 'At White House Behest, Postal Service Scraps A-Bomb Stamp', in *The New York Times* December 9, 1994: p. 31.

16 Tom Crouch, Director of the Air and Space Museum's division of aeronautics, cited in Ringle (1994).

17 Benedict Anderson, *Imagined Communities: Reflections on the Origin and Spread of Nationalism* [revised edition], New York and London: Verso, 1991.

18 Vera L. Zolberg, 'Remaking Nations: Public Culture and Postcolonial Discourse' in *Paying the Piper: Causes and Consequences of Art Patronage*, edited by Judith H. Balfe, Urbana and Chicago: University of Illinois Press, 1993.

19 See Wagner-Pacifici and Schwarts (note 1).

20 Tony Bennett, 'The Exhibitionary Complex' in N.B. Dirks et al. *Culture/Power/History: A Reader in Contemporary Social Theory*. Bennett goes beyond Foucault, seeing the 'archaeology' of modern institutions as connected with the emergence of the liberal bourgeois state. See also Wagner-Pacifici and Schwartz and Steven C. Dubin, *Arresting Images: Impolitic Art and Uncivil Actions*, London: Routledge, 1992. Michel Foucault, *Discipline and Punish: The Birth of the Prison*, New York: Pantheon Books, 1977.

21 Clifford Geertz's influential essay, 'Thick Description: Toward an Interpretive Theory of Culture' did much to open up debates around these issues. It is published in his *The Interpretation of Cultures*, New York: Basic Books, 1973.

Into the heart of irony: ethnographic exhibitions and the politics of difference

Henrietta Riegel

Abstract

The paper discusses the 'western' museum practices of representing culture within a dominant visual metaphor as an inherently political act which separates those who view the exhibit from those who are on display. The act of viewing is related to the acts of ordering, defining and representing according to the categories of the 'viewing' culture, and serves to deny shared space and time occupied by the representing and represented cultures, a process related to the anthropological construction of ethnographic distance in ethnographic texts. Two recent Canadian exhibitions which attempt to use irony to subvert traditional exhibit practices are analysed: *Into the Heart of Africa* and *Fluffs and Feathers*. *Into the Heart of Africa* attempted to mount a postmodern critique of colonial collecting practices, but its one-sided use of irony reproduced, for many visitors, the colonial relations of power that made it possible for one group to dominate another. The narrative structure of the exhibit was predicated on a relation of difference. *Fluffs and Feathers*, on the other hand, directly challenged the white visitor's power to view and define native peoples, by dialogically inviting visitors to try on alternate subject positions that help to fracture essentialist notions of self and culture. Thus irony, a risky trope, can lead to very different results in museum exhibitions depending on who it is aimed at and who does the aiming.

Museums[1] have a contentious history of the dual processes of collecting and display within a scholarly, and more recently, educational context. Under the guises of philanthropy, value-free knowledge and a certain patina of 'culture' and 'civilization', museums have made it their business to reproduce other cultures for the visual consumption of their visitors. These representations, however, like the museums that house them, do not exist in a sanctified space removed from political processes. While museum professionals do recognize this political aspect of museums, their concerns tend to focus on the content of exhibits, ie, *what* is on display, rather than on the modes of representation. It is this latter aspect of display that I concentrate on, in particular the trope of the postmodern day, namely irony. Irony is a rich and risky trope, with a long history of use in literature and in art. Its application to museum displays is a relatively new phenomenon, and relates to a recent critical, reflexive turn in museology. I will examine the use of irony in representational strategies in two recent exhibitions at the Royal Ontario Museum (ROM), *Into the Heart of Africa* (1989–1990), and *Fluffs and Feathers* (1992). Both exhibits are critical of museum practices, and use irony as part of this critique. In addition, I relate their representational strategies to a politics of difference, positionality and detachment common in museum exhibits. It is with these aspects of the politics of display that this paper is concerned.

Museums, ethnographic distance, and the politics of the view

Museum professionals spend a great deal of time concerned with displaying objects: they ponder wall colour, label type-face, lighting, gallery ambience, and a host of other technical elements. Whilst these elements are undoubtedly important to an aesthetics of display, they do not constitute a mode of representation in themselves and remain merely elements that contribute to this mode. Museums exhibit cultures from within a certain logic of representation. This logic makes a number of distinctions, the main one being between representation and reality. As Timothy Mitchell (1988) points out, the exhibition itself is constructed as a simulation of an external reality, with the reality and the representation clearly differentiated.

This nineteenth-century European separation, as described by Mitchell, extended to a whole host of other phenomena, including the city, the body and the landscape, so that everything appeared to be an exhibit of itself, the actualization of a plan. The world outside the exhibit came to resemble an exhibit, and people began to expect to see things in this way, as if each new scene were an extension of the exhibit. The 'real' world kept being pushed further and further back, so that reality became an effect of a system in which the world could only be seen and understood as if it were an exhibit.

This reinscription of the world as an exhibit was also the organization of a view for an outside observer, external to the system. As Mitchell (1988:58) writes (after de Tocqueville), 'The meaning is something made visible only to the outside observer, who stands apart and sees the world as a representation.' Of course, the position of the observer is not a neutral one, despite its seeming objectivity.[2] There is a certain authority with which one orders up and views the world, a power to name, define, classify and re-present. This appearance of structure is the result of an act of order and pattern, of imposition, as Mitchell clearly demonstrates with the example of the nineteenth-century colonization of Egypt.[3] It is at once a system of definition and of control.

Indeed, during the French colonization of Algeria, French photographers were unable to penetrate the veiled and haremed world of Algerian women. Instead, photographer's models were dressed up to resemble Algerian women and unveiled themselves to the photographer's (and the subsequent viewer's) gaze. In this way, the inaccessibility of Algerian women was overcome in the constructed space of the photographer's gaze. Through a substitution, French men could voyeuristically and vicariously enact their fantasies of Algerian women, denied to them in the colonial encounter. Algerian women thus became eroticized and exoticized through a process that rendered them up for view, a view that left French men removed from the display by the eye of the camera in a state of flux between fulfilment and non-fulfilment (Alloula, 1986). Again, as in Mitchell's example of the colonization of Egypt, the machinery which produces these representations can only re-present, making that which the gaze attempts to present or reveal elusive. Both examples demonstrate the authority and certainty with which these representations order up and render for inspection colonial subjects, a process that is *not* value-free and objective, neither is it unrelated to political processes – in these two cases a colonial enterprise.

The logic of representation described by Mitchell and Alloula clearly prioritizes the visual over the other senses. Stephen Tyler (1987) details how the visual sense is a key metaphor in 'Standard Average European' (Whorf's term) language and thought, and that thinking and knowing are reductively equated to seeing. When we think in abstractions, we are 'trafficking in representations' (p.155), and when, as anthropologists, we 'look at culture', we are examining it 'as if watching a bug' (p.156). The reason for the primacy of the sense of vision is its mimetic ability to provide 'true and accurate information about the external world' (p.157), as if what we see in front of us is indisputably more real than what, for example, we hear or feel. Within this visual metaphor, it is as if the world is assembled by our eyes for our minds.

Tyler argues that this metaphor of seeing is not universal, but rather is part of a particular cultural tradition. To return to museums, I would argue that the cultural tradition that prioritizes the sense of vision acts strongly in museums in the Western world. Indeed, as Barbara Kirshenblatt-Gimblett points out when she discusses what she calls the 'reciprocity of the museum effect' (1991:406–411), there is a splitting of the visitor's gaze between the display and the everyday world, making visitors spectators of themselves by comparing themselves to the exhibit. Furthermore, the museum experience[4] becomes a model for looking at other aspects of society for turning, as Kirshenblatt-Gimblett describes, the city into a series of ethnographic Others to be viewed and examined as exhibits (which sublimated a kind of social pornography and touristic slumming).

The organization of exhibits around a centre occupied by the visitor, as Mitchell indicates (1988:9), concurs with the current separation of visitors from the objects they view in museums. Not only can visitors not touch most objects, they are also encouraged to remain mentally detached. Only their vision touches the objects. And this is also evident in the arrangement of objects in an exhibition as if the visitor is embarking on a journey, described by Mieke Bal (1992:561) as:

[T]he space of a museum presupposes a walking tour, an order in which the exhibits and panels are to be viewed and read. Thus it addresses an implied 'focalizer' whose tour is the story of the production of the knowledge taken in and taken home.

It is the visitor who is in motion, and the objects, and by implication the relationships they embody, are all curiously lifeless. In fact, Kirschenblatt-Gimblett calls museums 'tombs with views' (1991:416).

Thus we have two sets of distinctions here, the first between the representation and the reality, and the second between the representation and the visitor. The position that the visitor occupies, that of the observing eye, excludes him/her from the order of the exhibit and emphasizes the separation of the exhibit from the reality it supposedly portrays (Mitchell, 1989:223). What this suggests to me is that the mechanism that both separates the viewer from the representation *and* simultaneously equates the eye with the mind has the effect of distancing the museum visitor from the exhibit. This distancing takes the form of a personal, emotional and intellectual disengagement.

I also argue that museum visitors expect this cognitive distance from an exhibit, although they may not always take it up. I assisted in a visitor study of an experimental contemporary history exhibit, called *Shau Platz Süd West*, in Stuttgart in the summer of 1992. The exhibit featured the immediate post-war period during which several smaller provinces were joined into the larger province Baden-Württemberg. The exhibit deliberately had no text panels or labels, and immersed visitors into fantastically recreated scenarios from that time period. For example, one section of the exhibit reconstructed a bombed out cellar, and another depicted the plight of the 'Displaced Persons' rather graphically with graves in an eerie, oppressive room. A common complaint about the exhibit was that visitors felt too 'close' to the exhibit, that it brought back a whole host of unpleasant memories of the time during and after the Second World War. These visitors stated that they had come to the exhibit because they wanted to learn and read more about a time in which they had lived, a time they felt was important to know about for younger generations of Germans, but that they had not anticipated re-experiencing the emotions attendant to those events. It was a shock to find *themselves* on display, and several elderly visitors would, after the interview, begin talking about their own unpleasant experiences and memories, some of which they had locked away for decades. This was not, they felt, what an exhibit should do; rather, an exhibit should educate. These visitors, then, clearly separated personal emotions from museum education.

Many visitors say that they go to museums to learn about other cultures, and grant the museum a certain authority to accurately document and depict those cultures. Museums like the ROM exude authority. The architecture is monumental, the technical aspects of exhibits are superbly executed. Even (or especially) the gift shop aesthetically displays its wares in an atmosphere of luxury and connoisseurship. People look to museums as the arbiters of 'high class' taste, a source to be relied upon when it comes to matters of culture (Kelly, n.d.). They also look to museums for information, for, as Da Breo writes (1990:104), 'a history lesson at a glance, a confirmation of actual life as documented and preserved for our value-free absorption.'

These history lessons relegate other cultures (and mark them as 'Other' cultures) to an unspecified past, even when these groups exist in the present,[5] and equate temporal distance with objectivity. This is one of the results of strategies that Johannes Fabian calls 'allochronism', a denial of coevalness. He defines this as:

> . . . a persistent and systematic tendency to place the referent(s) of anthropology in a Time other than the present of the producer of anthropological discourse (1983:31).

This denial of a shared time and space transforms the participative aspect of ethnographic fieldwork into observation. The anthropologist thus becomes a viewer of another culture, a culture that 'holds still like a *tableau vivant*' (p.67). Thus the anthropologist's own experiences in the field, experiences that are rooted in a particular time and space and that take place under conditions of shared communication with other people are transformed into an ethnographic writing that contradicts the particularity of the fieldwork and creates a position of distance from these same people (p.71). There is thus a relationship between the construction of cultural difference and ethnographic distance.

Ethnographic museum exhibits can be considered a form of ethnographic writing. They are also the products of processes of encounters with other peoples, encounters which are subsequently re-produced into discourses conveying information about other cultures who are distanced, through rhetorical, stylistic and linguistic strategies (see Fabian, 1983). Participation is converted into observation, classification and order, resulting in a 'petrified relation' (Fabian, 1983:143). These allochronic strategies also confer authority to museums over the cultures they represent, and over visitors who expect to receive information objectively from museums. Thus we see that the dominant mode of reproduction in which museums are located denies a shared space between visitors, museum professions and the people whose cultures are on display. This denial of shared communication is a political act.

Into the heart of irony

Recent museological scholarship has become increasingly concerned with the ways in which museums display culture, construct difference, and produce relations of power (Ames, 1992; Karp and Lavine, 1991, Karp et al, 1992). Importantly, the museum itself is now viewed as an object of study, as an 'artefact of our own society' (Ames, 1992:44). As Karp and Lavine (1991:1) declare in their opening sentence to their ground-breaking book on museum display, 'Every museum exhibition, whatever its overt subject, inevitably draws on the cultural assumptions and resources of the people who make it.' This is, perhaps, not an earth-shattering statement, but it does indicate that museums professionals are seriously thinking about the organization, role and relationships of museums to their communities, and no longer locate themselves outside of social processes and structures. Thus museums not only reflect culture, they also help make it.

The politics of representation and voice have become a central issue for museums, likewise for anthropology. It should be of some concern to anthropologists to note that more people learn about anthropology from museums than from universities (Ames, 1992:139). Museum exhibits can thus be considered as very public forms of ethnography. Some of the critiques of museums stem from the fact that they control, interpret and impose classifications onto other peoples' histories. It is precisely these sorts of critiques that lead museologists to look more closely at the ways in which museums display other cultures. It is with this aim in mind that I examine two recent exhibits at the Royal Ontario Museum, one of the most prestigious and well-known research museums in Canada. I will concentrate here on two of its recent exhibits that attempt to critique museum practices. Significantly, both exhibits employ irony as part of their critiques.

From November, 1989, to August, 1990, the ROM hosted one of the most controversial exhibitions ever shown in Canada. Entitled *Into the Heart of Africa*, the exhibit was guest-curated by anthropologist and African specialist Jeanne Cannizzo, who drew on the ROM's existing African collection for the exhibit. Originally entitled *Into the Heart of Darkness*,[6] reminiscent of both Joseph Conrad's 1902 *Heart of Darkness* and Georg Schweinfurth's 1870's travel book *The Heart of Africa*, the exhibit was meant to be a self-reflexive critique of the colonial collecting practices of the museum. The exhibition became the centre of heated protests some four months after it opened, spearheaded by a group called the Coalition for the Truth about Africa, and caused both the curator and the museum great distress. Ultimately four other museums which were to receive the exhibition after the ROM cancelled.

Some of the controversy stemmed from the ironic strategy used to expose the colonial underpinnings of the collection. Cannizzo had deliberately decided to concentrate the exhibit on the histories of the African objects at the ROM and the colonial contexts in which they were acquired, mainly through Canadian soldiers and missionaries who collected the material as trophies and souvenirs of their experiences in Africa. The collection itself was quite piecemeal, and would not have lent itself well to a substantial exhibition focusing on a particular group or topic in Africa (Schildkraut, 1991:23). Cannizzo (1991:150–51) states that her aim was to mount a postcolonial critique of the collection:

> The collection seemed to me an ideal one with which to address the sometimes voiced complaint by African scholars that North American museums and art galleries have not really acknowledged the consequences of the colonial period.

Cannizzo also drew on recent anthropological critiques of ethnographic writing and the construction of knowledge of other cultures (cf. Clifford, 1988; Clifford and Marcus, 1986; Fabian, 1983; Marcus and Fischer, 1986). She too regards the museum as 'a cultural text, one that may be read to understand the underlying cultural or ideological assumptions that have informed its creation, selection, and display (Cannizzo, 1991:151). This critique of anthropology is clearly evident in the introduction to the exhibition catalogue:

> Anthropology is frequently described as a kind of dialogue between the ethnographic other and the cultural self. This characterization is meant . . . to suggest the 'fictional' nature of anthropology, for the work is generated in the interaction of the anthropologist's own cultural preconceptions and ideological assumptions with those of the people among whom he or she works. As such, the dialogue reveals something of the other as well as the self (1989:11).

Cannizzo then relates a similar museological concern with representation to this trend in anthropology by regarding museums as fictions, dialogues and as texts, referred to as 'reflexive museology'. She stresses the ideological assumptions behind the collecting which led to the museum acquiring the objects, and traces the relationships embodied in these objects in terms of the various contexts in which they have been located.

Running alongside this critical objective of the exhibit is another more celebratory one, namely, to display 'the rich diversity of African cultural practices and artistic traditions' (Cannizzo, 1991:150). This aim is evident in the catalogue's beautifully photographed objects which provide a glowing testimonial to the beauty of African objects. The accompanying descriptions lack reflexive commentary and thus are not critical of the practices of collecting *these* objects. Indeed, a certain reluctance to criticize too strongly is evident, as Schildkraut (1991:20) points out, the exhibit 'was meant to criticize colonialism (but not particular colonialists), missionaries (but not particular missions), museums (but not necessarily the ROM).'[7]

I will examine here the use of irony in the exhibition catalogue and in a later article written by Cannizzo to evaluate the extent to which irony promoted or discouraged a postcolonial critique of the ROM's collecting practices. As I have already mentioned, there are, in fact, several aims of the exhibition articulated by Cannizzo: to critique colonialism in general, to self-reflexively deconstruct museum collecting practices, to trace the different contexts in which objects have acquired meaning, and to celebrate the beauty and diversity of African peoples through their material culture.

The texts of the catalogue and the exhibition fall short of actualizing Cannizzo's aims in many respects. Irony is used often in the catalogue to question the authority of the written texts, particularly those portions of the text that are reproduced in quotation marks. This particular form of irony fits under the category of verbal irony, having double signifying power, ie having one signifier and two signifieds (Hutcheon, 1992:32). This is an unexceptional and standard definition of irony, that it is, in other words, a 'double-layered or two-storey phenomenon in which there is always some kind of opposition between the two levels' (Muecke in Knox, 1972:54), or even more basically, 'literally saying one thing and figuratively meaning the opposite' (Sperber and Wilson, 1981:295). This type of irony can often be unsettling, as Marcus and Fischer (1986:13) write:

> . . . [I]t is a self-conscious mode that senses the failure of all
> sophisticated conceptualizations; stylistically, it employs
> rhetorical devices that signal real or feigned disbelief on the
> part of the author toward the truth of his own statements . . .

The text's method of using verbal irony is not so explicitly disturbing. This is evident in its description of the motivations of nineteenth-century Canadian missionaries in the catalogue:

> Their vision . . . was to replace 'paganism' with Christianity,
> the slave trade with legitimate commerce, and 'barbarous'
> customs with their own form of civilization. Seeking glory on
> spiritual battlefields no less dangerous than the secular ones
> where Canadian soldiers fought, many of them with their
> health and lives for their beliefs (1989:15–16).

One is left with the impression that these missionaries were brave and adventurous, rather than colonizers intent upon destroying another culture's way of life. This impression overrides any 'unsettling' feelings that the text is drawing attention to and critiquing these missionary activities.

This is even more apparent when one reads the following paragraph in the catalogue, that refers to the fact that these soldiers and missionaries 'brought back many souvenirs and trophies of their journeys into the heart of Africa', where there are no quotation marks at all to indicate that these collecting practices could be quite unethical. This ambiguity is reinforced by the use of quotation marks for direct quotes which do not appear to be ironic at all. Thus, the use of quotation marks for direct quotes that are, at times, meant ironically, and at other times simply to copy a statement written in the past, leads to ambiguity about which kinds of marked text are endorsed by the museum and the curator, and which kinds are meant to critique the statements themselves.

One of the greatest sources of ambiguity is the intentional ironic juxtapositions of images and written text in the exhibit. For example, the catalogue has a photograph with the caption 'Mrs. Thomas Titcombe offering "a lesson in how to wash clothes" to Yagba women in northern Nigeria about 1915'. The following page portrays an intricate African-made straw hat, which, if taken ironically, would point to the fact that African women were already quite adept at making textiles, and probably already knew how to wash them (Da Breo, 1991:105).

An image that caused a great deal of uproar in the exhibition was a reproduced and enlarged picture from the front page of a nineteenth-century newspaper in London, depicting a white man on horseback thrusting his sword through the shield and into the heart of a black man. Part of the caption reads, 'Lord Beresford's Encounter with a Zulu',[8] with the word encounter not marked as being ironic. According to Cannizzo (1989:86; 1991:154), this image was supposed to be juxtaposed against the African weapons in that room, and was intended to show the partiality of museums to collect African weapons and to stereotype the Zulu as being fierce warriors. This juxtaposition presumes that visitors will give the same signifying weight to images and written texts, which is not the case with most visitors who read very few of the text panels and labels. Thus, playing verbal ironic captions against negative images may not question the image at all, it may indeed reinforce the image.

The ambiguous use of irony in the catalogue and in the exhibition point to its potential political overtones. The intentions of the curator and the interpretations of the visitor do not always overlap, and the linking of the one to the other by overt markers is not that easily accomplished. This is the risk of irony (Fish, 1983:176). The choices of strategies of exposition are political in themselves, not only in what they convey.

Linda Hutcheon (1994:22–24) characterizes the exhibition as having postmodern 'possibilities', rather than presenting a post-colonial critique. In its ambiguous use of irony, it refuses to offer a substantial and unequivocal critique of colonial practices of conquest. Rather, it ultimately undermines its oppositional potential by refusing to state explicitly the museum's position in the narrative itself. However, the exhibit also fails in its incomplete use of postmodern strategies. It does not have, as Hutcheon (1994:26) points out, 'the postmodern dialogic museum mode' because it never presents African voices directly in the exhibit. Colonial practices underlying the collection are presented through the voices of Canadian soldiers and missionaries, thus offering no directly voiced opposition. By not presenting the colonial encounter in dialectical and dialogical terms, textually the authoritative voice of the museum predominates, leading one away from questioning whether or not the museum problematizes its own collecting practices.

In addition, visitors are not led to question the strategies of representation by the exhibition itself. Irony as a strategy is not made problematic in the exhibition. In fact, the irony is predicated on rather standard lines. These verbal forms of irony have often been levelled with the critique of being too élitist, too sophisticated for all to understand. These forms of irony are for those in the know, those lucky few who somehow innately recognize 'the critical spirit of self-consciousness, of dialectical inquiry' (Chamberlain, 1989:100), and those lucky few who have received enough scholarly training to read Kierkegaard in the original Danish. This sets up a distinction between 'competent' and 'incompetent' readers (see Dane, 1986), and places the burden of the 'correct' ironic reading firmly with the reader.

Into the Heart of Africa has been criticized as being 'too subtle' for most visitors to understand on the grounds that it was a scholarly exhibition for scholars (see Jones, 1993:211). I, for one, think that in comparing Cannizzo's stated objectives and her later explanations with the actual ironies in the exhibit, it is evident that there are no clear and consistent markers of irony. And furthermore, just because some visitors objected to the exhibition does not necessarily mean that they did not *get* it.[9]

For me, the issue leads back to a consideration of the mode of representation itself. I argue that the particular form of irony used, namely verbal, is a type of irony that relies upon an intellectually distanced stance on the part of the visitor. This distance is unquestioned in the exhibition. The interpretive difficulty seems to be with those visitors who cannot accept the distanced position required by the text in order to read it as verbal irony. It seems to me that those visitors who felt an emotional or political affinity with the images and objects on display (it is significant here that both black groups and the descendants of the missionaries were offended by the exhibition) did not dispassionately stand back and interpret the exhibition as if it were an intellectual exercise. Thus the type of irony used reinforced the mode of representation typical in museums instead of critiquing it. It was predicated on the visitor being mentally differentiated and detached from the subject of the exhibition. The failure of the irony indicates that construction of differences and distance in exhibitions is problematic and political in itself.

Fluffs and Feathers: dialogical stereotypes

How can irony be used differently in museums? Is it possible to use irony in a manner that does not reinforce the dominant mode of representation? It is with these questions in mind that I examine a recent travelling exhibition at the ROM called *Fluffs and Feathers*, an exhibition originally produced and exhibited at the Woodlands Cultural Centre (WCC) in Brantford, Ontario, in 1988. The WCC serves six native communities from two different cultural groups, the Iroquoian and the Algonkian. In 1992 a travelling version of the exhibition was mounted at the ROM in a 'collaborative effort' (exhibit text panel).

After the widely-publicized protests of the Glenbow Museum's 1988 exhibition, *The Spirit Sings*, a Task Force on Museums and First Peoples, jointly sponsored by the Assembly of First Nations and the Canadian Museum Association, was formed to study and make recommendations in order to develop better working relationships between museums and aboriginal groups in Canada (Nicks, 1992:88). Bringing *Fluffs and Feathers* to the ROM from WCC in 1991–2 was one of the first attempts to put the Task Force Report (1992) into practice.

The process of reconstructing *Fluffs and Feathers* at the ROM was fraught with problems. The exhibition, according to native curator Deborah Doxtator (1993b), was designed specifically for a native community in order to show how the process of constructing images of native people works. However, when this critical message is exhibited within a large Western institution, it takes on an irony of its own, the irony being the contradictions inherent in, as Doxtator (1993b) puts it, 'The ROM trying to represent us represent them.'

Fluffs and Feathers is located on the first floor[10] of the ROM at the back of the museum. To reach the exhibition, one has to negotiate a long, narrow corridor and pass the magnificently displayed Chinese exhibition before reaching the far side of the museum. Doxtator (1992a) notes the irony of the placing *Fluffs and Feathers*, consisting of what she calls 'junk' that people had found in their homes, next to the beautifully-lit and presented East Asian Gallery, as if the objects in *Fluffs and Feathers* were 'real and had a value as art' instead of just being the funny, everyday objects that they are to their owners.

The entrance to *Fluffs and Feathers* presents a colourful, well-lit visual focal point, a large roped-off teepee. In addition, there are recognizably 'native' artifacts in a glass case: a small totem pole and a feathered headdress. These objects create an 'ethnographic' ambience. Visitors tend to look at several exhibitions in one day, so here is another 'culture' for them to look at and consume (visually).

In the following sections the ethnographic frame becomes challenged. The space is disjointed, historical objects are displayed without any seeming chronological order, and blank walls are juxtaposed with areas of massed objects. The impression created is that the objects are haphazardly arranged.[11] A further juxtaposition is set up, one that opposes 'real' and 'authentic' objects with reproductions and enlarged photocopies. Many of the objects belong to the realm of popular culture, for example sheet music, movie posters, popular books, postcards, plastic totem poles, toy cowboy and Indian figures, cigar cases and sports pennants.

It should be noted that popular material culture is rarely exhibited in museum displays, unless they have some special historical or sacred significance. And yet, the objects in *Fluffs and Feathers* are displayed in an elegantly labelled, beautifully lit manner, like the objects in the East Asian Gallery. The division between 'popular/kitsch' and 'fine/sacred' is thus brought into question, and the mechanisms of display become obvious. The jarring physical juxtapositions do not allow one to step back into an undefined past to contemplate another culture; rather, they serve to accentuate ambiguity and construction. The official, decisive, non-native voice of the museum breaks.

It is especially significant that these objects of popular culture are familiar ones to visitors, evoking memory and nostalgia. Nostalgia, according to Kathleen Stewart

is a cultural practice, not a given content; its forms, meaning, and effects shift with the context – it depends on where the speaker stands in the landscape of the present (1988:227)

In the present of the exhibition, the familiar objects stand out. They are not exoticized by being related to important events in the past. There is no removal of distance or time from these objects to render them mysterious. As Fred Shroeder (1981:7) writes:

Distance lends enchantment, and the rarity and remoteness of the everyday lives and the commonplace things of earlier times guarantee their value in the minds of the moment. Everyone respects a pioneer log cabin, an Abraham Lincoln campaign banner, a colonial recipe book, and an early edition of the *Sacred Harp* hymnal, but a Winnebago recreational vehicle, a *Who Can Beat Nixon?* board-game, a Cuisinart food-processor manual, and an Anita Bryant Christmas album do not win our reverence, however much they may be part of our daily lives.

The memories evoked by these objects are recent, familiar ones. The exhibit is thus placed firmly within the world of the visitor, not of the museum. Native people are not 'exoticized' by a separation in time and space from white people.

The middle section of the exhibition presents a narrative turning point. There is a platform with a mirror and native costumes which visitors can try on. They can then stand beside the cardboard cutout figures of a chief and his family and post against a highly artificial painted backdrop. One can, in a sense, 'try on' another culture. This is a liminal moment in the exhibit, where one can become reflexively distanced from one's own experiences in order to comment on them (MacAloon, 1984:11). Barbara Babcock (1984:108) defines this as an ironic double moment, ironic not in the sense of a 'true and false meaning', but in the sense of a 'double play', an interplay between social criticism and comedy.

It is apparent at this stage of the exhibition that this is *not* an exhibit about an ethnographic group, i.e. 'Indians', as suggested in the beginning of the exhibition, but rather is an exhibition that shows on an experiential level how stereotypes are created and what it feels like to have a negative stereotype applied to oneself. Crucially, the first mirror allows visitors to see themselves dressed up as native people, at a point in the exhibit where the authoritative narrative voice set up by the ROM is being questioned by a native counter-voice.

In the final section of the exhibition is a series of photographs of native people, a pair of beaded sneakers and a feathered sweatshirt. The photographs are at eye level, and the final one is not a photograph at all, but a mirror where one is confronted with one's own face. Indeed, the second mirror is as pivotal to the exhibition as the first one. It is empty, on the one hand, and reflects everything, on the other. It thus symbolically returns the visitor to him/herself, journey completed, lesson learned. Again, there is a movement in narrative voice.

It is clear that the mode of representation in *Fluffs and Feathers* diverges from the usual one at the ROM. The exhibition is about negative and harmful white stereotypes of native peoples, and yet, this message is not portrayed in a confrontational manner. In fact, the tone of the exhibition is amused and ironic, a form of irony that Linda Hutcheon (1991:5) characterizes as 'Irony Humorous', which gently subverts through jokes, and at times slips into 'Irony Demystifying', a somewhat more critical form. This is consistent with Babcock's notion of irony as a double play.

The strategic use of irony makes the exhibition relational and dialogic. Instead of merely telling visitors that stereotypes are dangerous to those groups who are stereotyped, the exhibition invites visitors to enter into a dialogue with another identity in order to experience[12] these messages on their own. In doing so, it does not revert to an essentialist position on identity. It does not construct native people and white people as polar opposites. Neither does it compare, through 'authentic' objects, native cultures in the past to native cultures in the present as if the present were somehow less 'real' due to its contamination with 'white culture'. Rather, culture is constructed as an 'ongoing human invention' (Linnekin, 1991:5) whose representations are situated historically.

The issue of a true and authentic culture that is unique to native people is avoided in the exhibition through the juxtapositions of 'authentic' and reproduced objects and through particular appropriations and reappropriations of popular culture (for example, the beaded sneakers).[13] The exhibit goes beyond 'displaying cultural properties which are taken (tautologically) to prove the existence of the entities said to have created or possessed them' (Handler, 1993:35). Rather, it plays with the notions of fixed identities by creating a space of shared communication within which visitors can become involved in the process of the exhibit, instead of standing back and visually consuming the exhibit.

Within the exhibition are representations of representations of representations (for example photocopies that show how white people represent native people, all within the representational system of the ROM), bouncing back against each other in a state of 'mimetic excess', defined by Michael Taussig (1993:254) as 'an excess creating reflexive awareness as to the mimetic faculty'. Mimetic excess in the exhibition creates an unstable subjectivity, rather than, as in *Into the Heart of Africa*, a politics based on difference. Taussig's notion of mimetic excess describes the drifting in and out of identities induced by the mirrors and the juxtapositions of the exhibit, a mimetic excess that is, as Taussig (255) describes it:

. . . a somersaulting back to sacred actions implicated in the puzzle that empowered mimesis any time, any place – namely the power to both double yet double endlessly, to become any Other and engage the image with the reality thus imagized.

Irony as contamination

In this final section, I would like to draw up the threads of the analyses of the two exhibitions. As I have shown, both exhibitions use irony as part of their critiques of museum practices. *Into the Heart of Africa*, however, does not extend its critique to the logic of the representation itself. Its use of irony depends upon a standard definition of irony that replicates the mode of representation dominant in museums. This mode makes a number of distinctions: between representation and reality, between visitor and exhibit, between the visitor and the 'Other' on display. Through strategies of distanciation, other cultures are thus placed in a different time and space than that of the exhibition, facilitating a politics based on cultural difference that borders on an essentialist view of culture. Indeed, in order to read the irony intended by the curator one must separate oneself from the culture on display.

Fluffs and Feathers, on the other hand, subverts the mode of representation by taking it to excess, by displaying representation upon representation upon representation. This is achieved through a form of irony that juxtaposes, that arranges objects into disorder, that goes beyond what visitors expect from museums. It is thus able to establish a space that is more dialogical. This has to do with the use of an irony that does not critique directly; rather it mocks, and throws our representations back into our faces. We lose, in a sense, the stability of a fixed subject position.

The dominant mode of representation in museums is, to quote Kathleen Stewart (1991) 'decontaminated', because it is based on a logic and theory that 'sees its object from a decontaminated distance' (395). Decontaminated theory attempts to define its objects and thus essentializes them. One of the ways out of this mode would be to 'contaminate' it, to interrupt and reenergize it by tracking its forms and modes. This contamination is dialogic, in the Bakhtinian sense of self/other relations of simultaneity, of shared existence and multiplicity of perception (see Holquist, 1990). Contaminated theory constructs an interpretive space which makes possible countervoices – 'backtalk'.

It is this critical potential of irony that comes from speaking within the system that I take to be a form of 'backtalking'. As Stewart writes (1991:411):

> It is not a superficial attention to form that rushes to discover the cause or explanation but an immersion in form in which the elements that produce meaning become known in the act of using them, manipulating them, and repositioning them in another version.

If irony is used in this manner in exhibitions, it can thus interrupt and contaminate the entrenched system of representation dominant in museums. This is then a way of problematizing representational strategies through representations themselves.

Marcus and Fischer (1986:14) discuss the implications of using irony as a mode of description:

> The task, particularly now, is not to escape the deeply suspicious and critical nature of the ironic mode of writing, but to embrace and utilize it in combination with other strategies for producing realist descriptions of society. The desirability of reconciling the persistence of irony with other modes of representation derives in turn from a recognition that because all perspectives and interpretations are subject to critical review, they must finally be left as multiple and open-ended alternatives.

Thus, irony can be used to open up interpretive spaces by offering several viewpoints. This is also a risky move, as is evidenced with the exhibition *Into the Heart of Africa*, where instead of creating a shared communicative space, the ironic strategies played into rather than against a politics of difference. This is a dangerous game for museums to play, but it can be an inordinately productive one for museums who want to create shared spaces of communication with their publics.

Acknowledgements

I would like to thank Kenneth Little and Linda Hutcheon for suggestions on earlier drafts of the paper.

Notes

1 I restrict myself to a discussion of ethnographic museums in this paper, although some of my remarks can also be applied to art galleries, historic sites, fairs and amusement park displays.

2 Neither, I might add, is the position of the 'observer' one that is necessarily taken up by all visitors, as point made by Mitchell when he described a group of Egyptians visiting the exhibit of Egypt who objected to the representation of the bazaar.

3 See also Kenneth Little, 1991, on the effects of this visual system of representation and order by African tourist safaris on the Kenyan landscape, animals and peoples.

4 This museum experience is, of course, a generalization, and can be and is contested in different kinds of exhibitions and museums, and importantly, by visitors.

5 This issue came to the fore in the widely-publicized boycott of the Glenbow Museum's 1988 exhibition celebrating Canada's native cultures. The instigators of the boycott, the Lubicon Cree of northern Alberta, who at the time had a long-standing unsettled land claim with the federal government, objected to, on the one hand, having their material culture celebrated in the exhibition, and on the other hand having their culture actively destroyed by the major sponsors of the exhibition, namely Shell Oil and the Alberta government.

6 The exhibition title was changed prior to its opening due to negative reactions from a focus group (Cuyler Young, 1993:175).

7 Indeed, considering that the African collection at the ROM was handed down to them through the bequests of these same missionaries, it is understandable that the critique of their activities would be tempered.

8 It is significant to the later interpretations of this image that Lord Beresford is named and the Zulu is not, and also that it is Lord Beresford that is having the 'encounter', and not the Zulu.

9 Schildkraut (1993:20) points out that many critics felt that the use of white voices, ironically or not, was unacceptable, and asked 'whether an exhibition on the Holocaust from the point of view of the Nazis would be acceptable'?

10 Temporary exhibitions tend to be placed on the first floor, but if one looks at the arrangements of exhibitions by floors at the ROM one notices a curious vertical arrangement, as if one were ascending into the higher reaches of 'civilization': prehistory and native peoples in the basement, China on the ground floor, and Greece and Egypt on the top floor. Does this mean that contemporary native people have moved up in the schema of things if they are shown on the ground floor?

11 This is to some extent true, as rather late in the installation they realized that not all the objects could travel to the ROM.

12 This is not to say that 'experience' is an unproblematic apprehension of the world (see Joan W. Scott, 1992).

13 For more on the invention of culture see Gable, Handler and Lawson, 1992; Handler, 1988; Hanson, 1989; 1991; Levine, 1991; Linnekin, 1991a; 1991b.

References

Alloula, Malek, (1986), *The Colonial Harem*. Trans. Myrna Godzich and Wlad Godzich, Minneapolis: University of Minnesota Press.

Ames, Michael M., (1992), *Cannibal Tours and Glass Boxes: The Anthropology of Museums*. Vancouver: UBC Press.

Babcock, Barbara A., (1984), 'Arrange Me into Disorder: Fragments and Reflections on Ritual Clowning,' in John J. MacAloon (ed.), *Rite, Drama, Festival, Spectacle: Rehearsals Toward a Theory of Cultural Performance*. Philadelphia: Institute for the Study of Human Issues.

Bal, Mieke, (1992), 'Telling, Showing, Showing Off.' In *Critical Inquiry* 18 (3):556–94.

Cannizo, Jeanne, (1989), *Into the Heart of Africa*. Toronto: Royal Ontario Museum.

Cannizo, Jeanne, (1991), 'Exhibiting Cultures: "Into the Heart of Africa" ' in *Visual Anthropology Review* 7 (1):150–60.

Chamberlain, Lori, (1989), 'Bombs and Other Exciting Devices, or the Problems of Teaching Irony' in *College English* 51 (1):25–36.

Clifford, James, (1988), *The Predicament of Culture: Twentieth-Century Ethnography, Literature, and Art*. Cambridge: Harvard University Press.

Clifford, James and George E. Marcus, (1986), *Writing Culture: The Poetics and Politics of Ethnography*. Berkeley: University of California Press.

Cuyler Young, T., (1993), 'Into the Heart of Africa: The Director's Perspective,' in *Curator* 36 (3):174–88.

Da Breo, Hazel, (1990), ' "Into the Heart of Africa" '. Exhibition review in *Culture* 10 (1): 104–5.

Dane, Joseph A., (1986), 'The Defense of the Incompetent Reader,' in *Comparative Literature* 38:53–72.

Doxtator, Deborah, (1992a), Museum Studies Lecture, Toronto, January 15.

Doxtator, Deborah, (1993b), 'The Rebirth of a Native Exhibit Inside a White Institution: *Fluffs and Feathers* Goes to the ROM.' Paper presented at the Canadian Anthropological Society annual conference, Toronto, May 8.

Fabian, Johannes, (1983), *Time and the Other: How Anthropology Makes its Object*. New York: Columbia University Press.

Fish, Stanley, (1983), 'Short People Got No Reason to Live: Reading Irony,' in *Daedalus* 112 (1):175–91.

Gable, Eric, Handler, Richard and Lawson, Anna, (1992), 'On the Uses of Relativism: Fact, Conjecture, and Black and White Histories at Colonial Williamsburg,' in *American Ethnologist* 19 (4): 791–805.

Handler, Richard, (1988), *Nationalism and the Politics of Culture in Quebec*. Madison: University of Wisconsin Press.

Handler, Richard, (1993), 'An Anthropological Definition of the Museum and its Purpose,' in *Museum Anthropology* 17 (1):33–6.

Hanson, Allan, (1989), 'The Making of the Maori: Culture Invention and Its Logic.' In *American Anthropologist* 91:890–901.

Hanson, Allan, (1991), Reply to Langdon, Levine, and Linnekin, in *American Anthropologist* 93 (2):449–50.

Hill, Tom and Nicks, Trudy, (1992), *Task Force Report on Museums and First Peoples. Turning the Page: Forging New Partnerships Between Museums and First Peoples*. Ottawa.

Holquist, Michael, (1990), *Dialogism: Bakhtin and His World*. New York: Routledge.

Hutcheon, Linda, (ed.), (1992), *Double-Talking: Essays on Verbal and Visual Ironies in Contemporary Canadian Art and Literature*. Toronto: ECW Press.

Hutcheon, Linda, (ed.), (1994), 'The Post Always Rings Twice: The Postmodern and the Postcolonial', to appear in *Textual Practice*.

Jones, Anna Laura, (1991), 'Exploding Canons: The Anthropology of Museums,' in *Annual Review of Anthropology* 22:201–20.

Karp, Ivan, Mullen Kreamer, Christine and Lavine, Steven D. (eds), (1992), *Museums and Communities: The Politics of Public Culture*. Washington: Smithsonian Institution Press.

Karp, Ivan and Lavine, Steven D. (eds), (1991), *Exhibiting Cultures: The Poetics and Politics of Museum Display*. Washington: Smithsonian Institution Press.

Kelly, Robert F. n.d. 'Culture as Commodity: The Marketing of Cultural Objects and Cultural Experiences.' Unpublished.

Kirshenblatt-Gimblett, Barbara, (1991), 'Objects of Ethnography,' in *Exhibiting Cultures: The Poetics and Politics of Museum Display*. Eds. Ivan Karp and Steven D. Lavine. Washington: Smithsonian Institution Press.

Knox, Norman, (1972), 'On the Classification of Ironies,' in *Modern Philology*, August: 53–62.

Levine, H.B., (1991), Comment on Hanson's 'The Making of the Maori', in *American Anthropologist* 93 (2):444–6.

Linnekin, Jocelyn, (1991a), 'Culture/*Kastom*/Tradition: Theory and Politics in Cultural Representation.' Paper given at the annual meeting for the Association for Social Anthropology in Oceania, March, 1991.

Linnekin, Jocelyn, (1991b), 'Cultural Invention and the Dilemma of Authenticity', In *American Anthropologist* 93 (2):446–9.

Little, Kenneth, (1991), 'On Safari: The Visual Politics of a Tourist Representation.' In *The Varieties of Sensory Experience*. Ed. David Howes. Toronto: University of Toronto Press.

MacAloon, John J., (1984), 'Introduction: Cultural Performances, Cultural Theory,' in *Rite, Drama, Festival, Spectacle: Rehearsals Toward a Theory of Cultural Performance*. Philadelphia: Institute for the Study of Human Issues.

Marcus, George E. and Fischer, Michael M.J., (1986), *Anthropology as Cultural Critique: An Experimental Moment in the Human Sciences*. Chicago: University of Chicago Press.

Mitchell, Timothy, (1988), *Colonising Egypt*. Berkeley: University of California Press.

Mitchell, Timothy, (1989), 'The World as Exhibition,' in *Comparative Studies in Society and History* 31 (2):217–36.

Nicks, Trudy, (1992), 'Partnerships in Developing Cultural Resources: Lessons From the Task Force on Museums and First Nations,' in *Culture* 12 (1):87–94.

Schildkraut, Enid, (1991), 'Ambiguous Messages and Ironic Twists: *Into the Heart of Africa* and *The Other Museum*,' in *Museum Anthropology* 15 (2):16–23.

Schroeder, Fred E.H. (ed.), (1981), *Twentieth-Century Popular Culture in Museums and Libraries*. Bowling Green: Bowling Green University Popular Press.

Scott, Joan, (1992), 'Experience', in *Feminists Theorize the Political*. Eds. Judith Butler and Joan W. Scott. New York: Routledge.

Sperber, Dan and Wilson, Deirdre, (1981), 'Irony and the Use-Mention Distinction,' in P. Cole (ed.), *Radical Pragmatics*. Academic Press.

Stewart, Kathleen, (1988), 'Nostalgia – A Polemic,' in *Cultural Anthropology* 3 (3):227–41.

Stewart, Kathleen, (1991), On the Politics of Cultural Theory: A Case for 'Contaminated' Cultural Critique, in *Social Research* 58.

Taussig, Michael, (1993), *Mimesis and Alterity: A Particular History of the Senses*. New York: Routledge.

Tyler, Stephen A., (1987), *The Unspeakable: Discourse, Dialogue, and Rhetoric in the Postmodern World*. Madison: University of Wisconsin Press.

Seeing through Solidity:
a feminist perspective on museums

Gaby Porter

Abstract

Applying poststructuralist and feminist theory to museums, this chapter traces the gendered relations of representation in museums. The author takes the relation of text, author and reader from poststructuralist studies and translates these to the museum forms of exhibition, curator and visitor. She examines the relations between men and women, masculine and feminine as they are constituted in museums, tracing a series of gendered, hierarchical oppositions. These are central to the ways in which museums organize their identity, space, collections and exhibitions to make meanings. She concludes that the roles of women as they are represented are relatively passive, shallow, undeveloped, muted and closed; the roles of men are, in contrast, relatively active, deep, highly developed, fully pronounced and open. Together, these provide a thread for the museums in the stories and narratives they construct. The author addresses the challenge of applying abstract and theoretical 'readings' to museums – where the collections appear to resist such readings through their concrete and solid presence, and where the prevailing professional culture is empirical and anti-theoretical. This challenge was also her own, as a museum worker struggling to develop a theoretical critique. Finally, she describes exhibitions in Britain and northern Europe which are more productive, diverse and open to re-reading. They are interdisciplinary and irreverent, breaking new ground in museum exhibition-making, developing new methods, forms of expression and themes.

Gaby Porter

> Our previous history is not the petrified block of a singular
> visual space, since, looked at obliquely, it can always be seen
> to contain its moments of unease. (Jacqueline Rose, 1986,
> *Sexuality in the Field of Vision*)

Rose's allusion to history as a petrified block, material and solid,
resonates with history as found in museums – the residues and
solid, hardened traces of histories of which their collections are
formed. Because they are full of such things, museums themselves
appear to share these material and physical characteristics, and to
escape or resist critical readings which might suggest that they are
other or less than solid, certain, and complete. Museums have not
received the attention of those who might look 'obliquely', and
with a different perspective: one which unsettles the certainty of
the museum discourse and suggests that these solid histories and
arrangements can soften to become more flexible and malleable.
Feminist critics, in particular, have focused on other media such
as history, television, cinema and magazines and have overlooked
or avoided museums. Even with people who have undertaken
feminist criticism in, say, literature or technology, my proposition
of a feminist critique of museums may be met with surprise or
even mild dismay: 'well, I actually *liked* that museum . . .'. Until
very recently, few people have undertaken critical research about
museums, and there have been few occasions where they have
come together with people working in museums to share and
openly explore critical issues of representation, sexual difference
and identity or cultural diversity.

Like many others entering museum work, I had no awareness
of such critical issues, nor a theoretical or practical grounding in
material culture studies. While working in different museums, I
increasingly felt that their displays and collections did not represent the histories and experiences of women as fully and truth-
fully as those of men. I sought to understand more fully why and
how this happened: eventually, I registered as a part-time postgraduate student to undertake research on the representation of
women in history museums in Britain.[1] My goal in this research
was programmatic, to increase and improve the representation of
women in museum displays and collections. Initially, I felt that
this could be achieved simply by adding material which reflected
women's experience in the past to the collections and displays. As
I studied further, I began to understand that the differences
between the histories of men and women as represented in the

museum lay at much deeper levels. I recognized that the whole structure of museums – abstract knowledge and organization as well as concrete manifestations of buildings, exhibitions and collections – was built upon categories and boundaries which embodied assumptions about men and women, masculine and feminine (Porter, 1987). As a further step, I recognized that these assumptions about men and women were interdependent and relational; they could not be anchored by reference to any 'real' men and women but were constructed, positional and constantly in the making (Porter, 1991).

In this chapter, I describe the broad approach and conclusions of the research which I undertook. I address the challenge of applying theory in museums, where people are strongly anti-theoretical, or empirical, in their practice and approach. This challenge is greater because a theoretical reading is difficult to sustain when the museum is such a complex, layered text of space, things, texts, images and people; its sheer scale and persistent physical presence constantly threaten to topple fragile concepts of subjectivity and positionality. This challenge was greater for me because I chose to use a feminist approach, with its equivalent tensions between the abstract, theoretical concepts and the material, physical body – anxious to avoid any appeal to biology and essences, yet struggling to maintain a concept of femininity which is always and only abstract and positional. I question whether theory, and the theories which I used, helped or hindered my intention at the outset, to effect change in museums. I employed poststructuralist and deconstructive methods, where the temptation has been to allow the endless play and deferral of meaning and to avoid any closure. I also examine the benefits and costs of such engaged research, where I have been both 'inside' the museum text as curator/author, and 'outside' the text as reader. Is such research of greater benefit than 'academic' research; and what are the costs and consequences for the professionals involved? Finally, I suggest some directions for feminist exhibition-making.

Theorizing museums

The focus of my research was not history itself, but representation: not the content of displays and collections, but their production and meaning. My concern was not whether something is true, but how it comes to be true in the museum text. Thus in my research I challenged the traditional, humanist and empirical, ways of thinking and working which permeate the professional framework and everyday practice of museum workers. Theory became central to my work, providing the tools to move beyond the obvious and evident presence of these displays and collections and to develop a critical understanding of the processes and relations through which they are constructed and maintained.

The theories which I used for this feminist critique of museums were not themselves new: they are, broadly, structuralist and post-structuralist and developed most fully in literary criticism and cultural studies, particularly in visual and popular culture such as advertising, films and magazines. (For example, in the work of John Berger, 1972 and Judith Williamson, 1978; also of Ros Coward, 1984; Jacqueline Rose, 1986 and John Tagg, 1988, among others.) What was new was that I applied these theories to museums, taking the relation of text, author and reader and translating these into the museum forms of exhibition, curator and visitor. Museums claim to show the past as it really was – to re-present history. In this simple claim, the medium of the museum and the process of making collections and displays are rendered invisible in a relationship of authenticity and truth. Many museum workers believe that the 'real thing' they are dealing with carries intrinsic, essential and universal truths – material facts. Their professional codes and day-to-day practice are built on the premise of objectivity and neutrality, eschewing bias or influence. This practice is empirical – attributing concepts and knowledge to common sense and experience. Empiricism posits itself as obvious and natural, and rejects theory as distorting or, at best, unnecessary. Critics since structuralism have put into question such a practice: from this critical perspective, the 'obvious' and the 'natural' are not givers of meaning, but are produced within a specific society by the ways in which that society talks and thinks about itself and its experience. In such a critique, the realist text depends as much as any other text on an underpinning theory or ideology, despite its apparent invisibility or transparency. It is intelligible as 'realistic' precisely *because* it is familiar, recognizable and taken for granted: it reproduces what we already seem to know. Thus, in the realist text of museums, empiricism is not a sufficient response to, or defence against, critical analysis.

The term 'structuralism' derives from Ferdinand de Saussure's linguistic studies in the early part of this century. His work demonstrated that the meaning of signs is not intrinsic but relational: each sign derives its meaning from its difference from all the other signs in the language chain. Thus structuralism insists on the primacy of relations and systems of relations. Saussure's work was taken up and applied in other areas from the middle of this century: in scientific, social, anthropological and cultural studies. In such studies, structuralism displaced nineteenth century empiricism, which gave ontological primacy to objects, with a 'theory of relativity'. Whereas empiricism stressed the endurance of objects and materials, in the new theory the only endurances are structures of activity (Culler, 1981:141).

Saussure located meaning in the language system, but saw it as single, fixed, prior to its realization in speech and writing. Critics since Saussure have taken his underlying concern with relations further to suggest that meaning is constantly changing. These poststructuralist critics disregard the conventional respect for the authority and intentions of the author, the hierarchy of text and reader. They insist on the autonomy of the text and show how conflict between the reader and the author/text can work productively to expose the underlying premise of a work and to release new meanings and interpretations in the text.

The move from structuralism to poststructuralism has been associated with the work of the French philosopher Jacques Derrida. Moving from a focus on speech to a concern with writing and textuality, Derrida saw all meaning as produced by a dual process of difference and deferral. This process is, respectively, spatial and temporal: meaning is never fully present but is constructed through the potentially endless process of referring to other, absent signifiers; through the interplay of presence and absence (Derrida, 1976). The effect of representation, in which meaning is apparently fixed, is only temporary and retrospective in its fixing.

If meaning is constructed in the text through the interplay of presence and absence, then it may also be deconstructed. Deconstruction locates meaning in texts and their relation with other texts. It is based on the premise of hierarchical oppositions, in which one side of the opposition is the key concept in relation to which the other is defined negatively. Deconstruction works to reverse these oppositions and, in doing so, is able both to show how discourses achieve their effects and to displace their systems. It is both subversive *and* productive, releasing new and unintended meanings. Precisely *because* meaning is incomplete and contradictory, it is open to challenge and redefinition.

Gaby Porter

In developing a critique of museums, I took the relation of text, author and reader from poststructuralist studies and translated these into the museum forms of exhibition, curator and visitor. In developing a feminist critique, I examined the relations between men and women, masculine and feminine, as they are constituted in the museum. I examined these gender relations[2] as hierarchical oppositions, central to the ways in which museums organize their identity, collections, space and exhibitions to make stories and meanings, both shaping and shaped by notions of masculinity and femininity. I used the position of a woman reader in order to reverse these oppositions, reading against the grain of the text to reveal its sexual codes, assumptions and omissions. From this position, the museum text no longer appears sexually neutral and full with meaning, but restricting and narrow. I read 'as a woman', not with reference to any essential qualities or experience of women, nor in the belief that my conclusions were limited to women; rather, as a position of otherness, at the margins of the text, to explore what is not represented, not shown and not said. This position reverses the usual hierarchy of dominant/masculine and subordinate/feminine to demonstrate that conventional interpretations are limited and limiting.

I traced the gendered identities of 'man' and 'woman', masculinity and femininity in such relationships as subject/object; self/other; progressive/static; public/private; production/consumption; culture/nature. Underlying all of these are the associations of active/passive and male/female. In museums, and in this discourse, 'woman' becomes the background against which 'man' acts. These representations are formed around idealized and stereotypical notions of masculinity and femininity, which are rendered as 'real'. I concluded that, as produced and presented in museums, the roles of women are relatively passive, shallow, undeveloped, muted and closed; the roles of men are, in contrast, relatively active, deep, highly developed and articulated, fully pronounced and open. 'His' existence and ascendance depend on 'her' presence and subordination. Together, they provide a thread for museums in the histories and narratives which they make. The critical project is thus to deconstruct the whole process in which these notions are both given and giving meaning, and to build new ways which are more productive, diverse and open to re-reading.

Museums use sexual identity and difference as a firm and persistent referent on which to build the narratives of exhibitions.

Yet feminist critics have drawn on psychoanalysis to unsettle the notion that sexual identity is certain and complete; rather, they suggest, it is hesitant and incomplete. Following this thread, I looked for the placing of sexual difference in the narrative of museum exhibitions; and at the moments of unease – the hesitations, contradictions, unconscious slips and awkward silences – in that narrative. Much of what we present as knowledge in collections and exhibitions is speculative – yet, when attached to material, physically evident, objects, it 'reads' as known, certain, authoritative. From the psychoanalytic perspective, these speculative attributions and ascriptions may be seen as projections – imbuing the environment and/or other people with an aspect of the self which is disowned, either because it is unconscious, unknown, or because it is suppressed. Sexual identity and difference are so strongly charged with meaning, and vice versa, in museum narratives, precisely *because* these identities, for each of us, are incomplete, unsettled and unsettling.

For the psychoanalyst Jacques Lacan, masculinity and femininity were fictional, constructed identities – the result of social and symbolic, rather than biological, difference. The symbolic order is achieved in the passage from the imaginary – the relationship between mother and child – into the symbolic – the recognition of the father and his law. The child passes from a maternal, natural or experiential, bond into a symbolic order of resolution and closure, rational and cultural, with its own laws and taboos. For boys, this journey is one of transition, separation, rejection: male identity is formed through a split and maintained through suppression and discontinuity. Rationality is established through the exclusion of the feminine: the knower (subject/masculine) splits himself from the known (object/feminine) and establishes dominance over it/her. At the same time, 'he' idealizes the lost 'mother' – eternal, ahistorical, feminine, with a child at her breast, and also available to men. For girls, the journey is one of inversion and loss: recognition of and subjection to an order in which she has no position in her own right, but only in relation to men. For Lacan, the negativity of the feminine is a symbolic and psychical necessity.

For both men and women, this journey is never perfected but always remains partial and precarious. Subjectivity is always in the making. As in Derrida's critique of textuality, Lacan states that meaning can only occur in specific locations and in a relation of difference from other locations. The mechanism of desire, rather than the principle of difference, prevents any final fixing of meaning: the individual is driven by desire for control, satisfaction and completeness which can never be achieved. The subject is never fully in command of his/her identity: rather, a complex network of conflicting structures *produces* the subject and its experiences.

The value of psychoanalysis to feminism is that it offers a specific account of sexual difference, and describes the psychic law to which we are all subject, but only in terms of its failing. If representations serve to maintain a particular and oppressive mode of sexual recognition, they do so only partially and at a cost.

Applying this analysis in literary texts, critics have traced women and the feminine as the necessary frontier between man and chaos: as 'the limit of the symbolic order [they] will share in the disconcerting properties of *all* frontiers: they will be neither inside nor outside, neither known nor unknown' (Moi, 1985: 167). Applying the same analysis in museums, women and the feminine can equally be seen as the boundary and frontier. In museums, knowledge and collections are split into disciplines and hierarchies of classification; specimens are separated from their context, isolated from other specimens, and dissected into individual parts; the parts are ordered and brought together with other parts into new associations and groupings. All these methods are presented as objective, neutral and rational, their goal to create completeness and a comprehensive historical and material record. From a critical and feminist perspective, these practices appears to construct and maintain the male order, with women at its margins. At first, representations of women and the feminine may seem haphazard and inconsistent, frustrating to those who wish to follow their traces in the material culture, but arbitrary. With closer inspection, through detailed study of the application of such methods in specific examples and case studies, I traced the ways in which these representations are different for activities and modalities associated respectively with the masculine or the feminine, to the relative disadvantage and marginalization of the latter. In exhibitions, in the selection and preparation of items from the collections and in classification systems, women and the feminine become, literally, the frontiers by which space and knowledge are defined: they are the more distant and imprecise elements, in the background and at the edges of the picture. The figures and activities in the foreground, more fully developed and with greater consistency, are those of men and the masculine attributes. 'Reading' across museums, to compare different types of museums and different subjects (industry/technology, social history, the media), I noted the discontinuity *between* them: positioned at the margins of each, representations of women did not 'fit' together coherently, whereas those of men were relatively congruent. I noted that, throughout, representations of women and the feminine are generally vague and idealized. Where narratives and incidents or materials relating to women do not 'fit' these ideals, they are couched in terms which show discomfort and unease: for example, where women worked in heavy and male-dominated industries (Porter, 1991); where they continue to do paid and unpaid domestic work; where women are independent of men. In these places, the terms of the representation may become more sharply focused, shrill or humorous; or they may appear to deny women and the feminine altogether so that these have to be teased out from oblique references in other messages and materials. At the same time, the expressions of a feminine identity and subjectivity in different terms than these is almost inaudible/invisible and scarcely articulated as 'woman' searches for a language which 'she' can use in order to express herself. This may come through more puralistic forms of representation which recognize and suggest the complex and contradictory formation of identity, and which explore the interior, immaterial life of the symbolic, emotional and imaginary as well as the exterior, material world of events and things.

In the research which I undertook, I acknowledged that museums are changing: that the materials and methods which they use are bringing people into a closer relationship with museums, and identification with the histories on display. But I argued that the ways in which museums communicate and connect with their visitors are ultimately constrained by the underlying premise of empiricism. This positions the reader/visitor as consumer, who gazes at the finished product and appreciates the creativity of the maker or the authenticity and truth of the setting. The mode of address is declarative; the process of production is mystified or suppressed.

Instead, I proposed that the poststructuralist approach produces a more dynamic and productive culture: it turns the reader/visitor from passive consumer to active producer of meaning, and sees meaning as constantly being made afresh. Its form of address is interrogative, inviting response and dialogue. Through drawing attention to the processes of production, and making them visible, the critical approach suggests that things can be made again, and made differently: that meanings are plural and negotiable. Applying this approach to museums, they can uncover the processes of selection, acquisition, ordering and arrangement of collections, which underlie the public expressions of identity and exhibition. Through presenting themselves as workshops and studios rather than shrines, and supporting others to use their tools and methods with different outcomes, museums can become the sites for active and creative production, the presentation and exchange of diverse viewpoints, and the dynamic (re)interpretation of collections and histories.

The museum as 'text' – entangled in complexity

In 'reading' the museum exhibition as representation and text, I confronted its complexity – its many layers of production and meaning. These reside in (at least) the exhibition themes; the physical layout of space and design; the sources and choices of objects, images, texts and other materials; the position, condition and presentation of these elements; the light, movement, sounds and smells created in the exhibition. The exhibition is produced and meaning is made also at the point when visitors enter it: in the expectations that they bring with them; the way that they enter, move around, use and leave the exhibition space; whether the exhibition is at the beginning, or the end, of a longer visit or whether it is the main purpose of their visit; whether they have opportunities to discuss or comment on the exhibition with museum staff. This complexity at the level of the exhibition is compounded by the complexity of the museum as a much larger system of production: its objectives, resources, constitution and hierarchical organization; the function and physical separation and devolution of departments and disciplines; the competing demands and pressures to raise visitor numbers and income, and to care for collections; the staff, the role of external specialists, consultants and opinion formers. In choosing to analyse the museum process through detailed research and case studies, I found it difficult to decide where to pitch the research project: which site and materials to select? which staff to interview? I initially pitched these at the level and in the area of my own professional position – at the level of the exhibition; the curators and interpreters who worked with collections and made exhibitions; the collections and research materials; visitor studies when available; published accounts and articles. As the research programme developed, my questions and the objects of study became broader and deeper, to place these exhibitions, people and materials more firmly within their institutional framework and context. With so many different layers and facets to the project, I easily became overwhelmed by detail and description, losing sight of my vision and analysis. This was compounded because, in all of the projects studied, research files and background materials were lacking and I conducted personal interviews in order to collect the data which I felt was essential to the study. In these interviews, especially, immediate concerns, constraints and problems – of people, buildings, collections and resources – were brought to my attention. It was difficult to step back from these 'causes' and to sustain a more abstract and less personalized analysis and overview: to 'read' and write at another level than the familiar, descriptive and chronological, cause-and-effect account.

Similarly, in using a feminist critique, I struggled to maintain a reading based on masculinity and femininity as fragile constructions, and to resist the appeal to experiences and essences, to biology and the body, to 'real' women and men – as subjects in history, as museum staff and as museum users or visitors. The studies from which I drew inspiration lay outside the museum sector, with culture as it is constituted in language, writing and the image – areas with a less solid and immediate physical presence than museums themselves and the collections with which they work. I was more familiar with the realist terms and goals of those striving towards a feminist practice in museums: to expose the gender-blindness of existing work and to reveal and represent other realities in which women were both visible and active. Just as the physical presence of collections and museums threatened to topple my analysis, so the flesh-and-blood beings of men and women seemed at times to overwhelm and intrude into the notion that gender is socially and symbolically constructed, not physically determined.

As feminist studies of technology, environmental and medical issues have developed, the domain of cultural studies has broadened to include studies which link the material and physical world with the symbolic and imaginary dimensions of identity and culture, showing that things both give and are given meaning through the interactions and movements between the concrete and the abstract (eg, Ormrod and Cockburn, 1993; Traweek, 1988). These move away from the notion of text and textuality, and are more immediately applicable to material culture studies. Yet museums are more than this: they work on the 'received' material culture and make stories with it: thus both directions in cultural studies are helpful in making a critical analysis of museums.

I return to the question: did theory, and the theories which I used, help or hinder my project to effect change in museums? I believe that the development and application of a theoretical analysis shifts the terms and scope of any such project. Rather than looking for opportunities to 'add' women and the feminine to museums and museum practices, theoretical analysis emphasizes that the feminine and the masculine are interdependent and relational, and must be addressed together. Through the theories which I chose to use, I saw that the museum project is not simply to arrange and re-arrange histories and things which are already fully formed and cast, but to make meanings through the choice, placing and displacing of histories and things. The project thus becomes less determined and constrained; more complex and challenging; ultimately, more creative and fluid. From the critical perspective, the realist project – to achieve a more accurate and life-like representation of reality – seems limited in its scope and tied to the terms and expressions of the existing discourse. The critical project suggests new languages and releases new possibilities for museums, which I shall explore in the final section. First, though, I explore the advantages and disadvantages of engaged research.

Standing both inside and outside the museum text

While undertaking this research, I continued to work in museums and in the specific areas of work which were the subject of my study. There were many strengths in this. I understood the 'building blocks' through which the whole structure of museums – knowledge and expertise, professional and public – is constructed, and maintained an overview of a complex and changing field. The research itself, and my work in museums, were strengthened because I moved constantly between research, reflection and writing, and the application of theories and hypotheses in everyday practice: testing whether a particular analysis can be sustained, revising or refining the analysis as a result. The more dubious benefits are: that I was able to access some materials and sources for case studies which are not easily available to people without contacts in museums; and that, because I speak with professional knowledge and experience, my work is less easily dismissed as 'ill-informed' or irrelevant than critiques which are offered by people working outside the profession.

There were, however, disadvantages in my position as both 'inside' and 'outside' the museum. I was very close to the situations which I was studying: as I explained above, I often felt overwhelmed by detail and individual circumstance. I was seen by colleagues to be excessively critical of the people, and institutions, which I chose to study. In the absence of a critical culture and open forum for debate, many museum workers are unfamiliar and uncomfortable with the experience of being exposed to criticism: they see it as personal and counterproductive or destructive. In the initial, 'realist' phase of my work I received support and encouragement from others working in museums – particularly from women, individually and in the network of Women, Heritage and Museums – which compensated for the more negative responses to my work. However, many of these same people began to feel bemused as I moved towards a more analytical and theoretical project. I began to speak a different – and unfamiliar – language; I focused on issues which were less immediate, contained and actionable, more diffuse and beyond their control.

At the same time I faced the practical difficulty of doing research part-time while working full-time, and in relative isolation. I always felt on the edge of academic study, not quite or only just understanding the theories; not able to keep up with leading edge/relevant theories and studies; constantly interrupted, so that I was unable to dwell with the theories and ideas for long enough to work them through fully. I also worked very slowly, and was worried that my work would be superseded at the intellectual and theoretical level before I completed it. (These same worries surface again as I write this chapter.) The people who supported and sustained my journey into theory were on the outside/edge of museums, in cultural and critical studies, particularly in the field of visual representation; latterly, in technology studies; and my supervisor and fellow postgraduate students. Through publishing material in the early stages of the research, my work became known and I was invited to visit and speak at museum events in northern Europe. In Sweden, Denmark and Germany, I discovered and heard of different possibilities for museums which connected with my work: investigations into theory and detailed research into museum collecting and interpretation; fresh approaches to collecting, and to themes and methods of display, which in their turn placed new expectations on museum visitors and built new relationships with them; strong attention to exhibition-making as the synthesis of form and content; and a willingness to experiment and take risks in public and touring exhibitions. These visits gave me renewed energy to continue my research, and new ideas to invigorate it. Some of the projects were particularly relevant to my research findings and the implications for museum practice: I describe them below.

Putting theory into practice: some feminist exhibitions

Those exhibitions which I call 'feminist' call into question many of the things which are taken for granted in conventional museum exhibitions: they are irreverent and interdisciplinary in both the forms of knowledge and the methods of display which they employ. Rather than accepting the dualistic notion that knowledge or science forms the content of exhibitions and art provides their shape and presentation, the makers of such exhibitions synchronize and blend these elements into an integrated whole. They work across the divides and disciplines of art and science, social history and natural history, work and home. They choose to make exhibitions around abstract, immaterial and integrating themes more than linear, typological and chronological sequences; they do not hesitate to use feelings and emotions as a point of departure. Such exhibitions draw on and mix different forms and conventions – historical and contemporary, 'found' and constructed, factual and fictional. They are often impermanent – with a much shorter lifespan than the ten or fifteen years expected in most museum displays.

Because they are organized around themes which are lateral rather than chronological, such exhibitions may produce plural, and often contradictory, discourses and representations. For instance, in many museums 'period room' displays are used as set pieces to declare and illustrate a historical period, and to demarcate it from another. They are an exhibition convention, bringing together collections of the same period and style into a generalized arrangement, rather than a specific case study based on fieldwork and detailed research. Such displays are rarely used to make contrasts between social classes and circumstances. At the Geffrye Museum in London, however, the temporary exhibition *Putting*

on the Style (1990) constructed roomsets from different homes in
the 1950s to explore the expectations and lives of the people who
had lived in these homes: a council flat, a room in a lodging
house, an architect's home. These stories were not text narratives
set apart from the displays, but were articulated and given shape
in the choice and detailed arrangements within each display.
Here, the home was not a static set piece, standing for a historical
period and a generalized 'working class' or 'middle class' family,
but a more dynamic place for investigation of other, more personal, messy and sometimes painful stories (Macdonald and
Porter, 1990). The permanent exhibition at Hull, *The Story of
Hull and Its People*, uses a time-based linear structure, but one
which explores stages in the life cycle from birth to death, rather
than using historical periods or centuries. The exhibition traces
these stages in the lives of individual people in Hull, choosing
personal histories drawn from the last two centuries; these are not
the histories of public figures and notable people, but the histories
of people whose lives are often not recorded or recognized
(Kavanagh 1994:373).

The examples cited above begin to unsettle some of the
assumptions of mainstream exhibitions while using similar forms;
they do so through thoughtful exploration of their subjects and
collections, from different perspectives and with different voices.
In Denmark and Sweden, I visited exhibitions which use a new
language, different from any in Britain: more impressionistic and
abstract, yet at the same time more provocative and expressive.
Such exhibitions are unashamedly personal and subjective: their
makers use personal material and histories not to flesh out or
substantiate the official histories and narratives, but as the point
of departure.

The Women's Museum in Aarhus, Denmark, is explicitly political in its purpose, critical of mainstream museums in their presentation of women as subjects in history, and seeking to create new
forms of history and expression. Jette Sandahl, a former member
of the collective directorate, describes this:

Turning to museums as mirrors of identity, women must fade
into the background and freeze in passivity. The founders of
the Women's Museum thought, however, that museums were
uniquely qualified and equipped to fill just the opposite
purpose. Material collections give museums an unequalled
opportunity to provide counter-images, to de-naturalize, to

de-mystify the present order. As a museum we wanted to
accentuate the dimensions of change and choices in history,
to convey a sense of power to intervene in history, to influence decisions and affect the direction of development.
(Sandahl, 1993)

Many of the staff are not trained in museum work and not
bound by its conventions and limitations. Many work at the
museum on temporary employment schemes, giving the museum
an active base and network in the local community, which con-
tributes to every aspect of the museum:

This embeddedness manifests itself in untraditional types of
audiences, in the kind of exhibitions done by the museum as
well as in the kind of objects donated to the collections. We
are entrusted with the improper objects and stories, the
shameful and private objects, the hopefulness, the grief, the
cynicism, the shadow selves, the knowledge that is usually
hidden or kept back. (Ibid)

The museum has mounted over thirty exhibitions since it was
established in 1982, always about women; they may be concerned
with women's experiences – such as mothering – or seen from
women's perspective – such as the exhibition in 1993, *At Night*.
Every element of these exhibitions, from the choice of themes to
the specific voices of text and orientation of models and figures,
transmits the overall message and viewpoint of the exhibition.

Many exhibitions are concerned with the working lives of
women, and show women's skills – even where these are difficult
to convey through the usual 'language' with which museums communicate work. For example, in one exhibition, the producers
chose to emphasize the work of women in a household to extend
the useful life of everyday things – darning stockings and clothes,
repairing china and furniture. The clothes were encapsulated in
plastic and hung in a room with light shining through them –
emphasizing that they were worn through almost to the point of
transparency. In another exhibition, about changes in housework,
exhibits focused on the different skills and senses which women
employed before mechanization and automation: preserving food
(Figure 1); choosing different woods to create different oven tem-
peratures; testing heat with their hand or arm; smelling to judge
the freshness of food.

© The Editorial Board of The Sociological Review 1996

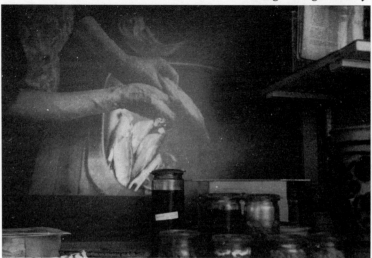

Figure 1 *An element of the 'Housework' exhibition at the Women's Museum in Aarhus, Denmark.*

In the exhibition *At Night* (1993), feelings and associations common to women were explored: fear; desire and pleasure; dreaming; nursing the very young and very old; working at night, in factories and theatres. The exhibition began in a small dark room with the sounds, smells and animals of the night: an owl, a nightingale and a wolf. Visitors then passed through a town gate, symbol of locking the night out and locking people in to the town. In a stark white 'room of fear', harsh high-pitched sounds were triggered by people's movements. The floor was painted with a geometric pattern in black and white, and a bicycle lay across it; on the walls, small perspex boxes contained small tools and weapons which women carried with them for protection, and their testimony (Figure 2). In the room of caring, a chair was placed in the centre of a dark room. Screens on each side of the chair half-hid objects behind them: a coffin and a crib respectively. Near the chair were a book, knitting, a cup, a jug and towels and cloths – things used to pass the hours and to nurse the sick (Figure 3). In the dark room of love at the end of the exhibition, classical sculptures were juxtaposed with anatomical teaching torsos to suggest the shift from romantic love to explicit and physiological sex. The exhibition ended with the wolf in bed.

At the Museum of Work in Norrköping, Sweden, any kind of work can become the subject of an exhibition. Museum staff have mounted exhibitions about social workers; office cleaners; people

Figure 2 *The 'Room of Fear' in the Exhibition at Night.*

Figure 3 *The 'Room of Caring' in the Exhibition at Night.*

living in an institution: all these have called for different approaches to collecting and exhibition-making. The museum's inaugural exhibition, *Sixth Sense*, (1991–94) cut across different kinds of work and was concerned with the interaction of the material world and immaterial world, explored through the different senses of sound, sight, touch, taste and smell. In the exhibition, produced by Eva Persson, the different experiences of rich and poor, skilled and unskilled, rural and industrial, men and women were juxtaposed in eloquent and powerful arrangements; there were many objects to hear, see, touch and smell but few words or texts (Persson, 1994).

In her exhibition work at the Museum of Work and at the Swedish Travelling Exhibition Service (Rikstutställningar), Persson wanted to create a new kind of exhibition, shifting from 'a scenic to a sculptural language . . . where form and content are one' (Persson, 1994:170). Whereas the scenic arrangement is static and two-dimensional, the sculptural exhibition is seen in the round; the structure is an integral part of the exhibition. This led her from chronology to space as the underlying principle for exhibitions.

In the exhibition *Sixth Sense*, Persson conceived installations such as that on 'Taste', concerned with the extremes of famine and wealth in Sweden in the 1860s. A row of stepped tables, laid with linen, silverware, china, glass and dishes for three set courses of a dinner held by a local grain merchant, were interspersed with rifles pointing out of the window. On the last of these tables, a paving sett lay among broken dishes; slogans were painted on the wall and window behind. In a showcase nearby, a handbill calling for a strike was laid on similar setts (Figure 4). In another part of the exhibition, 'Smell', huge anthropomorphic shapes suggested the connections between the nose and the brain; on each of these, a decorated perfume bottle stood which, when sprayed, emitted a smell – anything from spice to machine oil (Figure 5). Visitors

Figure 4 *The Sixth Sense Exhibition; 'Taste'.*

Figure 5 *The Sixth Sense Exhibition; 'Smell'.*

were encouraged to enter another exhibit which described how the sense of smell may not protect workers from lethal inhalations. In the semi-darkness of this cylindrical structure, a skeleton lay hunched on a central plinth. Around the walls, small glass phials were labelled with the names of substances which have no smell but which have been identified as toxic and lethal substances in the workplace. At the centre and end of the whole exhibition (Figure 6) was a series of screens with contemporary

Figure 6 *The centre of the Sixth Sense Exhibition.*

photographs of women working in Norrköping. The 'uniformity of the photographs, and a conveyor belt effect, lit by bluish neon lighting [were used] in order to emphasize the soul-destroying work which annually inflicts thousands of industrial injuries' (Persson, 1994:180).

In these exhibitions, the themes are matched with equivalent forms and methods of exhibition-making: open, fluid and flexible in their arrangements; more sculptural than scenic in their forms. Factual forms such as documents and testimony may be mixed with obviously fictional and fantastic forms such as artworks. They may use light, movement such as turntables or conveyor belts, projected sound and images, to create an ambience of shifting, changing states.

These exhibitions are unashamedly personal, too, in the relations between exhibition-makers and exhibition visitors – stimulating conversation and exchange; encouraging identification or differentiation. They avoid the unequivocal, categorical statement and didactic presentation of most museum exhibitions (Sandahl 1995).

The most remarkable of these exhibitions have been temporary – using the greater opportunities that short-term exhibitions provide for exploring themes and issues, less driven by the institution's collections and the drive to get material out from stores and on show, or responding to it by providing more frequent changes of the material shown. This rhythm and cycle of exhibition-making provides greater opportunities to explore, experiment and learn for exhibition makers and visitors than the conventional practice of 'permanent' displays with a life of five, ten or fifteen years. It acknowledges that things are 'of their time', and change/are changed over time. Its disadvantage is that these exhibitions are, like women's traces in the collections of museums, marginal and less enduring: the chances to learn from them may be marginalized or 'lost' within institutions as their circumstances change; or overlooked by other professionals because they do not recognize such short-term projects as a valid alternative. Thus the visible record and tangible legacy of museum work may omit these bold, challenging and suggestive projects.

Notes

1 I completed a postgraduate degree at the Department of Museum Studies, University of Leicester in 1994 (Porter 1994). I wish to acknowledge the guidance and encouragement given by my supervisor, Dr Eilean Hooper-Greenhill,

and the support of my employers while completing the research, the National Museum of Photography Film and Television/National Museum of Science and Industry, and the Museum of Science and Industry in Manchester.
2 I use the term gender to refer to the social and cultural meanings attached to the biological differences between men and women.

References

Berger, J., (1972), *Ways of Seeing*, London, Penguin.
Cockburn, C. and Ormans, S. (1993) Gender and Technology in the Making, London: Sage.
Coward, R., (1984), *Female Desire*, London, Paladin.
Culler, J., (1981), 'Semiology: the Saussurian legacy' in Bennett, T., Martin, G., Mercer, C. and Woollacott, J. (eds), *Culture, Ideology and Social Process*, 129–44, London: Batsford.
Derrida, J., (1976), *Of Grammatology*, Baltimore: John Hopkins University.
Kavanagh, G., (1994), 'Looking for ourselves, inside and outside museums', *Gender and History*, 6:3, 370–5, Oxford: Blackwell.
Macdonald, S. and Porter, J., (1990), *Putting on the Style: Setting up Home in the 1950s*, London: The Geffrye Museum.
Moi, T., (1985), *Sexual/Textual Politics: Feminist Literary Theory*, London: Methuen.
Persson, E., (1994), *Utställningsform: I Kroppen på en Utställare 1967–1993*, Stockholm: Carlssons.
Porter, G., (1987), 'Gender bias: representations of work in history museums' in Carruthers, A. (ed.), *Bias in Museums*, Museum Professionals Group Transactions 22: 11–15.
Porter, G., (1991), 'Partial truths' in Kavanagh, G. (ed.), *Museum Languages: Objects and Texts*, 103–17, Leicester: Leicester University Press.
Porter, G., (1994), 'The representation of gender in British history museums', unpublished thesis, Leicester: Department of Museum Studies, University of Leicester.
Rose, J., (1986), *Sexuality in the Field of Vision*, London: Verso.
Sandahl, J., (1993), 'Tangled up in love: the Women's Museum in Denmark', *European Museum of the Year Award News*: 9.
Sandahl, J., (1995), 'Proper Objects among Other Things', Nordisk Museologi, 2, 97–106.
Tagg, J., (1988), *The Burden of Representation*, London: Macmillan.
Traweek, S., (1988), *Beamtimes and Lifetimes: the World of High Energy Physicists*, Cambridge, Massachussetts: Harvard University Press.
Williamson, J., (1978), *Decoding Advertisements*, London: Marion Boyars.

Decoding the visitor's gaze: rethinking museum visiting

Gordon Fyfe and Max Ross

Abstract

This chapter reports preliminary findings from visitor research being executed by one of the authors in a conurbation of the English Midlands. The fieldwork consists of fifteen in-depth interviews administered at a random sample of households and with a total of circa 35 subjects. The report places the research design in the theoretical contexts of class, culture and locality, presents data from three interviews and provides a detailed analysis of one interview. The data suggest:
(1) that local museums are mediators between identity and structure;
(2) that museum meanings are diversely determined in relation to the class trajectories of subjects;
(3) that museum visiting is to be understood as a social relationship rather than as an attribute of individuals and
(4) that subjects readily conceptualize locality and identity through the visual vocabulary of museums and heritage sites.

Public viewing

Spectacles pushed above eyebrows, the expert grasps the pot, rotates it in hand, examines the base, gives it up to the gaze of the camera and pronounces the history of its manufacture and distribution. A moment of silence follows on this, 'The Antiques Road Show', a popular BBC television programme in which people offer up their antiques to the judgement of experts. For each weekly episode the show visits a district, town or city and invites locals to submit their treasures. A typical episode begins with a camera shot of queues at the venue, perhaps a civic building, each of which goes forward to an appointed expert in painting, furniture, ceramics, toys etc. A camera gives sight of the people outside where the queues stretch back out of the building coalescing as one: a conveyor belt of parcels, packages and shopping bags each concealing questions.

The silence is broken, as expertise calls for answers. 'Where did you get it? How long have you had it? How much did you pay? Do you know how much it is worth?' The encounter between expert and owner yields its story of place, time, artefact and consumption. Like the antiques each story is fabricated, for the artefact is not only an object of universal interest to experts: its meaning is determined by its local passage through markets, places and households. The owner will have to do well, craft a good story. 'Uncle Charlie picked it up in 1946 for 2/6d.' 'It's been in the family since the 1920s . . .' 'One of my aunts brought it back from India.' 'It's been hanging on the wall since I was a child and I've begun to wonder what it is.' 'An old lady gave it to my mother who had cleaned house for her over many years . . . she showed her two and this is the one my mother liked.' The houses and the *noblesse oblige* of affluent aged employers, family attics, old suitcases and pokey antique shops of a previous generation are among the settings for these mini-dramas.

The variety of stories may be resolved into a limited number of plots. Common themes are family, craft skills, market and place with two narratives dominant. On the one hand the stories are of inheritance and family, about being an old family. The owner's family has possessed the object for generations. And on the other the stories concern the commodification of consumption, they are myths of the triumph of use-value over exchange value: 'but you'd never want to part with it'! Each viewer is invited to return to the realities of the market – what is it worth, for what market value should the antique be insured?

The programme is of interest for a sociology of heritage and museums. As a long running 'soap' it testifies to a popular interest in the associations between family, heritage, place and artefact. Its vitality flows from its location at the intersection of expertise, unofficial knowledge (Samuel, 1994) and ignorance. Running through the series is the frisson of discovery where an owner, who professes belief in the worthlessness of an heirloom, is rendered speechless by the revelation of its great value.

One story concerns the owl jug which belongs to the City Museum and Art Gallery in Stoke-on-Trent. Stoke-on-Trent is a conurbation in the English Midlands, also known as the Potteries. The owl came to light at a Northampton Road Show in 1990 where it was identified as a rare example of late seventeenth century Staffordshire slipware. The owner who judged it to be worth £5 was given an estimate of £20,000–£30,000 by the Road Show expert. The owl had apparently been acquired from a Birmingham antique shop in the 1930s and long resided on a domestic fireplace where it served as a flower pot. The owl, or Ozzy, as it became popularly known, was acquired by the Museum at auction – an event that received the notice of national newspapers. Today visitors are known to arrive at the Museum and ask to see the owl which, reproduced by the Museum as advertising copy, has acquired the status of a ritual object. In 1994 Ozzy made a guest appearance when the Road Show visited Trentham Gardens in Stoke.

Figure 7 *'Ozzy the Owl'. Late seventeenth century Staffordshire slipware: City Museum and Art Gallery, Stoke-on-Trent. Reproduced by kind permission of the City Museum.*

Ozzy is a condensed symbol; for some of the Museum's visitors he is a distallation of the meaning of the Potteries and his location is signposted. Such artefacts express the mechanical solidarity that one finds in the Potteries where deep historical associations with a manufacturing trade have tended to counter the centrifugal forces of modernization. Stoke-on-Trent is a twentieth century federation of six older towns which have extensive associations with pottery production and a declining coal industry. They are Stoke-upon-Trent, Hanley, Burslem, Longton, Fenton and Tunstall. In the late twentieth century the old pottery towns continue to be *foci* for expressions of fierce loyalties and strong identities.

Yet the Potteries is changing. It is true that Stoke-on-Trent remains a world centre for pottery production and that, by national standards, the working population is *relatively* working class and homogeneous in its composition. However, concentration of capital and the globalization of production have altered industrial patterns and accelerated dilution of the *conscience collective*. The district has experienced patterns of industrial decline, restructuring and consumer revolution that were given a spurt by the Thatcher years but already evident in the 70s.

Such transformations place museums in uncertain situations. What is their role in interpreting social change? What version of the collective experience is to be told in the face of fragmentation? Whose gaze is to be accommodated? Does everyone want to see the owl? If local museums interpret place, whose sense of place are they to acknowledge? There is, as Hooper Greenhill (1995) argues, a curatorial dilemma in that museums are increasingly enmeshed in what can be the competing claims of diverse audiences, public accountability and consumer culture.

The Potteries study:

This chapter considers the ways in which interpretations of the world, particularly as they relate to class, leisure and place, are associated with museum visiting. The data flow from visitor research currently being carried out by one of the authors, Max Ross, in Stoke-on-Trent. Subjects were selected randomly as members of fifteen households, contacted, visited and interviewed at length on the topics of social background, leisure time, lifestyle, community and locality. The households were selected to be representative of local class differences; data from three interviews are presented here. The project has been conceived as an inquiry into the way in which identity and structure are mediated by experiences of the museum.

The method deployed in the research differs from much of the work carried out into museum visiting both by museum professionals and by sociologists. The post-war history of museum visitor research has been dominated by one-sidedly quantitative methods, by questionnaire surveys and behaviourist methodologies (Lawrence, 1991/1993). However, as one scholar has observed: 'a more flexible model of research that moves beyond demographics into interpretive or ethnomethodological understandings and methods is required' (Hooper-Greenhill, 1988:12) if we are to understand the dynamics of museum meanings. This is a direction in which museum visitor research is moving.

Rather than being asked to provide answers to closed questions the interview subjects have been invited to reflect at length on their lives, their uses of non-work time, their social backgrounds, consumption, living in Stoke, and their senses of place and time. Whilst the object is to find out how museum visiting might or might not be interwoven with other aspects of their lives as consumers of places and spaces, the topic of museum visiting has, as far as possible, been left to the subjects to introduce in the first instance. Following Billig (1992), who explored the dynamics of popular monarchy, subjects are being interviewed together as households by means of open-ended discussions. So far the field-work has failed to turn up a non-visiting household though there are non-visitors and lapsed visitors. It is necessary, as Merriman (1991) shows, to break with primitive contrasts between visitors and non-visitors which tend to aggregate the never visited and lapsed visitors. The data suggest the importance of conceptualizing visiting in relation to the life cycle.

The aim is to see if a museum gaze can be detected, to excavate the classifications that order subjects' narratives of family, lifestyle and leisure. How do subjects read the museum and judge its works? What makes museum visiting so compelling for some people and perhaps not so for others? The question of the museum as a regime of signification is problematic for social and cultural theory in that it has tended to gloss over audience interpretation, assuming that ideology and content may be 'read-off' the social relations of the text's production. How different social groups and subjects 'read' museums, according to the range of cultural experiences, needs and desires they bring with them is an aspect of cultural representation and reproduction that is underdeveloped in museum visitor research – though not, it should be said, in media research and cultural studies theory. A concern with audience 'decoding' (Hall, 1980) as intrinsic to the making of meaning is foregrounded as central to a theory of museums.

In this project data analysis has been guided by three principles.

First, class is conceived as at once economic and cultural. Bourdieu and Darbel (1991) challenge interpretations which treat art museum visiting as an effect of economic differences (perhaps construed as occupational identity) which ignore the cultural capital which is a prerequisite for a visit experienced as enhancing a visitor's identity. Visiting is not an attribute of individuals or of classes understood as aggregates of individuals; it is a cultural strategy through which class is produced. This project is concerned with how class is lived in relation to the museum and with how class is produced through the medium of the museum visiting.

Second, the use of in-depth interviewing at households means that class emerges not as a univocal theme of male occupation but out of different gendered class memories and personal experiences. Household members (with the exception of one subject who was interviewed alone) give different emphases or contradict each other in what are plural accounts of museums, cultural practice and identity. Third, where possible, the strategy has been to allow subjects to determine the importance of museums in their lives rather than leading them to the view that museums are or should be significant for them.

Class, place and gaze

An important subject for social theory is the social organization of physical dispositions and capacities (Hirst and Woolley, 1982; Shilling 1993). Whilst the subject of visual capacities remains comparatively untheorized in sociology (Fyfe and Law, 1988; Chaplin, 1993) strides have been made in understanding how class and gaze are associated in contemporary societies. This association is clearly of importance in understanding museums. Urry has pioneered research into class differences in modes of looking (Urry, 1990, 1995). He identifies prevailing visual dispositions which are found amongst contemporary tourists as they engage in the activity of consuming places, *viz.* the romantic gaze and the collective gaze. Where the former celebrates a solitary, personal and spiritual engagement with sights such as Alpine mountains or the English Lake District, the latter is compelled by the collective, carnivalesque experience of, say, a crowded seaside beach (Urry, 1990: 45–6).

Urry's concept of the gaze is partially informed by Bourdieu's concept of the 'habitus'. The habitus constitutes the frame of reference, the underlying dispositions, grammar or mental schema, through which individuals are oriented to action as embodied actors. The world view of a group is not only consciously articulated, it is tacitly expressed in modes of bodily organization including touristic looking of the kind that Urry identifies. Thus, museum visiting is a social practice which varies between groups in terms of their underlying dispositions to look. The theoretical significance of the museum is partly that it is a meeting point of the social organization of visual capacities and the visualization of social relations.

For Bourdieu, class formation entails the struggle for assets by groups who occupy determinate positions within a field or social space: a social field is a field of struggles between groups who continuously seek to augment their assets. Amongst the assets mobilized in struggles for power and privilege are economic and cultural capitals. Classes are not fixed in place; they are characterized by trajectories as they move through the field to win or lose advantage. Moreover, whilst a class is objective in that it is at any moment positioned differently to other classes, it is culturally constituted in that advantage and disadvantage are mediated by class habituses. Thus, museum visiting, particularly art museum visiting, is a strategy by which some people accumulate cultural capital and others do not. Family socialization into museum visiting may constitute a mechanism of social reproduction – that is a mechanism through which the privilege of cultural capital is transmitted from one generation to the next (Bourdieu and Darbel, 1992).

The habitus of the dominant class is sacralized by the art museum which institutionalizes the distinction between a Kantian aesthetic and a popular aesthetic. Bourdieu's point is that aesthetic distinctions are not innocent in relation to class, they are judgemental media through which boundaries are established within the social space of class struggle. The Kantian, or pure aesthetic, entails an orientation of distanced assessment in relation to art which is at once a refusal of the immediacy of popular art. The former celebrates form over content, the latter content over form; these are related encodings of a struggle for distinction which is an aspect of class formation. Where the former has its centre of gravity amongst intellectuals, cultural workers etc., who monopolize élite cultural production, the latter is most closely associated with the working class, with those who are least able to distance themselves from necessity.

Analyses of class formation in Britain have forged ahead under Bourdieu's influence to build on the notion that class is cultural process (Allatt, 1993; Crompton, 1993; Prout, forthcoming; Savage et al., 1992). An important turn in this work has been towards class formation as it is interwoven with place (Bagguley et al., 1990; Savage et al., 1992; Urry, 1990, 1995). Earlier work (Elias and Scotson, 1965/1992) explored processes of inclusion and exclusion as they related to meaning, locality and migration. Underlying this research was an emphasis on the balance of power as a key to understanding the social production of meaning. As with Bourdieu there was an emphasis on the field of competition but there was an additional emphasis on the flux of shifting balances of power which might be quite uncertain in their outcomes for both the private troubles of individuals and the public issues of collectivities (Mills, 1959). More recent research on place has established that social space and physical space are two facets of the meaning of locality and that class formation is interwoven with migration (Savage et al., 1992).

Habitus and class trajectory

In common with others (Bellaby, 1992; Martin, 1981; Urry, 1990) we have found Mary Douglas's (1971) classic distinction between grid and group to be of use in theorizing the habitus as it mediates the relationship between identity and structure. The distinction is between two dimensions of social ordering. Group refers to strength of boundaries; it concerns the extent to which group identity is strongly or weakly articulated through rituals and symbols. Our concern is with the consumption of local museum artefacts and heritage as this may relate to belonging. Grid concerns the extent to which the social is finessed and nuanced as rules ordering relationships between individuals through time and space. Thus, there is the subjects' propensity to map their places within local networks through their encounter with artefacts such as museum displays, memorable buildings and discovered objects. Where strong group confers certainty of who belongs and who does not, grid enables subjects to say: 'I am here and not there in the scheme of things'.

Douglas's structuralist approach in anthropology was closely associated with developments in sociology and particularly with the pioneering work of Basil Bernstein (1971). In the 1960s

Bernstein's work on the cultural coding of power developed our understanding of the relationship between the symbolic order and the distribution of power as it was affected by economic and social restructuring. In recent years British sociology has interpreted the relationship between modernization and class formation, particularly middle-class formation in terms of the concepts of code, grid and group (Martin, 1981, Urry, 1990). We have found it useful to view Bourdieu's distinction between a Kantian aesthetic and a popular aesthetic through the matrix of grid and group. Douglas provides a more subtle formulation of the cultural grammars of our subjects than can be accommodated by Kantian/popular alone. On the other hand, accepting strictures about the absence of dynamics in the grid/group thesis (see, eg, Bellaby, 1992), Bourdieu's concept of a field of class struggle allows us to account for the moves which subjects are making along grid and group.

The place and the museums

The sample frame included both Stoke-on-Trent and the contiguous market town of Newcastle-under-Lyme. The working class is, in national terms, disproportionately represented in the city's population and this is reflected in key features of the social structure – the relatively small proportion of the population located in affluent households of single or childless couples. A comparatively large proportion is resident in old, often Victorian, housing stock whilst a pattern of outward migration has produced housing estates in which the elderly tend to be, by national standards, over-represented. Stoke is characterized by a strong sense of place. it is perhaps symptomatic that the crime least feared in Stoke is bother or threat by strangers (Evans, 1993:235).

Stoke is sandwiched between the Staffordshire Moorlands to the East, to which residents including our subjects turn for leisure activities and local tourism, and Newcastle to the West. Newcastle is a comparatively affluent town with established middle class districts; it has significantly higher proportions of its households located in professional, managerial and technical occupations than Stoke. Despite proposed changes in local government boundaries which would have absorbed it into Stoke and which were a source of anxiety for one of our households, Newcastle continues to enjoy autonomy from its larger neighbour. The town is not without its share of declining staple industries, especially in mining, but throughout the twentieth century economic development has included more by the way of light industry.

There is a complex of museums and heritage sites which interpret industrialization and deindustrialization and whose development is an aspect of the local economy. There is the City Museum and Art Gallery in Hanley which displays a world class collection of ceramics. It is known locally for other displays including its Spitfire and the community history reconstructions of early twentieth century life: including an elementary school room, fish and chip shop, pharmacy and a working class domestic interior. Other industrial museums include the Gladstone Pottery Museum in Longton, the Etruria Industrial Museum and the Chatterly Whitfield Museum of Coal Mining which recently closed. In Newcastle there is the Borough Museum noted for its fully scale display of traditional town centre shops where locals may recognize the names of recently extinct local family businesses. Two museum displays, the shops at Newcastle and the community history reconstructions at Hanley are much remarked upon by the interviewees.

The three households

Three households are discussed here. Two represent different fractions of the middle class whilst one is working class; two are located in Stoke, one in Newcastle. All contain museum visitors although the members' lives of leisure and work are constructed differently in relation to museum visiting.

The Cartwrights live in Newcastle; they are a second (and possibly third) generation middle-class family of four: Mrs Cartwright has origins in the locality. Mr Cartwright comes from outside the district although he has lived in Newcastle for many years. He is 50, university educated in electronics in which field he is employed by a medium sized corporation outside the district. Mrs Cartwright, aged 41, is a teacher and graduated from a local university. The children, Wayne and Fiona, are both at a local independent secondary school. On the mother's side the family have long been in the district and both her grandfathers were local shop keepers.

The Cartwrights are strong on grid. Museum and heritage site visiting are regular activities; they are means through which the family construct their lifestyle and past museum visits are readily recalled. The Cartwrights convey a tremendous interest in how things work, they want to know the rules; their world can be ordered and they look across to Stoke with anxiety to a world of inner-city uncertainty. They have a strong sense that the world can be ordered, that the past and the natural world are open to rational inquiry according to known principles and that they can place themselves within a cosmology.

The Cartwright's class trajectory is one in which attachment to local group is becoming attenuated. They are affiliated to local cultural institutions and to the Church. They are concerned about the decline of their market town, they see commercial development as being given priority over a local primary school. They have a romantic sense of loss through change, of expropriation by national corporations of local control over economic and political decision making. For them group is evaporating and they are unable to find it appropriately expressed in the policies of the local council. The Cartwright's response to proposals for amalgamation between Newcastle and Stoke is hostile and they anticipate leaving the district if they materialize. Where others may look across the Stoke and see *Gemeinschaft* they observe inner city decay and the threat of the unknown.

Ms Brown is in her mid-twenties, teaches a humanities subject in higher education and has migrated to the district from the South. Her co-ordinates are those of weak group and weak grid. The interview data suggest that career and academic specialism have drawn her away, though not estranged her from her parents: 'that's the way our experiences and interests differ really'.

As a professional, as a middle class newcomer to the district, she has a strong sense of being an outsider in a provincial town and is critical of, though prepared to endorse, some developments in the local museum. Her class trajectory reflects a broader pattern of middle-class formation through migration from the Southeast (Savage et al., 1992:132–85). She and her partner (not interviewed) are good neighbours, keeping an eye on next door when the people are away. However, leisure, friendship networks (concentrated in the South East) and the demands of work mean that Ms Brown and partner (also an academic originating outside the district) have a national, even international orientation in their lifestyles which Ms Brown sees as difficult to classify. There is no typical weekend; weekends are shaped in accordance with the requirements of travel and work.

On arriving from London, Ms Brown experienced a sense of estrangement: 'I actually hated the place, I couldn't bear it . . . I used to think it was just a big – the whole area of the city was just sort of – bricked up with red brick, and somewhere along the line there – every sort of three hundred yards or so there just might be a really tiny little spy-hole . . .'.

She wants to stand on the edge: '. . . we're [self and partner] very much on the fringe, we like to be on the fringe, we don't want to be swallowed up in completely trivial, irrelevant community issues'. Her viewpoint is not static; there is an accommodation with locality that comes with several years of residence: '. . . but I think, slowly, over the years, I think I'm getting to know people a bit better – erm – that brick wall's just starting to crumble'. And there are positive developments at the Museum associated with its curating of the fine arts. The museum's art gallery has improved from its humble, provincial origins: 'It was very much sort of local artists, paintings of the city and that was about it basically, no new sort of, erm, contemporary art, or sort of nineteenth century art . . . nothing particular actually got into the gallery'.

The third household consists of Mr and Mrs Grainger; they are aged 65 and 61 respectively. Mr Grainger's father was a haulage contractor; Mr Grainger was a lorry driver until illness forced him to give up work. Mrs Grainger was a skilled operative in the pottery industry and comes from a line of pottery workers. They have two children who form separate households. Their daughter who, they say, loves museums, lives on the other side of the conurbation and a son works in the pottery industry. The daughter visits the library and the museum with Luke, her six year old son (the Central Library and the City Museum are adjacent to each other). Mr Grainger takes the lad out independently and regularly to the City Museum: 'I always have a walk round the museum, especially if I've got Luke with me, coz' he'll always say, are we going round the museum? And I'll say, yes, go on then, and away we go'. They have visited other museums in the district although most of the visiting is done by Mr Grainger. Mrs Grainger has a disability that prevents her visiting but it is also clear that she is not so committed as her husband. Moreover, as we note in the next section, Mrs Grainger's evaluation of the City Museum differs in part from her husband's.

The couple are strong on group/grid. They draw the boundaries of community sharply whilst they can readily map individuals and buildings onto time and place.

Mrs Grainger: 'Oh, it's – but you've got to live here to understand it, it's really – I mean, people round here – they're good! I mean, when you've had, we've had bad times haven't we, one thing and another? They always support you, we've had some support in that club – they all rally round you – they know you! And you don't get that much. This community, it's a good community round here isn't it?'

The couple belong to a Working Men's Club; Mr Grainger is a self consciously Hanley man and is keen to talk about 'old Hanley'; he is conversant with the architecture of the six towns, familiar with the 'good old buildings' – Hanley market, Burslem School of Art, one of the old town halls. They don't particularly like Newcastle, it's Hanley for them: 'we go to Burslem occasionally, but mostly we're very much local people, we support local things . . .'.

They live close to the City Museum in Hanley and they remember the 'old museum' with its distinctive odour of Mansion House Polish. For Mrs Grainger, who has only visited the new museum once, it is the 'old museum' that is recalled from her school days; there are memories of stuffed animals and 'that smell'. For Mr Grainger the Museum is the natural place to send unusual finds: a keen gardener, he has discovered a beetle and submitted it to the Museum – a satisfying experience as he recalls receiving an explanation that it was 'uncommon' but not 'so uncommon'. The Museum is to be noted, amongst other things, for its Spitfire fighter aeroplane (the real thing). Mr Grainger readily moves from reflections on his period of National Service in the Army to the shared technology of Spitfire and the engines of armoured vehicles.

Possessed of a strong sense of community, the Graingers also display a high degree of internal differentiation in their awareness of place. Mr Grainger easily maps the Potteries in relation to himself, his family network and his acquaintances through time and space: knowledge of local characters, buildings, changing street names are the raw materials of his conversation. Where the Cartwright's local knowledge is subtended by the oral tradition of the family's class memories and by the local histories of expertise, the Graingers are masters of a spontaneous capacity to classify the local. They are natural informants (the sociologist has been beaten to the door by a local historian and author).

Interpreting social history galleries

During the three interviews the topic of the community history display at the City Museum and the shops at the Newcastle Museum emerged. However, the displays had different meanings for the three households.

Ms Brown has a negative view of the City Museum's community history gallery and neither is she very excited by the ceramic collection: 'if I walk through the ceramics section I go through quickly – very quickly!' (laughing). The community history display is singled out as boring, static, uninspiring, and irritating: 'if everyone's seeing constant models of someone in – the nineteenth century pub, and it doesn't change – it becomes boring!' For Ms Brown this is a 'sociological' aspect of the City Museum that does not represent her in 'any way'. Although she has an intimate knowledge of the City Museum her grasp of the wider heritage trail emerges as shaky: she knows the Newcastle Museum ('of course') and has visited the Gladstone Pottery Museum but there has been no visit to the Chatterley Whitfield Mining Museum: 'I'm not into mining'. Her knowledge of the Etruria Industrial Museum seems sketchy and she asks for confirmation of the name of the Wedgwood Factory Museum.

What matters most is the fine art side of things, which connects with her professional needs as a researcher and teacher. She needs new ideas, new perspectives and looks to the museum for these, not for affirmation of local community and certainly not for inclusion in its way of life. Her habitus leads her to evade classification; there is a sense that she is a classifier looking in on community – she defines herself by evading the sociological gaze.

Mr Grainger also picks out the City Museum's community history section. Deeply embedded for generations in a local community, its shared forms of association in leisure and labour, Mr Grainger reaffirms ties of belonging in his visits – ties of family, place and community. For him, decoding the City Museum entails an implicit historicism that is not a formal body of knowledge but rather a set of implicit associations with locality: 'I've been there with them [daughter and grandson] when they've been to exhibitions – not too long ago, about "the way we were" – they've got a mock set-up of an old street, when I was a kid, and I went up and they'd got it more or less spot on, how I remember it . . . very good!'

Mr Grainger's perspective contrasts to that of Ms Brown. For him meaning, value and identity derive from the particularity and embeddedness of local culture and institutions: '. . . see they had a week of local history up there [the museum] . . . there's a separate bit with an old pub and the old off-licence, and the chip shop, and the average kitchen, how it would be, you know . . .'. There is a contrast with Mrs Grainger who, it should be recalled, does not visit the museum, and has perhaps had a different experience of the kitchen to her husband: 'I've seen 'em in my life, well you [Mr Grainger] went in that time they'd got the old mangles and the washtubs and that there . . . but you've seen them in reality . . . why go to a museum and see 'em?' Perhaps closer in her gendered class identity to the drudgery of community, her decoding resonates with Ms Brown's.

Lastly, the Cartwrights were readily drawn to social history displays of the museums they had visited, locally and elsewhere. Asked what was the appeal, Mrs Cartwright replied: 'I think, they are putting a picture into your mind, of what it might have been like – erm, I mean, you get that particularly at the "Shambles" in York, which is more . . . little close streets, narrow streets of close shops – but that's it – you can imagine what it might have been like . . .'.

Mr Cartwright drew a contrast between the 'small shop mentality' ('It's a more intimate level') and the modern supermarket. The contrast is seen as an historical shift in the social relations of retail: an older ethos of personal attention and skilled service having given way to a more depersonalized form. Shopping has become an individualistic leisure pursuit, with a tendency 'to waste time – looking at things, instead of getting someone who's knowledgeable to sort it out straight away'.

For Mr Cartwright the display evokes an old order of craft retail in which things can still be done properly and which is resistant to consumerism. Mrs Cartwright shares her husband's celebration of the small shop but her gaze is refracted through memories of class and a personal nostalgia emerges: 'I have an interest in shops because both my grandfathers were, erm, well – one grandfather was a manager at Edward Mason's, which was a local greengrocers', and the other one had his own paper shop and grocery shop, and – in those days – it sounds as if it was a hundred years ago, but it wasn't – people used to drop their order through the shop door, and it was delivered to them, and it was all done on a very local basis.'

A number of points may be made concerning these evaluations of museums. It is apparent that museum visiting is not an attribute of individuals so much as a social relationship that is interwoven with dynamics of households, families and life-histories. Each household has established its own partnership of looking with the museum world. The partnerships are momentary fixings of grid and group as this is cut through by the dynamics of class, gender and community formation. Households produce their identities and place themselves in relation to community partly through the medium of museum visiting.

For Ms Brown, with a professional interest in producing and transmitting cultural capital, museums are properly sites for a tradition of the new that cannot be satisfied by static displays of social life. She visits museums with friends but the demands of a competitive and individualized professional life are dominant in her cultural appropriation. At the Grainger household there is only one visitor, Mr Grainger, whose museum interests are shared with daughter and grandson on their visits to the household. Here museum interests express the dynamics of family rather than household whilst Mrs Grainger's non-visitor's evaluation of the social history display may have something to do with disability, gender and her experience of working-class domestic labour. The Cartwrights have a strong collective interest in museums; they revel in reconstructions of social history. Their interest is probably informed by different middle class strands in their class background, but is also associated with the cultivation of an active, inquiring mode within the household. The Grainger household is a forcing-house for curiosity.

The Cartwrights, the museum and cultural classification

We turn to a consideration of the Cartwrights with a view to exploring further the social production of their museum visiting. The questions are: what makes museum and heritage site visiting so compelling for this family? What is the underlying grammar of their gaze? How do their cultural practices relate to their class trajectory?

The Cartwrights engage in a range of cultural, hobby and sporting activities. There is an interest in making music and playing tennis but the family do not go to spectator sports. They are readers with a strong interest in history. As parents, Mr and Mrs

Cartwright know that educationally things can go wrong and see the provision of a supporting environment as crucial for their children. Mr Cartwright has a sense of life as an educational project; learning is an activity not completed with the end of schooling or with graduation, never completed.

The Cartwrights are oriented towards the British countryside and the locality though some foreign travel is in evidence. Accumulation of cultural capital is achieved partly through the consumption of heritage and locality. Through this and countryside tourism they have passed onto their children a consuming curiosity about how things were in the past. This curiosity relates to self-identity and empowerment. Discovering the local past is a personal project of self-identification insofar as to 'find that you're part of something else' is to gain a sense of self-knowledge: to the extent that this past 'touches you', 'it touches your life', 'it's where you live'. In addition, such place-bound knowledge can be empowering in a political sense, with regard to the relationship between local community and a state which they perceive as distant and hostile. The family have been on a series of tours of the locality guided by a local historian. The initial impulse behind this activity was: 'to find out why this house is here and what these roads are all about'.

They display familiarity with local museums; they are experienced visitors, they are members of the National Trust and they have enrolled their children in a process of learning about the community and its past. They are fond of their nearest local museum, the Newcastle Borough Museum, and seemingly less keen on the City Museum and Art Gallery in Hanley. Their visiting is in part an educational strategy. However, it is more than a struggle for cultural capital, for this family-strategy is interwoven with a sense of eroded community. Their habitus is structured by a loss of community, particularly as the locus of economic decision making shifts outside the locality. At the same time they have a sense that the world can be opened up to rational understanding and the certainty of strong classification. This habitus is complexly structured in a way that may have something to do with the multi-polar relations of the household – towards different class histories and futures. They are a local middle-class household with a class trajectory that may lead them, should they move elsewhere, to become cosmopolitans (Frankenberg, 1966). A habitus of weak community/strong grid is the key to their museum gaze.

Community and identity

There is a contradiction in the Cartwright's identifications of place and community. Whilst they have a sense of what community might be, it is not located in the present. Their gaze is into Newcastle's past as a market town and across Stoke to the Moorlands on the eastern side of Stoke. The Cartwright son observes: 'We're definitely not city'. For his mother Stoke connotes inner city decay and Toxteth (a Liverpool district where rioting occurred in the early 1980s). They are aware of Newcastle's social problems but Stoke has become the Other to their Newcastle. Newcastle town centre, in common with other market towns, is experiencing a decline exemplified in the ugliness of a well-known and now empty supermarket buildings. For the Cartwrights Newcastle *is* a market town whose boundaries are threatened by external corporate interests which are facilitated by the local council.

The family's sense of place gravitates towards a prudent, local shopkeeper's view of the world: a conservative identification with the provincial commercial virtues embodied in the ethics of the traditional middle classes. This habitus may derive from the family connection on the mother's side, with local retail and from their relative social and geographic stasis. Nostalgia for a community is bound up in memory with the earlier days of retail – the ethos of good service that acknowledged the value of the local neighbourhood and the individual consumer, affirming both in their irreducible particularity.

The Cartwrights, *pace* Elias (1983), have a dual-front class situation so far as their sense of place is concerned. On the one hand they resent the effects that large capitalist retailers have on Newcastle but feel powerless to influence the local planning and political processes including the proposed integration of Newcastle into Stoke. And on the other they face towards the unknown that is Stoke, a place they would probably prefer not to visit and in which, as local knowledge has, it car drivers are prone to get lost. It may be a sense of this compression between large capital and derelict Stoke that leads them to cultivate their imaginations in relation to the past and to draw perhaps on family class memories of a vanished *petit bourgeois* Newcastle. Unlike the cosmopolitan Ms Brown, they are enmeshed in the locality through ties of background and children's schools. But they have an escape route which amalgamation with Stoke might lead them to take: with the children growing up and Mr Cartwright working in a city outside the Potteries there is the possibility of domestic relocation.

Shopping and classification

A theme initiated by and returned to by the Cartwright household is shopping. Whereas the boundaries of community are subject to erosion, shopping still offers possibilities for doing things correctly. The Cartwrights go to supermarkets, as one might expect, and it is clear that shopping is interwoven with their identity. Their attitude towards shopping reveals an identification with a certain supermarket ethos, an identification that is bound up with a sense of self and group identity. They exhibit confidence in handling the everyday semiotics of consumption:

Mrs Cartwright: 'We go to Sainsburys', and you think, oh, they're a different sort of people in Sainsburys' from what you get in Asda or Tesco, and you can actually – it's almost tangible – when you meet people individually there's not much difference, but grouped together there does seem to be a different – you seem to meet different sorts of people in different shops, and it's most odd!'

Mr Cartwright: 'It's true – the product mix says that as well, doesn't it?'

Mrs Cartwright: 'We don't go to Morrisons [a low price retailer] because we think it's really naff' (general laughter).

Their consumer choices are a source of self and other identifications. Both the social world and the world of goods are amenable to classification and it is noticeable that shopping offers the opportunity to affirm the strength of classification and to celebrate its possibilities for placing themselves and other individuals:

Mrs Cartwright: 'I think you get that in the staff as well, often, the, the – the attitude of the staff if they don't care and they can't be bothered, whereas perhaps in another shop they might remember you, particularly in Tescos. I always seem to see the same women – erm, I mean, I went to the fish counter this morning didn't we, and I said "where's Melanie", and I thought, this is almost small shop mentality.'

Gordon Fyfe and Max Ross

A Romantic ethic of active leisure and the embodied gaze

Participation in local walks and visits to historic sites is a means of 'finding out', an active approach to learning defined in contrast to formal, academic modes of inquiry. This active engagement is embodied in the sense that the Cartwrights reach out with their hands to grasp the world, to pull it in for inspection so to speak. Where Ms Brown's disposition is to hold the world at a distance the Cartwrights are anxious to be in there with the artefacts. The Cartwrights come close to Lash and Urry's characterization of middle-class tourists who yearn for a truthful nature; who are 'in search of a time when time space and culture were full of affective charge' (Lash and Urry, 1994:58). Theirs is a physical engagement which is seen as facilitating a special kind of experiential knowledge:

Mr Cartwright: 'It's easier to go on that type of activity than to do the research and read it up yourself – you find that with a lot of walks of life, I mean, you can read . . . but it's not the same as being there.'

The Cartwrights celebrate the power of objects, structures and locations which are perceived as signs of a living history, as possessed of a capacity for the communication of transcendant historical insight. Theirs is a Romantic gaze refracted through feeling, imagination and empathy; they focus upon the aura of original surfaces and authentic objects. In place of universalizing reason and Kantian distancing, they celebrate the particular and unique, the local and personal. The family's most recent holidays entailed a high concentration of visits to various attractions:

Mrs Cartwright: 'We only went for two days but we did quite a lot, didn't we? We visited an old abbey, the rescued horse we went to see, a windmill, Sizewell B. power station . . . a farm park, a vineyard – that sort of sums us up, doesn't it really?'

Asked how visits to these diverse sites summed up the household Mrs Cartwright replied: 'to find out really – how it all works . . . it's finding out – it's social history, isn't it?'

Academic history is found incapable of realizing some essential level of historical reality. Authentic structures and artefacts, on the other hand, are seen to have a power for direct and immediate communication. The mass-produced printed image is 'just a picture in a book, which doesn't mean anything', where the actual object itself may be read as tangible proof:

Mr Cartwright: 'I don't concentrate much on the manuscripts and documents from the past – I like to see – artefacts from the past – with – that have no equivalent in modern day.'

The documents that constitute evidence for the scholar of professional history, are viewed with indifference – there is a more palpable, living history adhering to the fragments and remnants of past material culture. There is a sense of the past that is there to be appropriated, not through scholarly distanciation, but through physical proximity: accessible to decoding through gazing upon, sensing, touching and intuitive imagining.

A rural romanticism pervades observations about community and locality. Conventional cultural oppositions between country and city are extensively invoked. There is the suggestion of a relation to history and culture enacted at a level other than the rational, relying not upon empirical indicators or intellectual enquiry, but upon tradition, 'family interest', an intuitive conservatism, empathy, the affectual and emotional potential in cultural practices and historical texts. These values are expressed as attachments to landscaped gardens, mountains, country houses and countryside and also through household mythology that constructs their own locality as a village community.

The Cartwrights value the hands-on experience of appropriating meaning from physical sites and objects. The motif of 'hands-on' signifies a gaze which can contemplate the world and get at it directly rather than through interpretive texts. For the Cartwrights nature is privileged over culture. Asked about memorable visits Mrs Cartwright replies:

'I'm just trying to think, when you [children] were at school, and they went down to the [Newcastle] Borough Museum where they were firing the old guns –'

Fiona: 'Oh yes! and everyone else –'

Mrs Cartwright: 'They were absolutely amazing!'

Mrs Cartwright: 'There was like a blunderbuss wasn't there, a huge thing –'

Mr Cartwright: 'They actually fired two of them –'

Fiona: 'Ooh, it gave you a headache!'

Wayne: 'They fired a lot more!'

Mrs Cartwright: 'There's something else which was only last year as well, which is to do with guns, was when we went to the civil war re-enactment – the battle –'

Wayne and Fiona: (in unison) 'Yes!'

Conclusion

This paper departs from visitor research as it is usually conceived – that is as a programme of closed questions that theorize visiting as attributes of individuals. The method has entailed in-depth household interviews in which subjects are asked to reflect on their life-style and their leisure patterns as these are interwoven with a sense of locality. The aim has been to provide a theoretical defence of the method and to give a preliminary report of findings concerning the structuring of the gaze.

We have found it productive to begin with the notion that class is cultural process in the sense that it entails the organization of bodily habits and capacities. Class cultures include the organization of visual capacities so that gazing is (to rephrase Bernstein) a means through which individuals learn the priorities of their social structure. Drawing on Mary Douglas the argument has been that the gaze issues forth from a habitus that is structured according to the grammar of grid and group. Grid and group are cross-cutting dimensions of classification in which actors seek to stabilize the uncertainties that flow from their situated experiences of modernity.

Class formation does not occur independently of place; as Savage et al. argue, it occurs partly through the medium of geographical migration. It follows that class trajectories entail strategies of placing and displacing as individuals and households produce themselves through the dialectic of established and outsiders (Elias and Scotson, 1965/1992). Visual interpretations of locality are aspects of that dialectic; class formation occurs partly through the medium of migration. Thus class formation occurs through the medium of locality to produce different types of gaze: local working class (the Graingers), outsider cosmopolitan middle class (Ms Brown) and local middle class (the Cartwrights).

These are are not fixed class identities; the subjects have life histories which are interwoven with the dynamics of socio-physical space. The research method has proved appropriate to tapping into the synchronic and diachronic dimensions of class, place and museum visiting. The subjects have spoken extensively of their current leisure activities and lifestyles. They have readily constructed their social trajectories in terms of museums; memories of class, childhood and school are readily museum memories. For the interviewees, it seems, museums are good to think with. The data begin to show how households might take up different *museum* positions within the socio-physical space that they inhabit and think of as the locality. The research may also suggest that modernity and identity entail a process of museumification, at least in this conurbation of North Staffordshire it may be so.

Acknowledgements

The chapter has had the benefit of discussions with Alan Prout, Mike Savage, Kevin Hetherington and Jeanette Edwards. The research has been supported by the ESRC in the form of a studentship awarded to Max Ross.

References

Allat, P., (1993), 'Becoming Privileged: the Role of Family Processes' in Inge Bates and George Riseborough, *Youth and Inequality*, Buckingham and Philadelphia: Open University Press.

Bagguley, P., Mark-Lawson, J., Shapiro, D., Urry, J., Walby, S. and Ward, A., (1990), *Restructuring: Place, Class and Gender*, London: Sage.

Bellaby, P., (1992), 'To Risk or not to Risk? Uses and Limitations of Mary Douglas on Risk Acceptability for Understanding Health and Safety at Work and Road Accidents' in *The Sociological Review*, vol. 38, no. 3, 465–83.

Bernstein, Basil, (1971), *Class, Codes and Control*, volume 1, London: Routledge and Kegan Paul.

Billig, M., (1992), *Talking of the Royal Family*, London: Routledge.

Bourdieu, P., (1984), *Distinction: A Social Critique of the Judgement of Taste*. London: Routledge and Kegan Paul.

Bourdieu, P. and Darbel, A., (1991), *The Love of Art: European Art Museums and their Public*, Oxford: Polity Press.

Crompton, R., (1993), *Class and Stratification: an Introduction to Current Debates*, Oxford: Polity Press.

Directorate of Strategic Planning (1993), *Newcastle-under-Lyme: 1991 Census, A Profile of the Borough's Population and Housing*, Borough Council, Newcastle-under-Lyme.

Directorate of Strategic Planning (1994), *Newcastle-under-Lyme: 1991 Census, Information on the Employment, Educational and Social Status of the Residents of the Borough*, Borough Council, Newcastle-under-Lyme.

Douglas, M., (1973), *Natural Symbols: Explorations in Cosmology*, London: Barrie and Jenkins.

Edwards, J., (forthcoming), *Born and Bred: Ideas of Relatedness and Relationships in late Twentieth Century England*.

Elias, N. and Scotson, J., (1965), *The Established and the Outsiders: A Sociological Inquiry into Community Problems*, London: Frank Cass.

Elias, N. and Scotson, J., (1994), *The Established and the Outsiders: A Sociological*

Inquiry into Community Problems (with new introduction by Norbert Elias), London: Sage.

Elias, N., (1983), *The Court Society*, Oxford: Basil Blackwell.

Evans, D.J., (1993), 'The Social Structure of Stoke-on-Trent: A Spatial Perspective' in A.D.M. Philips (ed.), *The Potteries: Continuity and Change in a Staffordshire Conurbation*, London: Alan Sutton.

Frankenberg, R., (1966), *Communities in Britain*, Harmondsworth: Penguin.

Hirst, P. and Woolley, (1982), *Social Relations and Human Attributes*, London: Tavistock.

Hall, S., (1980), 'Encoding/Decoding' in Centre for Contemporary Cultural Studies (ed.), *Culture, Media, Language*, London: Hutchinson

Hooper-Greenhill, E., (1988), 'Counting Visitors or Visitors who Count', in R. Lumley (ed.), *The Museum Time Machine: Putting Cultures on Display*, London: Comedia/Routledge.

Hooper-Greenhill, E., (1995), 'Audiences: A Curatorial Dilemma' in S. Pearce (ed.), *Art in Museums: New Research in Museum Studies*, vol. 5, 143–63.

Lash, S. and Urry, J., (1994), *Economies of Signs and Space*, London: Sage.

Lawrence, G., (1991), 'Rats, Streetgangs and Culture' in G. Kavanagh (ed.), *Museum Language: Objects and Text*, London: Leicester University Press.

Lawrence, G., (1993), 'Remembering Rats, Considering Culture: Perspectives on Museum Evaluation' in Bicknell, S. and Farmelo, G. (eds), *Museum Visitor Studies in the Nineties*, London: Science Museum.

Macdonald, S., (1995), 'Consuming Science: public knowledge and the dispersed politics of reception among museums visitors', in *Media, Culture and Society*, vol. 17, 13–29.

Martin, B., (1981), *A Sociology of Contemporary Cultural Change*, Oxford: Basil Blackwell.

Merriman, N., (1991), *Beyond the Glass Case*, Leicester: Leicester University Press.

Prout, A., (forthcoming), 'Performance, Habitus and Trajectory: New Directions in the Study of Class and Health'.

Samuel, R., (1994), *Theatres of Memory*, London: Verso.

Savage, M., Barlow, J., Dickens, P. and Fielding, T., (1992), *Property, Bureaucracy and Culture: Middle Class Formation in Contemporary Britain*, London: Routledge.

Shilling, C., (1993), *The Body and Social Theory*, London: Sage.

Policy and Information Group (n.d.), *Stoke-on-Trent in the Nineties: an Atlas of the 1991 Census*, Department of Planning and Architecture, Stoke-on-Trent.

Urry, J., (1990), *The Tourist Gaze: Leisure and Travel in Contemporary Societies*, London: Sage.

Urry, J., (1995), *Consuming Places*, London: Routledge.

Part III
Contents: Classifications and practice

The utopics of social ordering –
Stonehenge as a museum without walls

Kevin Hetherington

Abstract

This chapter takes up Malraux's discussion of the museum without walls and asks the question 'how might we think of the space of such a "museum"?' To answer this question the chapter draws on Foucault's analysis of heterotopia together with Marin's analysis of utopics. My aim is to show that the museum has always been a site of otherness that expresses a utopic practice that comes to shape a vision of the ordering of the social. Having made this argument in relation to the 'classical' museum, I then turn to the space of the museum without walls and suggest that it is also heterotopic but, in relation to particular sites, characterized by many different utopics that make the meaning of such a space uncertain, ambivalent and ultimately not representable in any unified way. To illustrate this I use the example of Stonehenge as a museum without walls. It is an impossible, unrepresentable space but one that also means a great deal to many different groups of people. Stonehenge is imbued with a myriad of different utopics all of which express different visions of the ordering of the social that are often expressed through forms of resistance to ways in which society, through the prism of such a site, is seen to be currently ordered.

What monstrous place is this? (*Tess of the D'Urbervilles.*[1])

Museums and social ordering

How might we imagine the space of the 'museum without walls'? (Malraux, 1954). Malraux's famous essay is, of course, about more than just museums. It is about the very nature of what we know as art. While at one level he makes the seemingly obvious sociological observation that there is nothing universal about art but that it is shaped by social context in the way that context interprets not only its own art but also all that has come before, his essay is also much more about representation and social ordering. This present essay is not about art but it is about social context and how we might think about the museum without walls and the spatiality of its mode of ordering (see also Law, 1994). For Malraux, the museum without walls is something that is brought about by the reproduction of art, notably through photography. There are clear resonances between his discussion of the museum without walls and Benjamin's ideas about the loss of aura which comes as a consequence of the mechanical reproduction of art (1973). For Benjamin, this was something to be celebrated, for the loss of aura made possible, he believed, new ways of seeing and new forms of resistance, important in the context of the era of fascism in which he was writing, that challenged the conservative authority of auratic culture. For Malraux, the museum without walls means that we now have a new context from which to view and to represent art and the possibility of new ways of seeing and representing being expressed in that art.

There are three spaces that Malraux deals with, at least implicitly, in his discussion of the museum and its relation to art. First there is a pre-museum space in which art exists in a localized social context such as in churches, private houses, palaces, gardens and so on. Secondly we have the classical museum which, as is well known, developed out of the numerous picture collections and cabinets of curiosities during the seventeenth and eighteenth centuries before being fully instituted as the museum 'with walls' from the latter half of the eighteenth century. Diverse collections of 'works of art' were brought together, in one space that provided that art with a whole new meaning and opened up new possibilities for representation within artistic practice. Finally, with the advent of the mechanical reproducibility of art, we have the museum without walls, which, for Malraux appears to be located in books. Indeed, the very essay in which he presents the idea of the museum without walls exemplifies, with its wide variety of photographs, what he is describing in the text and the different ways in which art can represent through the selectivity of photographic reproduction.

This idea is both illuminating and limiting. What Malraux shows quite clearly is that these different social contexts organize representation in art. Art is ordered and classified and becomes a form of ordering and classifying in a way that is linked to the space in which it is exhibited. But Malraux's essay is too limiting in seeing the museum without walls simply as books and indeed in his focus just on art museums (see also Crimp, 1985). We now have a whole range of other media to display reproduced art. The breakdown of the walls of the museum, partly as a consequence of forces of commercialization and the emergence of a heritage industry (see Hewison, 1987) and partly as a consequence of popular interest in sites of historical and cultural interest outside of the confines of the museum (see White, 1985), liberates the idea of the museum and returns it into a wider set of spaces (Negrin, 1993).

Clearly we cannot think of the museum without walls in the same way as we might the classical museum; but the two are not completely separate. As Malraux implies, we should not think of the museum just in terms of sites or buildings. Instead, the museum is a spatial relation that is principally involved in a process of ordering that takes place in or around certain sites or buildings. This emphasis on spatial relations can already be seen in Malraux's essay. The spatial trajectory in Malraux's account is one of ever more openness, from the private ownership of works of art, to private collections, to semi-public collections, to collections open to the public, to the final spilling out of cultural works into a generalized public over which the gatekeepers of the museum have less and less control.

Museums as spatial relations are, however, not just involved in ordering and classifying cultural works and artifacts, they are also expressions of the ordering of the social. They are already imbued with power-knowledge that derives from social context and within that context they produce distinct modes of ordering that involves an interplay of assemblage and deferral of social meaning through spatializing effects. It is this issue that I want to explore in this paper in the context of ideas about the museum without walls. I do not intend to try and offer a comprehensive discussion of the history of the various spatial relations of the museum and the different modes of ordering that it produces. Instead, I want to look at the contemporary spatiality of the museum as it is manifest in the idea of the museum without walls, again not generally but though one particular example, Stonehenge, through which the spatial relations of the contemporary museum without walls can be illustrated.

Stonehenge must be one of the world's most familiar sites. It is a megalithic circle of stones set in the chalk downland of Salisbury Plain about eight miles from the cathedral city of Salisbury in Wiltshire, England. It was built over an extended period beginning with an earthworks some 5000 years ago (Atkinson, 1987). What it was originally intended to be used for has never been conclusively determined although given the amount of time, effort and skill required in its construction and the archaeological significance of the surrounding area, it was clearly a very important site (see Chippindale, 1983; Atkinson, 1987; Bender, 1993). It is not the ancient Stonehenge that interests me here, however, but the modern Stonehenge and the significance it has had over the past 300 years. Stonehenge is an example of an uncertain site whose ambivalence is constituted by a multitude of meanings and ways of seeing that have become attached to it (see Balfour, 1979; Michell, 1982; Chippindale 1983; Chippindale et al., 1990; Bender, 1993). It is a site that has become of interest to many different groups of people all of whom have sought either to interpret its meaning or use it in their own distinct ways. As a cultural space, Stonehenge is centrally central within British Culture as a *World Heritage Site*, that has over the years often been used as a sign of nationhood and tradition as well as a significant archaeological site. However, it is also a site that can be described as centrally marginal, especially when we look at it in relation to the range of interpretations associated with the site's importance to an earth mysteries tradition (see Michell, 1982) and to the various carnivalesque practices associated with the site at the time of the summer solstice, from popular festivities during the eighteenth and nineteenth century to the Druids of the early twentieth and then New Age Travellers and their free festival held at the site annually between 1974 to 1984 (see Hetherington, 1992).

As a museum without walls this site can be seen as being constituted in a variety of different ways: as an important archaeological site (Atkinson, 1987; Chippindale, 1983); a Druidic Temple (Sebastian, 1990); an ancient astronomical instrument (Hoyle, 1977); a tourist attraction; a symbol of ancient Britain (Jones, 1990); a New Age site of worship (Michell, 1986); part of England's cultural heritage (Chippindale et al., 1990); a node in a system of ley lines (Devereaux, 1990); a place replete with UFO sightings; and the site of an annual free festival. The constitution of Stonehenge as a significant archaeological site and important part of English cultural Heritage over the past four hundred years, has, therefore not been without opposition. In addition to conflict over the recent use of the site by New Age Travellers for a free festival (see Hetherington, 1992), we have also seen in recent years controversy over plans to build a new visitors' centre and to open up the site and its surroundings to the public.

In looking at Stonehenge as an example of a museum without walls it is clear that we must begin by seeing such a museum space as a contested one. That contestation is focused principally on the issue of modes of social ordering. More specifically, conflict has been focused on how modes of ordering are represented within this particular site, notably expressed through attempts to show what the site means and what it should be used for. There are many actors in this contest: the managers of the site (English Heritage), the land owners (National Trust), archaeologists, Druids, Travellers, pagans, the Police, the County Council, tourists as well as the locals who live in the vicinity. They are all, in effect, 'visitors' to this museum without walls and whether they choose to be or not, their practices become a part of the social context that makes this site meaningful.

In looking at Stonehenge as expressing the spatial relations of the museum without walls and considering the relationship of that spatiality to the issue of social ordering, I want to suggest that we use two concepts to try and interpret the significance of its spatiality: heterotopia and utopics. This is not the first time that the concept of heterotopia, developed by Foucault, has been used in conjunction with museums (see Foucault, 1986; Delaney, 1992; Bennett, 1995). Meaning literally 'other places', heterotopia are sites of incongruous spatial relations that challenge the dominant space of representation within a society (see also Lefebvre, 1991). I would suggest that heterotopia be defined as sites of alternate order constituted through their incongruous character and their relationship to other sites within an established social spatialization.[2] The term utopics, which relates to the issue of utopia, has been developed by Marin principally through his deconstructive reading of Thomas More's *Utopia* (1984; 1992). Utopics, for Marin, derive from a spatial play of difference between ideas of the no-place, *ou*-topia, and ideas of the good-place, *eu*-topia that More brought together when he coined the term *u*-topia. While Marin has applied these ideas to a study of Disneyland (1984:239–57), the concept has not, to my knowledge, been used in the context of examining the spatiality of the museum. In the rest of this paper I aim to look at the spatiality of the museum firstly through a discussion of Foucault's concept of heterotopia alongside Marin's concept of utopics. I follow this by looking at the spatiality of Stonehenge as an example of the museum without walls before concluding with some comments about how such a spatiality and its relationship to the issue of social ordering might be applied more generally to the issue of the contemporary experience of the 'museum'.

Foucault, heterotopia and museum space

'Heterotopia' has becoming something of a fashionable word within cultural studies and cultural geography in recent years (see Teyssot, 1980; Connor, 1989; Soja, 1990; Delaney, 1992; Chambers, 1994; Lyon, 1994; Bennett, 1995; Genocchio, 1995; Hetherington, forthcoming). It is a word that has been much used but little theorized. While there are notable exceptions (see Genocchio, 1995), there has been little discussion of the uses of the concept outside of observations on Foucault's initial and rather brief comments (1986; 1989). While heterotopia are often invoked in the analysis of social space, it has tended to be Foucault's writing on the spatiality of Bentham's design for the Panopticon in his *Discipline and Punish* (1977) that has received more critical attention.

The term 'heterotopia' originally comes from the study of anatomy. There it is used to refer to parts of the body that are either out of place, missing, extra, or, like tumours, alien.[3] For Foucault, who makes many references to the metaphor of the social body in his work, there exist places of Otherness, heterotopia, non-discursive literary sites and actual sites of contrast whose existence sets up unsettling juxtapositions of incommensurate 'objects' that challenge the way we represent and especially the way our representations are ordered. Heterotopia have shock effects that unsettle establish modes of representing and ordering (1986, 1989).

It is in the juxtaposition of things not usually found together and the confusion that such representations create, that mark out heterotopia and give them their significance. Heterotopia signify, not through resemblance but through similitude, through a series of deferrals that are established between a signifier and a signified rather than with direct reference to a referent. Heterotopia, for

Foucault then, are sites that bring together heterogeneous collections of unusual things (or words), without allowing them a unity of meaning through resemblance. Their meaning is derived from a process of similitude which produces, in an almost magical, uncertain space, monstrous anomalies that unsettle the flow of discourse (1989: xvii).

Such sites can be seen to facilitate acts of resistance and transgression. However, there is another important but related role that heterotopia serve. They also act, for Foucault, as spaces for the means of alternative orderings through difference and Otherness,

> Either their [heterotopia's] role is to create a space of illusion
> that exposes every real space, all the sites inside of which
> human life is partitioned, as still more illusory . . . Or else,
> on the contrary, their role is to create a space that is other,
> another real space, as perfect, as meticulous, as well arranged
> as ours is messy, ill constructed, and jumbled. (1986:27)

Heterotopia are not easily located within a system of representation but neither do they exist *sui generis*. Heterotopia do not exist in the order of things, but in the ordering of things. They can be associated with both culturally marginal and central sites, associated with both transgressive outsiderness (see Hetherington, forthcoming) as well as 'carceral' sites of social control and order. In both cases, however, heterotopia are sites in which all things displaced, marginal, rejected or ambivalent are engaged and this engagement becomes the basis of an alternative mode of ordering that has the effect of offering a contrast to the dominant representations of social order.

Bennett has recently introduced his observations on the birth of the museum through a discussion of Foucault's heterotopia concept. His comments about heterotopia, while illuminating, are also somewhat brief and underdeveloped (1995:1-4). What Bennett does say however, echoing Foucault (1986), is that museums, as heterotopia, emerged out of uncertainty and incongruity and developed as distinct sites of social ordering mainly during the nineteenth century. The tension within heterotopia is seen here as that between chaos and order. Museums emerged, Bennett argues, as spaces of representation from the chaos of the cabinet of curiosities and its mode of ordering that sought to represent through spectacle and wonder. The museum in its 'with walls' mode is engaged with the ambivalence of this mode of representing and negates it by producing a space of representation whose mode of ordering is one that seeks to represent and classify in a more systematic and rational way (Bennett, 1995: ch. 1). Bennett also suggests that this mode of ordering, once it had neutralized the spectacle of the cabinet of curiosities into a more rational and discursive space, continued to be involved in a contest with a remnant of that spectacular mode of representing found in the carnivalesque festivities of the fair and the circus (1995:3). The identity of the museum, Bennett is suggesting, was constituted through an engagement with and negation of its Other. Both the museum and the fair are, for Bennett, engaged in different modes of exhibiting (1995:6; see also Altick, 1978). It is not only a question of the rational against the spectacular but also an issue of vocality that is involved here. The classical museum, an ordered architectural space that resembles the equally ordered space of its discourse (see Markus, 1993:171–212), seeks to impose a univocal mode of ordering over both the objects that it classifies, and through its pedagogic intent, over the subjects that make up its (supposedly passive) audience. It is, of course, questionable whether the museum ever fully succeeded in establishing this univocality. What is clear however, is the contrast with the spectacular mode of representation. The mode of ordering found in fairs, festivals and circuses invites, through its display of difference and Otherness, a multivocality or heteroglossian playfulness that allows spectators to become a part of the exhibition (see Bakhtin, 1984). Museums and organized exhibitions, such as the Crystal Palace in 1851, according to Bennett, sought to discipline and neutralize the power of spectacle and in doing so incorporated and negated its heteroglot and ludic powers through its own ordering and classifying processes (1995: ch. 2).[4]

The museum without walls breaks down the disciplinary powers of the classical museum. It opens up forms of resistance to the mode of ordering represented by that sort of museum. The museum without walls allows spectacular modes of exhibiting back in. The resistances that it produces however, should not be seen simply in terms of a transgression against the idea of the museum but as establishing its own modes of social ordering through its spatial effects.

The museum and the neutral

While we might describe the space of the museum as heterotopian in effect, the intention behind its development has always been more utopian in character. In terms of its spatial practice, we can say that the mode of ordering represented in the museum is an example of what Marin has called utopics (1984). The utopics of the museum and the ordering effects it establishes are made up of a play between assemblage and deferral of meaning within an uncertain space. Marin starts from a deconstructive reading of More's *Utopia* focusing on the play of difference between the ou/eu-topia that More introduced within this signifier. Marin's key concept is 'the neutral' which develops out of this tension of meaning within the term Utopia. For Marin, utopian discourse emerged out of the conjunction between feudalism and capitalism from the end of the fifteenth century to the eighteenth century in Europe, the time, we might add, when the museum came into being and left behind the cabinet of curiosities. This Utopian discourse is, for Marin, a polysemic figural discourse that derives its significance from the practices of a spatial play over this no-place/good-place ambivalence. It is, for Marin, through utopics that the significance of the neutral is revealed. To dream the Other, another world of the good life, the eu-topia, is to reveal its lack in the present. But this Other exists as ou-topia, an imaginary no-place that is not to be found except in a form of social critique. Utopics are the spatial practices that emerge from the vacillation between the no and the good in a neutral realm of pure difference. The neutral is what lies between these two poles of More's pun. It is neither 'the good' nor 'the no'-place. The neutral for Marin is both an 'Other place' and the 'Other of Place' (1984:13) The neutral is an impossible space, a realm of differànce as Derrida might have put it (1976), an endless deferral of meaning that derives from the unresolvable tension contained within this eu/outopia. What should now be clear is that Marin's 'neutral' has much in common with Foucault's 'heterotopia'.

For Marin, the discourse of Utopia reveals social conjunction as an example of the neutral,

> As [utopia's] organizing principle [social conjunction] is the
> centre of the structure and the rule of its coherence. It allows
> for the elements inside the whole system to be substituted.

This term designates the process at the very same time it
comes into being between the contraries. It ontologizes this
duration in the synchrony of an opposition it henceforth
masters and orders. The neutral will constitute the principle
of the conjunction of contraries, it will join them in their
very opposition, tying them together and dominating them, it
is the very contrariety of contraries. It allows each of them to
be contraries and at the same time escapes from the relation
that founds them. (1984:15)

The realm of the neutral stands outside as something separate but
also as a transition. The neutral stands apart, it constitutes sites
of difference within a process, a neutralization, and from this
emerges a new social ordering; a new form of sameness. The
process of utopics is what lies behind the idea of the museum.
The museum ontologizes the gap between the no and the good. It
is a space of the 'not yet' as Ernst Bloch might have called it, that
seeks to turn its 'not yet' into a 'there'. It creates a neutral heterotopic space that establishes a mode of ordering out of an
assemblage of the incongruous and Other which it seeks to represent and to order in line with ideas about the good. Through its
assemblage of the Other, the museum defers the difference of
other ways of representing or exhibiting that challenge its mode
of exhibiting and representing. The realm of the neutral is the
realm of social ambivalence. The neutral is the realm where social
ambivalence is engaged and then neutralized.

If this is the character of the spatial relations of the classical
museum then what of the museum without walls? I would argue
that its spatial relations still involve this play between utopic
practice and heterotopic or neutral space. In doing so they are
likely however, to produce a new spatiality and indeed new
modes of ordering themselves. However, the museum without
walls involves not one utopic practice like the classical museum
but many. It is a doubly heterotopic space, one that not only
orders through difference but through competing readings of that
difference. It is the very ambivalence and uncertainty of this
space, however, in contrast to the classical museum that allows
many voices to be expressed. It is also a contested space, a space
with many actors who all wish to project their ideas about society, their utopics, through its space. I will attempt to explore
these issues now through the example of Stonehenge as a museum
without walls.

Stonehenge and the museum without walls

The heterotopic character of a site such as Stonehenge is clearly apparent and derives from the fact that it has for a long time been seen as a site of mystery and uncertainty and open to interpretation. Its mysterious nature, owing partly to its ruined state (a state that suggests continuity with an ancient past as well as decay), the technological accomplishment in its original production, uncertainty over its original purpose and its age, have all gone in to promoting a heteroglossia of ambivalent and competing utopics, which still continue, being focused on this site. The openness to interpretation of Stonehenge has led not only to its continuing interest amongst archaeologists but also amongst those, such as Pagans and Druids, who associate themselves with those unusual interests and practices that Webb has called rejected knowledge (1974). As Michell suggests of the innumerable interpretations of Stonehenge:

> The vast literature on Stonehenge offers the widest conceivable range of answers, or guesses. Various authors have attributed it to the Phoenicians, Romans, Danes, Saxons, Celtic Druids, British aborigines, Brahmins, Egyptians, Chaldeans, and even . . . the Red Indians. Giants, dwarfs and supernatural forces were suggested by several of the pre-scientific writers. The post-scientific ones have added Atlanteans and extra terrestrials. It has been called a temple, an observatory, a memorial, a parliament, a necropolis, an orrery, a stone-age computer, and much besides. One might almost suppose that it was specifically designed to accommodate every notion that could possibly be projected onto it. For at Stonehenge no antiquarian cause is ever finally lost. (1982:22)

As well as being associated with mystery and forms of rejected knowledge, Stonehenge has, at least from the twelfth century been seen as a significant site and part of some of the key myths associated with British history. Geoffrey of Monmouth in his *History of the Kings of Britain* spoke of the rebuilding of Stonehenge by the wizard Merlin (Chippindale, 1983:23–4). After that time the site became intertwined with the stories of Boadicea, the history of the Ancient Kings of England, and with Arthurian legend.[5]

In addition to being important to those interested in earth mysteries and the ancient myths of Britain, Stonehenge has long been a significant tourist site. It begins to get reported in travel journals from the sixteenth century. Folkerzheimer, a Swiss tourist, was the first to mention a visit to Stonehenge in 1562 (Chippindale, 1983:29). The Stones have also been a popular site for artists like Constable and Turner (Chippindale, 1983: ch. 6; Chippindale, 1987), there are many watercolours, maps and sketches dating from the sixteenth century that depict Stonehenge. Within the nineteenth century it started to become a popular site for trippers as well:

> Stonehenge on a Victorian public holiday was a busy place:
> 'The pilgrim who goes there with his reverent mind full of
> Druids . . . undergoes a series of electric shocks . . . He never
> bargained for vanloads of uproarious humanity, dressed in
> all the colours of the rainbow, and in many others of aniline
> origin. They come, they crack jokes, they feast, and they sing
> the latest sweet things from the music hall repertoire . . .
> while a fusillade of ginger beer adds to the general rudeness.'
> (quoted in Chippindale 1983:173)

More recently, of course, it has been the New Age Travellers and their free festival at the time of the summer solstice who have been the main focus of attention. The free festivals began in 1974 and were quite small in size, attracting a few members of what was left of the counter-culture of the 1960s. They conceived the idea of free festivals as utopian spaces in which people might be free from the routines and values of 'straight' society as well as a form of opposition to the more commercial pop festivals that were happening at the time (see Clark, 1982; Hetherington, 1992). After unsuccessful attempts to hold free festivals in Windsor Great Park, Stonehenge was adopted as an alternative. Its mystery and the associations that it held with a supposed pagan tradition led to it being taken as a site whose shrine-like social centrality gave it new meanings, located in older ones, as a site whose alternative character and aura of mystery led it to being taken, especially at the time of the summer solstice, as a site that represented values and beliefs marginalized within industrial society (see Cohen et al., 1987). The New Age Travellers, who emerged out of this free festival scene in the late 1970s, people who chose a life on the road, continued to travel to the festival often in large convoys of vehicles in future years (see Hetherington, 1992; forthcoming). By 1984 it is estimated that 30,000 people were being attracted to the festival and amidst fears of damage to the site, drug-taking and the general carnivalesque atmosphere of the festival, the various authorities who had some interest in the site, most notably the police, decided to put a stop to the festival. In 1985, 1986 and 1988 violent confrontations and mass arrests followed. A four mile exclusion zone was imposed on the site and every year controversy as to whether Travellers should be allowed on the site at solstice time has continued (see Hetherington, 1992). Stonehenge has in recent years also become a political site for these groups; to gain access is to get one over on the State. As well as the Travellers, then, there are a number of official groups like the county council and the police who have taken an interest in the site from the perspective of their legislative or policing role. These groups might all be described as visitors to a museum without walls. It is not only pagans, Druids, Travellers, trippers and the police who have had a utopic interest in Stonehenge. It has also been a significant scientific site for some considerable time. There are also, therefore, some who still treat the site more like a museum in the classical sense; English Heritage, the managers of the site since 1984, The National Trust, who own the surrounding land, and archaeologists. While recent archaeologists have been meticulously 'scientific' in their study of the site this has not always been the case. Indeed the modern science of archaeology emerged out of the earlier pre-science of antiquaries which was fascinated with Stonehenge because of the mystery that surrounded it. It is of some importance, therefore, to try to disentangle some of the history of the reception of the site if we are to understand why all of these different groups now have a utopic interest in it.

It was in the seventeenth century that the first 'scientific' attempts were made to understand what Stonehenge might be. During this period, there emerged a growing amateur, 'gentlemanly' interest in science, especially in antiquities. It can be argued that a fascination with the ordered life of the ancients and nostalgia for an established ancient British cultural tradition developed against the backdrop of post-civil-war England and anxieties over the issue of social order (see Bauman, 1987). This led to the growing reputation of studies of antiquity and architecture, as sciences able to teach lessons about social stability anchored in a view of the past (see Rykwert, 1980). Inigo Jones, perhaps the most important architect of his day, wrote a book on Stonehenge, which included a number of drawings, all of which emphasized the supposedly ordered nature and symmetry of the stones so that Jones was able to interpret Stonehenge as based on a Vitruvian design and therefore a Roman building (Chippindale, 1983:57). Antiquarians around the beginning of the eighteenth century, notably John Aubrey and William Stukeley also made visits and documented studies of Stonehenge. They criticised Jones's Roman interpretation of the origins of Stonehenge. Instead, they were the first to suggest it was a temple built by the Ancient Druids, reflecting their interest in the Deist beliefs of the period and attempting to give Stonehenge a heritage that situated it in an early British civilization, indigenous and culturally sophisticated, that predated the Roman occupation (see Piggott, 1974).

The utopics involved here produced a novel understanding of the issue of social ordering. Stonehenge was a site that represented, for the architects and antiquarians, a possible resolution of the Hobbesian problem of order. They represented Stonehenge as a product of a sophisticated culture with skills available to overcome the challenges of nature, in conjunction with the ordered and stable life of the ancients that could be seen as counter to the contemporary uncertainties of modernity then just beginning to be felt in a time of social upheaval. Commentators like Aubrey and Stukeley, especially the latter (see Piggott, 1974; Chippindale, 1983), attempted to use interpretations of architectural design as a means of establishing a tradition based on a lost memory of happier and more stable times, by drawing on the neo-platonic ideas of the Renaissance, in conjunction with the practices of an emerging modern science to the excavation of ancient sites. Their fascination was with mystery and was originally intertwined with the search for a utopia based in the ordered past.

As the science most associated with Stonehenge, archaeology has developed its scientific methodology and become much more empirical in character. It has shunned this earlier interest in using the arcanum of hermetic mystery as a means of interpretation (see Chippindale, 1983), making such antiquarian interests appear as a form of outdated, naive, rejected knowledge, which has begun, subsequently, to attract those from an earth mysteries perspective (see Michell, 1982; Devereaux, 1990). It has however, retained a utopic that seeks to see the site in an ordered way, developed systematically over many years by its builders (Atkinson, 1987).

The recent interest in Stonehenge as a mysterious site has been associated with the fascinations of ley line hunting, numerology, paganism and UFO spotting (see Chippindale, 1983; Devereaux, 1990; Michell, 1982; 1986). For those associated with this earth mysteries tradition, and this would include many, though not all, New Age Travellers, Stonehenge is an 'authentic' space in which a utopic is developed which aims to recover an ancient wisdom on which, at least symbolically, new lives may be based. Just as Stukeley sought to use Stonehenge to represent British culture before the invading, destroying Romans came, so too, those in the earth mysteries tradition have used the site to challenge the idea of tradition and progress established by archaeologists and upheld by the National Trust and English Heritage.[6]

The incongruous character of this site, associated with its mysterious appeal, is, I believe, heightened by the fact that Stonehenge is a ruin. As Simmel suggests the appeal of the ruin lies in the return of nature to the work of art (1959). Art, in this case architecture, which aims through a heroic desire of the human will to triumph over nature, ends, ultimately, in the failure of decay. The aesthetic appeal of the ruin lies, according to Simmel, in the half revealed return of nature, reasserting itself as time, yet not having fully triumphed. The aesthetic appeal of the ruin is essentially tragic. In it, the original purpose of the human will to create and master nature remains visible but alongside the signs of its ultimate demise (Simmel, 1959). It is, perhaps, the aesthetic appeal of this indeterminacy associated with the ruin that adds to the powerful appeal of mystery that is associated with Stonehenge.

The ruin, however, is not unappropriable to the upholders of a utopics of order. Organizations such as English Heritage and the National Trust have used this aspect of the site to their own ends. Many of the stones, which have been excavated by archaeologists and which, over the centuries, have tended to fall, now have concrete foundations underneath them so that they will remain permanently upright but leaning 'precariously'. Since 1978 the central area within the stones has been closed to the public for fear that erosion will damage the monument. The ruin is replaced by a simulated ruin, a staged authenticity for tourists to appreciate the aesthetic wonder of the ruin that is not a ruin but a space preserved (see MacCannell, 1989: ch. 5).

A linear sense of continuity, constructed in terms of *English* heritage, is established by the managers of the site. One example of this can be seen when one visits the monument by way of the car park on the other side of the road.[7] The entrance to Stonehenge from the car park is via an underground tunnel beneath the nearby road, the A360. Access from the road is now blocked by high fences and is patrolled at night by private security guards. Along this tunnel are a series of pictures with dates and historical pictures leading back from the present through representations of key moments in English history and culminating in the stones themselves. One starts at the present and meets on the way familiar signs of Englishness: the Queen at her coronation; Henry VIII; 1066 (and all that); the Roman invaders and so on, until, finally one emerges out of the tunnel at the other end and is confronted by the starting point of English history, Stonehenge itself.

The appeal of ambivalence and marginality associated with the ruin, as well as celebrated by the proponents of rejected knowledge, has also been a source of attraction from within popular culture over several centuries and adds to the spectacle-like utopics of festival that has also become associated with the site (Clark, 1982; Hetherington, 1992). This utopic, embodied in the idea of the free festival, seeks not to create a staged authenticity and sense of Englishness but to try and bring an expressiveness and a sense of mystery to the site and to locate participants' lives in a 'magical' space that contrasts with the disenchantment of modern society (Weber, 1985).

Such opposition to seeing Stonehenge as a place for reverence of tradition is not new. There are irreverent instances, such as carving graffiti, which date from as early as the seventeenth century (Chippindale, 1983:33), and attempts by tourists to chisel off bits of stone, believing them to have magical healing properties, a practice that Stukeley greatly disapproved of (see Chippindale, 1983:72). A letter addressed to the editor of the *Times* by a 'vacation rambler' after a visit to Stonehenge in 1871, rather dubious in its claims it must be said, shows how the attachment of ideas of tradition and heritage to the stones were then prominent as was also the stone-chipping practice:

There were many visitors, and constant chipping of stone broke the solitude of the place. I overheard the following dialogue. A mechanic who had just drained a stone jar of beer ejaculated, 'If I had known there was to be no one to look after this place I would have brought a hammer and chisel.' 'So would I,' said, in reply, his companion. My object of writing to you, Sir, is to bring the matter before the notice of the proprietor, whoever he may be, and suggest that some means may be taken to preserve for future generations the most remarkable monument of antiquity in this island. (*The Times*, 14/9/1871)

And as Joseph Browne, the self-styled guardian of the Stones during the mid-nineteenth century, notes concerning alleged damage to the stones by two Scots:[8]

The wooden legg man saw them do it. These vandalls were furnished with ropes. The tenon of the great leaning stone after having stood the wear of centuries was broken on Sunday September 16th by some vandalls from Salisbury train on Sunday.

Stonehenge was also used as a site for sports, picnics and festivals that pre-date the contemporary free festivals by many years, indeed centuries, as is shown by a notice that appeared in the *Salisbury and Winchester Journal* July 2 1781:

On Wednesday the 4th July instant will be run a Race by six young men in sacks over Stonehenge Down for a Hat of 10s 6d value. The same day Eleven Pair of Gloves will be Played for at Cricket. The Wickets to be pitched by nine o'clock. Likewise a New Pair of Buckskin Breeches to be Wrestled for. The winner to spend 2s 2d. The same day a hat of One pound value will be Bowled for. He that gets the most pins in three bowls, to have the hat, if the money is bowled in; if not to have half the money that is bowled or pay the residue and have the hat. . . . No person to keep a booth or sell liquor, but the person who rents the ground. By order, Mr John Waters, Wm. Robertson. Running Horse, Amesbury. (*Salisbury and Winchester Journal*, 2/7/1781)

Yet it is not sports, but the heterochronia of the summer solstice that has attracted most attention over the years. The alignment of the stones has meant on the day of the summer solstice that the sun rises over the stones such that at the point when it has risen it lines up with the slaughter stone. It is uncertain when the practice of going to the stones to witness this event began; the earliest reference in visitors' books, kept by Joseph Browne, dates from the solstice of 1865, although it is known to have been witnessed by an antiquarian, a Dr. Thurnham, as early as 1858 (*Devizes Independent*, 28/9/1865). It is most likely that such an event was known by locals from much earlier time and, no doubt, without wishing to suggest my own interpretation of the site, it probably played some part in the construction of the stone circle in the first place.

The summer solstice is without doubt a symbolically significant time for this museum without walls. It was in the early part of this century that the solstice events began to get reported, emphasizing the eccentric and somewhat bizarre activities that occurred, notably associated with Druid ceremonies and indeed also with the mocking of their solstice ceremonies.

> The many who made a pilgrimage to Stonehenge on Tuesday
> night to see the sun rise on midsummer morning were
> rewarded by seeing a beautiful sunrise, and the early rays fell
> directly on the so called 'slaughter stone' the great flat stone
> in the centre of the circle of monoliths . . . Before midnight
> parties began to arrive at Stonehenge – including travellers
> from Bath and Brighton and as the morning wore on a large
> crowd collected. A low temperature prevailed in the early
> hours, but pic-nics and popular airs played on gramophones
> whiled away the time of waiting. Much amusement was
> caused by a party of military officers who, in garments of
> white sheeting and with false beards held a mock Druidical
> ceremony. No demonstration by the Druidical Order took
> place. (*The Times* 23/6/1922)

The popularity of the solstice event, and its carnivalesque atmosphere, continued into the 1960s,

> [T]he only violence was in the hour before midnight when
> beer bottles were hurled against the massive trilithons . . .
> The crowds began building up about 10pm on Tuesday.
> Slightly embarrassed spectators eyed each others clothes,
> many of which bore silent tribute to their wearers' imagina-
> tion . . . One youthful Beau Brummel wore a long blanket
> over his head, decorated with pheasants tail feathers. The
> rest of his outfit consisted of dark corduroy trousers, no
> socks, 'peep-toe' sandals and sunglasses . . . An amateur

contortionist gave an impromptu performance on a 15ft high pillar. (*Salisbury Journal* 23/6/1961)

In festivities such as these, one encounters the utopics of a spontaneous *communitas* and a carnivalesque practice that contests the utopics of Stonehenge as a site of order and reverence now represented in terms of the ideas of tradition and heritage. Festivals introduce a spectacular mode of exhibiting and representing to the site.

For the custodians of the stones and their chief examiners, the archaeologists, a utopic is established that attempts to represent Stonehenge through an ordering that implies continuity with what is ancient, stable and routine; sedimented in the past, a static space with defined boundaries aimed at excluding all that is strange. Stonehenge becomes a monument to the past rather than of the past. It represents the stability and order of tradition and something to be preserved for the future when more might have been discovered as to what it was originally for. The continuing intentions of groups like English Heritage and the National Trust to exclude New Age Travellers and their festival from the site can be seen as an attempt to preserve the idea of representation expressed in the museum against the spectacular modes of representing found originally in fairs and festivals and continuing in the carnivalesque tradition by those who treat the site as a museum without walls. The development of a new visitor centre and plans to open up the land around Stonehenge to the visitor and to do away with the road and the concrete bunker near to the stones are themselves spectacular; but this is a neutralization of the powers of spectacle in keeping with the mode of ordering associated with the classical museum and not a concession to the museum without walls.

For the earth mysteries people, New Age Travellers and all festival goers down the years, Stonehenge is represented through a utopic that is not embedded in the archaeological sediment of tradition, but in a new ordering of the present in a world in which the 'authentic' and the expressive aspects of sociality are seen to have been rationalized and routinized. The significance of the ruined nature of the site aids both interpretations. In the first instance the ruin is seen as something ancient and fragile and therefore needs to be preserved and venerated. In the second sense what is venerated is the sacredness of the site, seen as a place of worship and renewal, symbolized by the significance of the sun at the time of the solstice. In all of these cases, some old and some new, we can see that the ambivalent character of the site opens up the possibility of a number of different utopics, constituting Stonehenge as a contested space that can be seen as an example of the idea of the museum without walls.

Conclusion

In taking Stonehenge as an example of a museum without walls I have tried to show something of the significance of the spatiality of that site and the relationship of that spatiality to the issue of ordering as performed by the museum. Stonehenge, with its multiple, contested and incongruous meanings can be seen as a heterotopic space, a site that opens itself to the possibilities, through many forms of utopic spatial play, to ideas about alternate modes of ordering the social. The ideas about what society should be like, an expression of the beliefs, values and practices, lies behind the utopics of the many 'visitors' to the site. Clearly the utopics of the Travellers and festival supporters are different from those of the archaeologists, English Heritage, the police or day-trippers. They are also different from those of pagans and Druids, even though they may have more in common with the latter than some of the former.

I have given a general overview of some of the main utopics associated with Stonehenge. I have not had the space in this chapter to go into the details of all of them. The point, however, has not been to catalogue all of the different utopics found in this heterotopic space but to illustrate the usefulness of looking at the spatial relations of this site and to make some more general comments about the idea of the museum without walls.

Social actors are skilled agents who have their own outlook on the world and do not need that outlook to be established for them by the museum. While some might choose to accept the interpretations of culture that museums offer, others clearly choose not to and to adopt either a negotiated reading or indeed an oppositional or alternative one (see Ross, 1994). If, as Ross has recently suggested, the space of the conventional museum has shifted from one focused on performing a role of cultural legislation to that of cultural interpretation (1994; see also Bauman, 1987), two distinct utopics, I would add, that are both still engaged in modes of social ordering, then the museum without walls is a further extension of this trend. The museum has spilled out beyond its boundaries and while the principles involved in processes of social ordering still lie behind the idea of this 'museum', the multivocality of its audience is much more apparent. In the museum without walls, members of such an audience are not passive spectators, they are not even just active spectators, they are also would-be curators, trustees, interpreters and indeed exhibits in this contested, heterotopic space, over which they wish their own utopic to prevail. Of course, this is not always going to be an equal contest. Rights of access and the validity of specific interpretations in the context of wider social beliefs will continue to exist and influence such a situation.

By looking at Stonehenge as an illustration I have tried to show that the museum without walls is a heterotopic space that, though not necessarily democratic, invites participation through utopic spatial play in the ordering and articulation of culture. We do not need to resort to terms like postmodernism to explain such a phenomenon. The modernity of the museum, its heterotopic space and the utopic play that it expresses through ideas about social ordering, is still to be found in the museum without walls. The difference is that we can now begin to see that the mutlivocality of modernity, the producer of these varied utopics, is revealed through these different visions of how to order the social to be highly diverse, uncertain and ever changing. The classical museum sought to impose a vision of modernity through a control of all that it saw as Other. The museum without walls reveals that deferral and Otherness are at the very centre of the modern.

Notes

1 (Hardy, 1983:379).
2 For a more detailed discussion of the concept of heterotopia, see my forthcoming book *The Badlands of Modernity*, Routledge.
3 *Oxford English Dictionary, Volume VII* (Second Edition) (1989) Prepared by J. Simpson and E. Weiner, p. 91. Oxford: Clarendon Press.
4 On the ordering and negation of social ambivalence in bourgeois culture see also Agnew (1986), Castle (1986), Stallybrass and White (1986), Hetherington (1996).
5 Stonehenge is also provides the backdrop for the dramatic and tragic denouement to Hardy's *Tess of the D'Urbervilles* (1983).
6 Interview with TKI 3, Long term Traveller and festival organizer, interviewed 18/5/1991, Ross-on-Wye.

7 My visit took place in September 1991.
8 Two visitors' books are held in the library at the Salisbury and South Wiltshire Museum in Salisbury. I would like to thank the staff for letting me look at them. Joseph Browne who kept them was not officially employed by the Antrobus family that owned Stonehenge at that time. Instead he was the Registrar in Amesbury. Unfortunately there are very few visitors comments. Of interest is the entry on 5/6/1856 of Millard Fillmore a president of the United States, foreign royalty, 13//9/1853, a visitor from Australia on 8/8/1856, and from the United States as well as from all over Britain. There are also a few names written in strange lettering, I originally thought these to be in Greek but they are more likely to have been written by Druid enthusiasts in druidic runes! There is the example of picnics by large parties as on 28/6/1855 and of musical entertainments like brass bands 26/9/1855.

Bibliography

Agnew, J-C., (1986), *Worlds Apart: the Market and the Theatre in Anglo-American Thought*, 1550–1750. Cambridge: Cambridge University Press.

Altick, R., (1978), *The Shows of London*, Cambridge, Mass.: Harvard University Press.

Atkinson, R., (1987), *Stonehenge and Neighbouring Monuments*, London: English Heritage.

Bakhtin, M., (1984), *Rabelais and his World*, Bloomington: Indiana University Press.

Balfour, M., (1979), *Stonehenge and its Mysteries*, London: Hutchinson.

Bauman, Z., (1987), *Legislators and Interpreters*, Cambridge: Polity Press.

Bender, B., (1993), 'Stonehenge – Contested Landscape (Medieval to Present Day)', pp. 245–79 in B. Bender (ed.), *Landscape: Politics and Perspectives*, Oxford: Berg.

Benjamin, W., (1973), 'The Work of Art in the Age of Mechanical Reproduction', pp. 211–44 in *Illuminations*, London: Fontana.

Bennett, T., (1995), *The Birth of the Museum*, London: Routledge.

Castle, T., (1986), *Masquerade and Civilization*, London: Methuen.

Chambers, I., (1994), 'Leaky Habits and Broken Grammar', pp. 245–9 in G. Robertson, M. Mash, L. Tickner, J. Bird, B. Curtis, T. Putnam (eds), *Travellers' Tales*, London: Routledge.

Chippindale, C., (1983), *Stonehenge Complete*, London: Thames and Hudson.

Chippindale, C., (1987), *Stonehenge Observed: an Illustrated Essay Published for the Exhibition 'Visions of Stonehenge 1350–1987.'* Southampton: Southampton City Art Gallery.

Chippindale, C., Devereux, P., Jones, R. and Sebastian, T. (eds), (1990), *Who Owns Stonehenge*? London: Batsford.

Clark, M., (1982), *The Politics of Pop Festivals*, London: Junction Books.

Cohen, E., Ben-Yehuda, N. and Aviad, J., (1987), 'Recentering the World: the Quest for "Elective" Centers in a Secularized Universe.' *The Sociological Review*. 35(2): 320–46.

Connor, S., (1989), *Postmodernist Culture*, Oxford: Blackwell.

Crimp, D., (1985), 'On the Museum's Ruins', pp. 43–56 in H. Foster (ed.), *Postmodern Culture*, London: Pluto Press.

Delaney, J., (1992), 'Ritual Space in the Canadian Museum of Civilization: Consuming Canadian Identity', pp. 136–48 in R. Shields (ed.), *Lifestyle Shopping*, London: Routledge.

Derrida, J., (1976), *Of Grammatology*, Baltimore: John Hopkins University Press.

Devereaux, P., (1990), 'Stonehenge as an Earth Mystery', pp. 35–61 in C. Chippindale, P. Devereux, R. Jones, and T. Sebastian (eds), *Who Owns Stonehenge?* London: Batsford.

Foucault, M., (1977), *Discipline and Punish*, Harmondsworth: Penguin.

Foucault, M., (1986), 'Of Other Spaces.' *Diacritics*. 16(1):22–17.

Foucault, M., (1989), *The Order of Things*, London: Tavistock/Routledge.

Genocchio, B., (1995), 'Discourse, Discontinuity, Difference: The Question of "Other" Spaces', pp. 35–46 in S. Watson and K. Gibson (eds), *Postmodern Cities and Spaces*, Oxford: Basil Blackwell.

Hardy, T., (1983), *Tess of the D'Urbervilles*, Oxford: Oxford University Press.

Hetherington, K., (1992), 'Stonehenge and Its Festival: Spaces of Consumption', pp. 83–98 in R. Shields (ed.), *Lifestyle Shopping*, London: Routledge.

Hetherington, K., (1996), *The Badlands of Modernity*, forthcoming, Routledge.

Hetherington, K., (forthcoming), 'New Age Travellers: Heterotopic Spaces and Heteroclite Identities', *Theory, Culture and Society*.

Hewison, R., (1987), *The Heritage Industry*, London: Methuen.

Hoyle, F., (1977), *On Stonehenge*, London: Heinemann Educational Books.

Jones, R., (1990), 'Sylwadau Cynfrodor ar Gôr y Cewri; or a British Aboriginal's Land Claim to Stonehenge', pp. 62–87 in C. Chippindale, P. Devereux, R. Jones, and T. Sebastian (eds), *Who Owns Stonehenge?* London: Batsford.

Law, J., (1994) *Organizing Modernity*, Oxford: Basil Blackwell.

Lefebvre, H., (1991), *The Production of Space*, Oxford: Blackwell.

Lyon, D., (1994), *Postmodernity*, Milton Keynes: Open University Press.

MacCannell, D., (1989), *The Tourist*, Second edition. New York: Schocken Books.

Malraux, A., (1954), 'The Museum Without Walls', pp. 13–128 in *Voices of Silence*, London: Secker and Warburg.

Marin, L., (1984), *Utopics: Spatial Play*, London: Macmillan.

Marin, L., (1992), 'Frontiers of Utopia: Past and Present', *Critical Inquiry*, Vol. 19(3):397–420.

Markus, T., (1993), *Buildings and Power*, London: Routledge.

Michell, J., (1982), *Megalithomania*, London: Thames and Hudson.

Michell, J., (1986), *Stonehenge: Its History, Meaning, Festival, Unlawful Management, Police Riot '85 and Future Prospects*, London: Radical Traditionalist Papers.

Negrin, L., (1993), 'On the Museum's Ruins: a Critical Appraisal', *Theory, Culture and Society*, 10(1):97–125.

Piggott, S., (1974), *The Druids*, Harmondsworth: Penguin.

Ross, M., (1994), *Interpreting the New Museology: A Case Study of Museum Workers*, Working Papers No. 8. Keele University: Department of Sociology and Social Anthropology.

Rykwert, (1980), *First Moderns*, Cambridge, Mass.: MIT Press.

Sebastian, R., (1990), 'Triad /|\: the Druid Knowledge of Stonehenge', pp. 88–119 in C. Chippindale, P. Devereux, R. Jones, and T. Sebastian (eds), *Who Owns Stonehenge?* London: Batsford.

Simmel, G., (1959), 'The Ruin', pp. 259–66 in K. Wolff (ed.), *Georg Simmel, 1858–1918*, Columbus: Ohio State University Press.

Soja, E., (1990), 'Heterotopologies: A Remembrance of Other Spaces in the Citadel-LA', *Strategies*, 3:6–39.

Stallybrass, P. and White, A., (1986), *The Politics and Poetics of Transgression*, London: Methuen.

Teyssot, G., (1980), 'Heterotopias and the History of Spaces', *Architecture and Urbanism*. 121:79–100.

Webb, J., (1974), *The Occult Underground*, La Salle, Illinois: Open Court.

Weber, M., (1985), *The Protestant Ethic and the Spirit of Capitalism*, London: Counterpoint/Unwin.

White, P., (1985), *On Living in an Old Country*, London: Verso.

Maintaining boundaries, or 'mainstreaming' black history in a white museum

Eric Gable

Abstract

In this chapter, I explore ethnographically how enduring notions of racial 'identity' continue to make it unlikely that an ongoing attempt by America's largest outdoor living-history museum – Colonial Williamsburg – to tell stories about race relations in the antebellum era will be pedagogically effective. I focus on pedagogic practice among Colonial Williamsburg's 'frontline' because, while the professional historians ostensibly set historiographical policy and monitor historiographical product at Colonial Williamsburg, it is ultimately the dozens of guides who tell Williamburg's story to the visiting public. Moreover, I focus on the way guides talk about a particularly revealing topic – miscegenation – because it is a generally accepted argument among historians of antebellum America that the history of laws against miscegenation (which were codified in the eighteenth century), coupled with the history of their systematic violation, is at the root of the invention of distinct racial categories. To tell this story of 'kinship denied' at Colonial Williamsburg would have meant that a largely white audience and a mostly white 'frontline' would have had to rethink the category of race itself in ways perhaps more threatening to their 'identities' than to their ostensibly 'black' peers. In this chapter, I suggest that the way miscegenation remained a resisted topic at Colonial Williamsburg, reinforces, at the level of vernacular historiography, the very dichotomizing thinking about racial categories that the topic should have called into question.

Introduction

What happens when the professional historians who set educational policy at an American heritage site and museum commit their institution to teaching about black and white race relations

© The Editorial Board of The Sociological Review 1996. Published by Blackwell Publishers, 108 Cowley Road, Oxford OX4 1JF, UK and 238 Main Street, Cambridge, MA 02142, USA.

in the eighteenth century? This is what a new generation of historians did at Colonial Williamsburg, the largest outdoor living-history museum in America, in the late 1980s and early 1990s.[1] These historians were part of a movement generally known in the museum world in America as the 'new social history' – a movement with an interest in exposing class relations and conflict, and a desire to use history to effect positive political change in the present. At Colonial Williamsburg the new social historians were particularly interested in making slave-master relations and the lives of slaves more central to the stories they told their visitors, in order to rectify a longstanding inequity in the way Colonial Williamsburg portrayed America's collective past. This would be the new social historians' attempt to promote a kind of historiographical racial balance and, in the process, ameliorate racial tensions and misunderstandings in contemporary America.

How successful were they? In this chapter, I try to answer this question by focusing on the way guides at Colonial Williamsburg talk about miscegenation in the antebellum era. I focus on guides because, while the professional historians ostensibly set historiographical policy and monitor historiographical product at Colonial Williamsburg, it is ultimately the dozens of guides – the museum's 'frontline' – who tell Williamsburg's story to the visiting public. Guides, unlike visitors, spend months, even years, at the site. If anyone is to be influenced by the pedagogic messages of the new social history, it is they.

I focus on miscegenation because it offers a telling lesson in the failure of the new social history to ameliorate interracial misunderstanding at Colonial Williamsburg. It is a generally-accepted argument among historians of antebellum America that the history of laws against miscegenation (which were codified in the eighteenth century), coupled with the history of their systematic violation, is at the root of the invention of distinct racial categories. As such, professional historians are merely elaborating upon what has been an enduring theme among African–American intellectuals concerned with revealing the arbitrariness of racial boundaries. To tell this story of 'kinship denied' at Colonial Williamsburg would have meant that a largely white audience and mostly white 'frontline' would have had to rethink the category of race itself in ways perhaps more threatening to their 'identities' than to their ostensibly 'black' peers.[2]

Moreover to tell the story of miscegenation at Colonial Williamsburg would have been to perform one of the chief missions of the new social history – to reveal the historicity of the natural or taken-for-granted. Such a story needs to be written in the space between official laws and covert violations of the laws – and it is precisely this kind of story of a myriad traces, no trace necessarily complete in itself, that is the stuff of social history.

At Colonial Williamsburg in the early 1990s, after a decade of the new social history's dominance, miscegenation continued to be a topic which the majority of guides avoided. White guides resisted it by reverting to a historiography of 'just the facts' directly antithetical to the new social history. They did so by drawing a sharp contrast between themselves and a public they claimed was fascinated by the topic simply because it was eager for cheap thrills; they did so by distinguishing themselves from a minority of black guides who, they believed, played fast and loose with the facts in using the topic of miscegenation to 'get up on a soap-box.' In short, the way miscegenation remained a resisted topic at Colonial Williamsburg, reinforced, at the level of vernacular historiography, the very dichotomizing thinking about racial categories the topic should have called into question.

The site

Colonial Williamsburg is, at once, America's largest outdoor museum and a middle-sized corporation and resort (Handler, forthcoming; Leon and Piatt, 1989). This hybrid museum-corporation is divided into a 'for profit' or 'business side' which owns and manages two golf-courses and three hotels (catering not only to tourists but to corporate conventions), and restaurants. The 'business side' markets, sells, and licenses colonial-era reproduction furnishings, and manages an endowment approaching 250 million dollars in value. What is referred to as the 'museum' or 'education side' consists of a 175-acre complex of 100 gardens and some 500 restored or totally reconstructed structures meant to replicate Williamsburg, the capital of Virginia in the colonial era on the eve of the American Revolution. Of the hundreds of buildings, about fifty houses, stores, taverns and craftsites are open to the paying public. They include houses owned by the gentry such as the George Wythe house and the Peyton Randolf house, public buildings such as the Governor's Palace, the Courthouse, the Gaol, the Powder Magazine, and the Capitol, and craftsites such as the Anderson's Forge, the printshop, the silversmith's, a brickmaker's yard, and so forth. There are also research facilities, offices, and several museums within the museum (DeWitt-Wallace Decorative Arts Gallery, Abbey Aldrich Rockefeller Folk Art Center, James Anderson House archaeology exhibit).

During the years of our research, this popular tourist destination attracted roughly a million paying visitors a year, and earned and spent over 120 million dollars a year. During this period, the Colonial Williamsburg Foundation employed about 3000 people – most of them gardeners, waiters and waitresses, busboys, maids. About 500 of the total employees worked on the 'education side' – a handful of historians and archaeologists, curators and craftspeople, but mostly guides of one kind or another.

Most of the guide corps, or historic interpreters as they were called, wore period costumes, and all but a handful of them were white. There was also a small coterie of black interpreters in the Department of African–American Interpretation and Presentation (AAIP). The AAIP staff, all of them African Americans, was made up of a dozen fulltime, college-educated, historic interpreters, two administrators, and a secretary.[3] The fulltime people were responsible for leading daily a black history walking tour of Williamsburg, and for on-site interpretation at two exhibit kitchens. At these sites, they alternated between acting as if they were 18th-century slaves (called 'first-person' interpretation), and commenting on eighteenth-century slave life, as a twentieth-century museum employee (called 'third-person' interpretation). In addition, AAIP presented a variety of staged productions ranging from evening plays during the summer season to programs of storytelling, music, and dance.

The AAIP department had developed in conjunction with a shift in the general historiographical agenda at Colonial Williamsburg that began in the late 1970s. During that period, a group of 'new social historians' were hired to restore what was becoming an increasingly threatened institutional credibility (Gable and Handler, 1993; Horton and Crews, 1986). Critics argued that Williamsburg was, in effect, selling a bowdlerized past and kitsch artifacts of that past to a gullible audience. The common word was that Williamsburg was 'too clean' or that its story was 'sanitized' because it focused too narrowly on the 'silk-pants patriots' – the town's upper-crust – and what they consumed in the way of foods and furnishings, and too little on the rest of the colonial town's inhabitants, including the close to 50 percent of the population who were slaves.[4]

The new social historians were given broad leeway to refurbish Colonial Williamsburg – to make it more up-to-date and accurate historiographically. They wanted to tell a story of America's founding which was at once more critical and more inclusive. Central to this new accounting of the national past would be the lives of what came to be called 'the other half' – Williamsburg's black slaves. Initially, the AAIP department was formed to put black history onto the street, but by the time of our research the new social historians' agenda had become much more ambitious. Their goal was to 'mainstream' black history by making the story of the 'other half' an integral part of every story at every site in the reconstructed town.

'Mainstreaming' meant that sites which had once served as forums for talking about the lives of their white proprietors or inhabitants would now also be used to talk about the lives of slaves who lived and worked there. 'Mainstreaming' also meant (at least in theory) that the story of the 'other half' would not be left only to the Foundation's small coterie of black guides in AAIP, but it would now be expected that every guide would be able to talk about slave life in the eighteenth century.

Although the new social historians were ostensibly in charge of developing historiographical policy, they had to convince Colonial Williamsburg's various audiences and patrons that the changes they wanted to institute were (depending on the audience), historically, morally, and (to a lesser extent) economically correct.[5] To some audiences, they argued that the new story was to be an alternative to the story of the 'silk pants patriots', and that this would represent a paradigm shift. They pointed out that to tell about the past from the perspective of the slaves, or even the 'middling sort', meant that there would be less pedagogic space remaining for the older celebratory narratives (see Carson, 1981, 1991; Chappell, 1989). To other audiences, they argued that the new story would be an addition – just another facet of an ongoing institutional effort to bring the past to life in all its details.[6] In this sense mainstreaming would merely be an extension of a long term and generally ever progressing quest for ultimate accuracy.

If the new social historians had to make a convincing case for mainstreaming in terms of historical accuracy, they also wanted to claim that the new policy would be morally correct as well. Colonial Williamsburg had always presented itself as a shrine to American values, yet, as many of its critics pointed out, its 'devotees' or 'pilgrims' were largely white and relatively well-off economically. Colonial Williamsburg was, as some insiders put it, a 'Republican Disneyland'; yet, whatever the politics of its patrons, visitors, and board, the Foundation was also deeply committed to notions of melting-pot equality. Thus, the new social historians were able to use the institution's own discourse to argue that to include the story of the town's other half – to integrate, if you will, the town's reenacted and narrated past – would also be an ameliorative step in the present. The notion was that a 'mainstreamed' history would also be more attractive to black audiences. The notion was that Williamsburg could thus participate in black enfranchisement and assimilation.

Needless to say, the several ways that the new social historians justified their claims to have authority to change Colonial Williamsburg's story, generated their own potential contradictions. I will return to this issue in my concluding remarks. What I would like to note for now is that it is ultimately in this atmosphere of mistrust, by influential outsiders who could never believe that the museum would ever be 'dirty' enough and inertia, even resistance, by institutional insiders, that the new social historians instituted these new programs.[7]

Miscegenation at the Wythe House

Miscegenous unions are an enduring fascination for many Americans (Friedman, 1970; Hernton, 1965; Stember, 1976; Washington, 1970; Williamson, 1980). In their historical imagination such unions are exemplified by a standard scenario which has become a kind of archetype: an older white master takes a younger slave as a mistress and they have a child to whom, as social conventions require, the master pretends to have no substantive connection. Society's mistreatment of the slave mistress and the disenfranchised mulatto can become the symbols for the fundamental inequities of slavery itself.

Because this scenario has taken on the status of an archetype (and, indeed, because such unions occurred) almost every historical site in the American South where the scenario could possibly have been enacted accretes such a story as part of its 'public memory', its unofficial history (cf Gable, forthcoming). At Colonial Williamsburg, the Wythe House is the site which attracts such a story.

The Wythe house is an elegant brick building in the Georgian style. Ever since Colonial Williamsburg became a popular tourist destination this restored 'original' structure has had a peculiar attraction among those who wish to replicate in their own lives the upscale idyll that Williamsburg often represents. The Wythe house has been called the 'most copied house in America.' The edifice and its decor are emblematic of a certain widely emulated taste.

George Wythe is also an important protagonist in Colonial Williamsburg's ongoing narrative of a celebratory past. He is the only silk-pants patriot who actually resided in the colonial capital. A lawyer, he is famous as the teacher of Thomas Jefferson and as a signer of the Declaration of Independence. Like Jefferson, he is portrayed as a great enlightenment intellect whose polymath interests ranged from chemistry to moral philosophy. A champion of the good egalitarian principles that would make America great, he also managed to live the good and elegant life. Like Jefferson, Wythe was uncomfortable with the institution of slavery. And (unlike Jefferson) he acted upon this discomfort by freeing his slaves in his lifetime. After his wife's death he moved to Richmond (the new state capital) along with his newly freed cook, Lydia Broadnax, under whose care he continued to live along with a mulatto boy, Michael Brown, who Wythe took special pains to educate and to whom Wythe left property in his will.

It was Wythe's relationship to Broadnax that became the topic of the archetypical miscegeneous union during the period of our research. The general theme of miscegenation was projected onto the Wythe house by some visitors and by, as we shall see, black interpreters among the museum's frontline. At the same time, white interpreters – especially those working in the house itself – defended Wythe against such a story.

Miscegenation and the Other Half

On a two-hour walking tour called the 'Other Half Tour' AAIP guides used the Wythe house as backdrop to tell the story of the Black Codes – the laws that made interracial marriage a crime and, in a sense, made racial essentialism an official policy. On the 'Other Half Tour' a black interpreter would lead a group of twenty or so visitors (who'd bought a special ticket) on a stroll around the Governor's Palace green and its environs. The theme of the tour was the increasing segregation and disenfranchisement

of blacks as a group apart, beginning with their arrival as indentured servants (like any other indentured servants) in Jamestown
in 1619. The guides would stress that for much of the seventeenth
century blacks and whites intermarried, and that there were no
laws against this. They then gave a brief history of American
slavery, describing the horrors of the Middle Passage, and emphasizing, for example, that captive women were kept in the upper
level of the ship's hold for the sailors' sexual pleasure, while the
captive men were shackled together on the lowest deck 'as bal-
last.' Then, with the Wythe house behind them, they explained
the Black Codes. Here is an excerpt from one of several tours we
tape-recorded:[8]

> The law of 1662 stated that all children born to Negro
> women are bound or free according to the condition of the
> mother. So if the mother is free, the child is free. If the
> mother is a slave, then the child is a slave. Now previous to
> that the status of the child had been based upon that of the
> father. But once they moved, you could see a lot of intermar-
> riages taking place, a mulatto population coming about.
> They put a reversal on the law.

This interpreter spent the next five minutes or so on punishments
given slaves for various offenses – hog stealing, running away –
before returning to sexual relations.

> There was also a castration law. It was never really explained
> as to whether it was the actual act of raping a white woman
> but the law reads, 'for ravaging a white woman.' So it could
> mean just looking at one. So some people associate that law
> with the downcast look of male slaves so that they would not
> look into the eyes of white women. OK, you get that connec-
> tion? Any questions?

The interpreter then directed the tour group's attention to the
Wythe House, to recount the story of the recent widower, freeing
his slaves and moving to Richmond:

> He carried three persons with him: Lydia Broadnax, Ben
> who might have been Lydia's husband, we don't know for
> sure, and a mulatto boy by the name of Michael Brown.
> Now (the guide laughed here) George Wythe taught Michael

Brown Latin and Greek. We don't know why. (She rolled
her eyes and laughed again.) We don't know that either
because there's no documented evidence to say that it was his
child.

AAIP guides usually finished the story of Wythe and his slaves
with an account of the poisoning of both George Wythe and
Michael Brown by Wythe's nephew. They stressed that Brown
had been poisoned because Wythe had left part of his estate to
the mulatto boy. Such a bequest, it was implied, was further evidence that Michael Brown was Wythe's son.

Occasionally a guide went further. For example, one concluded
her version of the Wythe-Broadnax story with 'you won't hear
that inside the house.' When a visitor asked her why, she said
that according to museum researchers there was no documented
evidence, 'so they won't talk about it.' Another time a guide told
the poisoning story and then remarked that she was 'written up'
for telling people on her tours to go into the Wythe House and
ask the guides there why George Wythe taught Michael Brown to
read.

Miscegenation inside the Wythe House

When the AAIP interpreters suggested that white guides say the
specific story of Wythe's relationship to Broadnax 'is not documented,' they were alluding to a pervasive belief among them that
white interpreters used an apparent lack of documents to evade
the discussion of sensitive issue that made white guides uncomfortable. Indeed, as we were to discover, guides inside the Wythe
house tried their best not to talk about this issue even though visitors, irritatingly (as one guide put it), 'were always asking.' They
asked, so some guides told us, because they had been prompted
to do so by the 'Other Half' tour; or because they had read or
heard about Fawn Brodie's popular biography of Thomas
Jefferson, which sets out to prove that Jefferson had a liaison
with Sally Hemings and suggests a similar relationship for Wythe
and Broadnax; or, because they simply believed that such liaisons
must have occurred and that institutions like Colonial
Williamsburg would hide or 'whitewash' this fact because they are
(as a senior member of the research staff put it) 'a slick corporation'. As a senior interpreter explained:

Eric Gable

It's the Fawn Brodie syndrome. They're looking for something – that the statue of marble is actually made of clay.
That it will crumble. That those people are not as perfect as
they are portrayed.

In short, many guides in the Wythe House believed visitors
asked about Wythe's black mistress or mulatto son because they
wanted to puncture a hole in the façade the Foundation had
erected. Most interpreters simply refused to recognize such questions as legitimate. As one interpreter put it,

I don't talk about that, and I don't interpret any ghosts. I do
nothing with ghosts. All I say – they ask you, 'do you know
about the ghost that's supposed to be in this house?' And I
say, 'no, if it's not documented, I don't do things that aren't
documented.' 'Oh.' So they go off to somebody else to see if
they'll tell them.

To equate Wythe's miscegeneous union with a ghost story was
to dismiss it as the kind of myth the credulous public seems
eagerly to invent for any old house. To note that the public will
'go off to somebody else' alludes to the tenacity of such myths in
the face of their constant denial. As a rule, white guides portrayed themselves as disinterested defenders of the facts against
the mythologizing desires of a gullible public.

Thus white interpreters, generally claimed that, if they had the
facts to back them up, they would broach the topic of miscegenation (although some guides, in conversations with us, might be
uncomfortable talking about it in front of a racially mixed audience some of whom might find the topic 'embarassing'). But
'facts' had to be ones, as a lead interpreter put it, 'that you actually can tie to here.' To her, AAIP staff were ignoring particular
facts in favour of a 'message':

[they] want to talk about miscegenation at the Wythe House.
And they're using a particular example – you know, having
an affair with George Wythe, and they produce this slave
called Michael Brown. And they're [saying] Michael lived
there. . . . Well, Michael Brown wasn't even born when
George Wythe lived there. Michael was a freed slave who
was with George Wythe in Richmond. But there's no proof –
in fact, the facts, according to [a professional historian in

Colonial Williamsburg's Research Department], pretty much [say that] the child was not his.

In this conversation, another lead interpreter added that the historian had offered an alternative example to use. According to her, the historian 'went back to his books and came up with John Custis.' And since, as he averred, 'miscegenation is an important thing to talk about,' he suggested 'why don't people talk about Custis.' Custis had 'left something in his will' to a mulatto child and 'the townspeople of the time sort of accepted the fact that Custis had this mulatto child and cared very much for it.' The lead interpreter concluded:

That's the story we need to tell if we're telling the story of miscegenation. So I'm not thinking that's an evil thing to do. The story of miscegenation is worth telling. I mean, every newspaper ad you look at talks about mulattoes. They came because of miscegenation. So you've got to talk about the story.

'But,' she went on, 'you need something that you can talk about that's' – and she hesitated as she chose her next word – '*fair* to talk about. And the George Wythe story – particularly since Michael Brown wasn't even born until Wythe lived in Richmond – isn't the story to tell.' She, like the other lead interpreter, realized, however, that the problem with the Custis story, 'the better story,' was that Custis, unlike Wythe, did not have 'a site' at Colonial Williamsburg, so it would be much harder to bring him up in an interpretive presentation.

Miscegenation and the 'documents'

In this way interpreters – even those who would have counted themselves as deeply committed to the mission of the new social history – were able to recognize that while miscegenation was a legitimate topic in the abstract, it was harder to legitimate as a topic in the concrete circumstances of Williamsburg as a particular site. Unfortunately, it was not the topic of miscegenation that these senior interpreters taught neophyte guides in training sessions, but the distance between site and topic that became, inadvertently, their chief pedagogic message. One day of a several day training session we observed for the Wythe house was devoted to talking about black history on the Wythe house 'property.' The trainers never mentioned miscegenation, not even to provide their trainees with material with which to *counter* questions they might get about Wythe, Broadnax, and Michael Brown. But towards the end of the session, one of the trainees, a white male, initiated the following:

> *Trainee*: One question [he paused] – There's obviously a lot of, ah, interracial children. And it was incomprehensible to us, as 20th-century whites – if you have a child, even though the mother was black, you want to have some kind of emotional tie. Would that not – ?
>
> *Staff person*: I think that's a very interesting question to raise. There's no doubt there was miscegenation in the 18th century. And who was the law protecting in those relationships?
>
> *Trainee*: The white person.
>
> *Staff*: Exactly, exactly.
>
> *Trainee*: Sexual relations are prohibited. But it went on anyway. I mean, a lot of things that are prohibited happen.
>
> *Staff*: That's right. But your point as a twentieth-century person, of having an attachment to that child, and to the woman you had a relationship with, again, you're in a foreign country. You're looking at people at a time and a place that we really don't understand. And I think that undoubtedly there were close ties formed. The West Indies is a fascinating place to look at because a lot of your white slave masters, overseers, had black mistresses. And their relationships to slavery are somewhat different.

At this point in the conversation, a second trainee, an African–American woman (the only black house guide trainee at the time), entered the conversation: 'Any relationship between black and white in slavery time, I would think, would have been more rape than compassion.' The staff person agreed with her, but suggested that white men did not usually abuse their own slaves because they respected, or feared, the consequences from the monogamous slave husband. And, said the staffer, 'more often it was the overseer, or the planter from a neighbouring plantation.'

By shifting the topic of miscegenation to the West Indies or to an anonymous overseer, this staff member missed the opportunity to teach her charges how to make miscegenation a part of the interpretative agenda of the site. In short, trainers could be well-versed in the historiography of miscegenation, yet despite themselves, turn it into a pedagogically sterile topic.

But, as we were to discover, even when trainers felt that they had the documents to talk about miscegenation, they still felt that the topic itself was of little importance. Consider an interview we had with the staffer responsible for training mainstream interpreters to include black history. When we asked her about including miscegenation in the 'mainstream' interpretations in Williamsburg she said she thought it 'had to be addressed.' When we asked about the problems of documentation, she responded, 'I think that there's enough – we have historians who have looked at the documentation of the Old South, for instance . . . You'd never be able to [look at a specific site and talk about miscegenation] but what you have to do is to move to the documentation of the larger area and see what the trends are.' She discussed some of these trends – how the museum's historians find and interpret documents that show evidence of miscegenation:

> So I think that our interpreters need to deal with the sense
> that there was miscegenation but that it was extremely hard
> to document. . . . You know, it was very much an issue in
> the eighteenth century but it isn't the predominant issue to
> discuss about slavery.

For the chief trainer miscegenation may be a problematic topic because of the ambiguities of 'documentation', but fortunately, it is also not the 'predominant issue.' Thus, it is not surprising that even when white guides had a 'document' of miscegenation and on site they managed to rationalize why the topic was not appropriate.

At Wetherburne's tavern, for example, the curators had redecorated (in order to mainstream black history in what had hitherto been a white space) the interior of one of the public rooms with reproductions of posters requesting information on individual runaway slaves. The posters described the slaves' physical characteristics and some noted that they were 'mulatto.' When we pointed out to a lead interpreter that this 'document' would serve as a perfect entrée for talking about the paradoxes of antebellum miscegenation, he agreed, but noted that he never broached the topic:

I don't know that we, that myself, not having pursued that subject particularly. But on a lot of subjects such as this I don't know that there's much documentation to begin with. So rather than be on shaky ground or say something off the wall that you have no proof for – either one way or the other. It's not that we avoid it because its a touchy issue. If something isn't documented enough we'd rather not deal with it than make statements that we're not sure about.

When we reminded him of the posters, he added,

Now we do have some of the inventories listed mulatto and they're listed children, so we do know it happened. But other than that . . . [and he stops himself before changing directions] What is the point of it – you know, if we get into it? You know people are curious about it, but so what? You discuss it; it took place but what is that?

When we asked what would be the pedagogic point of talking about miscegenation at all, he replied,

It depends on what you were trying to do. If you were, let's say, if you were teaching black history, okay. And you were trying to prove, say, that the masters mistreated the slaves. They took advantage of the slaves. And so on. Then I could see you trying to find documentation and using that to says 'yes' this is true – you know – that they treated them as property.

But rather than continue with this thought he returned to the issue of 'documentation' in order to explain why such a pedagogic approach would be inappropriate:

What we try to do, as much as possible is, if there is information that exists, we try to present the facts without swaying people one way or the other. This is the way is was. This is what the documents or the diaries or the court records say. Come to your own conclusions. Rather than saying, you know, ah. And we frown on, when interpreters take it upon themselves to take an issue which they have a strong feeling and sort of . . . get on their soapbox and use their interpretation to the visitor as a means of making their own statement about an issue . . . We try to discourage that . . . If you want to make a point, you can find a document and forget about all the other documentation. But we try not to do that because we feel that it is not our role as inter-preters – to persuade people.

As the lead interpreter rationalized the foregone conclusion not to talk about something as 'factual' as the word 'mulatto' on the poster prominently displayed on the wall in Wetherburne's Tavern, he kept defending this decision by talking about 'docu-ments.' Although he recognized that 'documents' could be deployed selectively, it was always somebody else – somebody eager to get up on a soap box – who chose to use some docu-ments and ignore others. By contrast, he and other good guides like him kept personal feelings, politics, passion out of his recounting of the facts of history. As a result, they edited and censored without being conscious of doing so.

There are obviously many reasons why this guide does not feel that it is proper to raise the topic of miscegenation. Among them, the guide feels a certain lack of expertise. He is not black: misce-genation is not his subject. In this way he replicates, at the level of dividing up pedagogic terrain, one of the underlying goals of the Black Codes: to transform that blurred category, mulatto, into the property of the discrete and inferior 'other,' the black.[10]

A tale of two fictions

What struck us every time we interviewed white guides was how unselfconsciously they believed that they were merely disseminat-ing 'just the facts,' how unaware they seemed to be, that they were tailoring a story. By contrast, black guides were much more self-conscious in their deployment of documents in service of a story. This meant that they were purveying a more sophisticated historiography, but it also put them at a disadvantage. To see how the contrasting approaches played out, let's turn to two the-atrical performances that the guides put on at the Wythe House.

In the winter of 1991, in the midst of the deflected controversy about miscegenation, the house guides joined forces with mem-bers of AAIP staff to put on an evening performance called 'Christmas at the Wythe House.' Such performances were becom-ing more and more the genre of choice for bringing history 'to life' in a way that was at once 'educational' and 'entertaining.' The guides wrote a script based on 'documents' available to them and costumed interpreters acted this script as if they were George Wythe, Lydia Broadnax and so forth. 'Christmas at the Wythe House' took the form of an upstairs-downstairs drama meant to highlight the iniquities of slavery. The program began with an explanation of how 'first-person' interpretation works – that we would meet George Wythe and members of his household, that we would hear and see them but that we would be invisible. Our guide described George Wythe – 'a gentleman with a brilliant mind . . . a lawyer, a teacher, a scholar, a revolutionary.' The program ended with characters portraying Wythe and a friend of his, a visitor from England, engaged in a long discussion of the inequities of slavery, with each gentleman concluding that the system 'does not rest easy upon me.' When the performance was over, our guide reminded us that Wythe eventually freed his slaves.

Although the focus of the program was Wythe, the slaves, nonetheless, had important roles to play. From characters playing slaves, we learned of the hypocrisies of the masters' culture. For the masters Christmas had become less a time of spiritual renewal than of material gratification. The slaves noted that they gave cheap gifts to them while trying to squeeze more work out of them during the busy holiday season. As one slave puts it, Christmas is 'a trick to get us to do more work.' We also learned something of what is must have been like to be treated as property (the slaves are fearful of being 'sold off') and to be constantly at the beck and call of others, with little personal freedom for oneself (Charles cannot even visit his ailing relatives).

In the end, however, these glimpses of slavery through the eyes of the slaves merely served to foreshadow the master's disapproval of slavery. Indeed, in this depiction, Wythe was not even responsible for a system which he merely inherited. As Wythe put it, 'as we have it [slavery], and it appears that it will be a great long time before we can find a way to abolish the system, I think it is the least we can do for these people to treat them as humanely as can be.' The proof of Wythe's benevolence is in the coda: freed, Lydia chooses to stay with him as a paid cook.

About a year after our research at Colonial Williamsburg had ended the guides put on another evening program, called 'Affairs of the Heart,' at the Wythe House, although this time the performance was directed by an African-American. It is described in the visitor's program guide as a play that 'looks at the affects of gentry marriage on the household of the groom, William, and his intended bride.' The visitor is also told that they will 'meet William who has a child by his slave Rachael as he ponders his decision to marry and carry on his family name.'

Like 'Christmas at the Wythe House,' 'Affairs of the Heart' was plotted as an upstairs-downstairs story. The visitors enter the house, to find the young master of the house angry with his slave mistress because she did not 'present' herself with the rest of the 'household' to his bride-to-be. He reminds her that she will be moving with the 'boy' to the country house he and his new bride will occupy. She scolds him for not calling the 'boy' (their boy) by his proper name. She pleads not to be forced to move to the country house where she and her son will eventually be mistreated by his wife and his legitimate offspring once they find out who the boy's father is. She argues that if they find out the boy will never get his freedom as the master has promised. The master leaves without making a decision. And, later we learn, from the interpreter, that while masters sometimes manumitted mulatto offspring, often their wills were contested and subsequently overturned.

'Affairs of the Heart' is a story of kinship denied in the face of overwhelming social convention. It manages to introduce into Colonial Williamsburg many of the issues that the topic of miscegenation might raise. Particularly it holds out the possibility that were such offspring recognized in our collective genealogies, rather than erased, we would have inherited a very different notion of race today. But, in the end, 'Affairs of the Heart' delivers this message packaged in a form which reinvigorates the fact/fiction dichotomy which allows so many white guides simply to ignore the issue of miscegenation altogether.

Unlike 'Christmas at the Wythe House' the performance is specifically marked as a kind of fiction. As we read in the visitor's companion, 'William' and 'Rachael' are not representations of specific individuals, but are composites based, however, on documents – 'the Daniel Custis letters, and the eighteenth century diaries of Philip Vickers Fithian, William Byrd II and Landon Carter.' This textual self-consciousness about the distinction between 'document' and performative construction was carried over into the way the performance was framed on site. Before the visitors entered the Wythe House to listen to the slaves and masters talk on the eve of the wedding, the interpreter who would later answer the visitors' questions when they emerged from the house reminded them while the story was 'based on documents,' Rachael and William did not in fact exist. The interpreter warned us especially not to mistake the people we would meet in the darkened house for the 'real George Wythe and his household' we would be introduced to tomorrow should we visit the house during the day. She emphasized, 'So don't bother those folks tomorrow with questions about William and Rachael.'

If black interpreters feel compelled to advertise and be self-conscious about the 'composite' (that is, constructed) nature of the stories they tell, then white interpreters have been allowed to remain less so. 'William' speaks lines that paraphrase or quote directly the words of several diarists separate in time and space but all, more or less, of an era and of a certain class. By the same token 'George Wythe' in 'Christmas at the Wythe House' is also a composite. He speaks words lifted from letters George Wythe wrote, but he also quotes lines taken from dialogues his biographers have supplied him in books written (and based on recollections and on 'documents') after his death. Yet the status of this kind of (selective) composition remains invisible to the audience. When Wythe speaks, the implication is that we are hearing the past brought to life as closely to the real truth as is possible. Worse, the fictional Wythe of the evening performance becomes the real Wythe of daytime interpretation – a man white guides and visitors alike would be proud to identify with. As a guide put it, a man 'very liberal in his thinking, very ahead of his times, yet who owned slaves. Of course he freed them . . . during his lifetime and at his death.'

Conclusion

White and black frontline employees at Colonial Williamsburg talk past one another when it comes to how to interpret miscegenation in the antebellum era. Their inability to communicate reflects and exacerbates racial prejudice in a place dedicated to erasing racial prejudice.

White guides accept as given the immutability of racial categories. They are, we would say, so secure in an essentializing belief that whiteness and blackness are separate categories that they see the topic of miscegenation as a 'black' issue not an American issue, as a minor or marginal topic not a central one. They inevitably see any discussion of miscegenation as an attack (even if justified) on the reputation of morality of the white master. Needless to say, interracial procreation can only be perceived as 'knocking' white masters 'off their pedestal' if there is an inherent acceptance of racial difference and inequality. Finally, white guides find the topic not appropriate for specific sites at Colonial Williamsburg because there simply are no facts to link particular individuals to particular acts.

White guides use miscegenation to claim for themselves a kind of intellectual superiority vis-à-vis their black peers in AAIP. White guides portray themselves as open-minded and dispassionate purveyors of 'just the facts' while they accuse black guides of allowing their passions to govern the stories they tell. Meanwhile, many AAIP guides suspect their white counterparts of wilfully erasing historical truths in order to maintain a self-serving version of the past.

One result of this mutual suspicion, coupled with the way 'interpretation' is institutionally organized at Colonial Williamsburg means that miscegenation remains a marginal topic. 'Affairs of the Heart' ended up in the Wythe house, but in the evening, and unlike 'Christmas at the Wythe House,' as a carefully framed 'fictional' account whose audience was small and self-selected. As such the more potentially disruptive implications of an historical exploration of miscegenation – that racial categories in America were a cultural invention, a creation of legal codes, and that a legacy of these codes is an artificial racial essentialism which continues to dog Americans today – were not likely to come up as topics of discussion with any consistency. In the mainstream story white guides told during the day at the same site, George Wythe continued to be the focus. It is with him that 'you' the visitor were encouraged to imagine yourself drinking tea. Meanwhile you are also told about 'they,' the slaves out back, who therefore remained an ethnic and cultural 'other.'

Although we ended our research before 'Affairs of the Heart' became a part of Colonial Williamsburg's pedagogic landscape, it is not farfetched to assume that its existence would merely confirm the worst suspicions among white guides already suspicious of the AAIP and the stories they told. Again, they could be cast as purveyors of 'fiction.' Again, it could be pointed out that they were allowed to get away with this kind of epistemological sloppiness because the powers-that-be saw in this program the double possibility of 'entertainment' and of advertising their institution to academic audiences and liberal-minded funding agencies.

Now, the existence of racially polarizing suspicion and how this suspicion plays itself out is hardly unique to Colonial Williamsburg. In fact, one way of contextualizing the potshots guides took at each other over miscegenation is to see it as a local skirmish in what was being called at the time in wider public discourse 'the culture wars'. In the conservative or reactionary (labels are of course one terrain where the war is fought) version of the culture wars, a left-leaning intelligentsia (the infamous 'tenured radicals' who came of age in the 1960s) colonizes public culture institutions such as Colonial Williamsburg, and uses as its proxies groups at the margins in order to mount an assault on mainstream cultural values, among them the epistemological and moral foundations of the true and the good. Meanwhile, the yeoman middle resists this assault. It may be, then, that by constantly reiterating their allegiance to 'just the facts,' the white frontline employees were digging their heels in against precisely this kind of assault at Colonial Williamsburg. But it was our impression that the white guides' faith in a 'just the facts' historiography was at once more naively pervasive and less pointedly directed than a resistance model might imply. At Colonial Williamsburg at least, it seemed to us that the new social historians were conceding the terrain of the museum without being aware that they are doing so. And as for the yeoman middle (ie the frontline), they seemed to believe that they were obeying or imitating the historians not resisting them.

This raises the question of whether or not there is anything peculiar to the relationship between the professional historians at Colonial Williamsburg and the frontline employees that encourages (if unintentionally) this kind of thinking. What, ultimately, does the Colonial Williamsburg case tell us about how heritage and history museums in general – even when they are ostensibly run by revolutionaries – end up promoting a reactionary mindset?

As already mentioned, the new social historians compromised themselves by portraying what they were doing as just the latest in a long line of 'just the facts' historiographies. One result of the compromise the new social historians made was that the new social history remained a mere addition to rather than a replacement of an older historiography. In the older historiography, the goal was to recreate mimetically a particular object or person (cf. Blatti, 1987: Ettema, 1987). Just as Colonial Williamsburg tried to reconstruct the real George Wythe house, the museum tried to exemplify a real George Wythe – to make him come to life – by presenting edited bits of the words George Wythe spoke and artefacts 'like' the artefacts he owned and used. In social history, by contrast, individuals are used to illustrate a general point. One talks about 'a George Wythe,' a provisionally real person, but also, in a sense, a convenient entrée into a constructed account of the past. In doing this kind of history one is constantly made aware of the fictional quality of all historical accounts. Yet, it was the fictionality of 'the George Wythe,' that white guides habitually brought to life through the selective pasting together of artefacts and narrative (as, for example, in 'Christmas at the Wythe House'), that the new social historians never attempted to question.

Social historians did not try to make white guides aware of the essential fictionality of their mimetic enterprise.[11] And one reason that they did not do so is that the social historians felt compelled to compromise their message in order to get any play at all. Another reason has to do with the problem of intellectual authority at Colonial Williamsburg. The professional historians were constantly saying that they encouraged frontline employees to become actively engaged in the production of historical narratives and to do research. In turn, frontline employees liked to emphasize that they are indeed pursuing and disseminating historical truth as if they too were credentialed professionals. The Foundation, in short, idealized a kind of intellectual populism.

Unfortunately this comforting rhetoric let the professional historians off the hook, for we suspect that they, for reasons having to do with their own intellectual security vis-à-vis their peers in the academy, like to have as little to do with the frontline as possible (cf. Gable and Handler, 1993; for a similar argument see Ames, 1992). What impressed us most about the work the new social historians did (despite how sophisticated they could be with audiences of their peers), was how little guidance they offered to frontline employees. When we asked one of the guides in the 'team' assigned to redesigning the Wythe house, what were the historians' roles in the revision, he pointed out to the grape-arbor in the beautiful backyard garden: 'They sit over there; we do all the work over here.'

At Colonial Williamsburg, historians have opted to become absent or otiose authorities. What authority, then, takes their place? I can only sketch an argument here. I would suggest that white frontline employees' misplaced faith in 'the documented' reflects more than a simple replication of an older historiography in the absence of pedagogic guidance from their superiors, but also a kind of class or status insecurity that derives from their role as employees in this huge outdoor museum. Historical interpreters at Colonial Williamsburg occupy a particularly tenuous position; an institutional status hierarchy based on the control and display of what we might call, after Pierre Bourdieu, intellectual capital. Perhaps anxious that they were being judged by their ostensible superiors, the guides seemed to us to play at being caricatures of the historians. This meant that, on the one hand, many guides seemed always to be looking over their shoulders, worried that they might 'stray' from the known facts or commit an obvious falsehood. On the other hand, they were left pretty much up to their own devices. Programs like 'Christmas at the Wythe House' or 'Affairs of the Heart' had to pass muster with the historians but they were never critiqued or commended as narrative wholes. As a result, guides continued to act as if historiography were a job of disinterestingly collecting and reconveying 'just the facts' or what is 'documented' even when they were producing obviously ideologically motivated programs.[12] But they did so deeply anxious about their ostensible professionalism. I would suggest that it pleased these employees to find others in their midst whom they could accuse of playing fast and loose with the facts. At Colonial Williamsburg, black frontline employees are convenient scapegoats in these narratives of intellectual superiority (see Gable, Handler, and Lawson, 1992).

The upshot is that the topic of miscegenation and the issue of the historicity of racial boundaries this topic raises, remains at the margins of the mainstream story. I would argue that it remains so, in part, because of a selective deployment of the 'fact/fiction' dichotomy motivated by an uneasy class-resentment and in part because white middle-class Americans continue to believe in the fundamental impermeability of racial boundaries. And it is these messages that Colonial Williamsburg continues to deliver, even as it includes the black experience in its narrative of national identity.

Notes

1 This essay is based on research I did in collaboration with Richard Handler and Anna Lawson funded, in part, by grants from the Spencer Foundation and the National Endowment for the Humanities. Our research began in 1990 and spanned a two-year period during which we spent two summers at the site,

and two days a week during the academic year. Our goal was to make an ethnographic study of the museum as a whole, from its senior administrators to its junior historic interpreters, looking at how its messages were produced and consumed. Because this chapter is part of a collaborative research effort, I will generally use 'we' when referring to the researcher in the narrative.

2 Shirlee Haizlip (1994) writes a family saga around the theme of recovering the connections of kinship denied and reminds her readers: 'Make no mistake. I do not lust after whiteness. More often than not, I feel ambivalent about the white part of me and those circumstances, both known and imagined, that resulted in the mix. I am not really sure what the white portion of me means, if anything . . . How can I love it when it does not love me' (p. 14).

3 The staff swelled to twenty or twenty-five in summer when another twelve to fifteen part-time people – mostly high school and college students – were hired.

4 This critique has been with the museum virtually from its beginnings (cf. Bordewich, 1988; Cotter, 1970; Gable and Handler, 1993; Handsman and Leone, 1989; Huxtable, 1963; 1992; Leone, 1981; Van West and Hoffschwelle, 1984; Wallace, 1986a; 1986b; 1987; Wells, 1993).

5 In 1977, for example, some of the historians argued in internal staff meetings that the decline of visitation which they had experienced in 1976 was because the American public had lost interest in patriotic shrines. They argued further that this audience, precisely because it was 'middle class', would have a natural affinity for stories about Williamsburg's average inhabitants – its working people, its 'middling sort'. During the period of our research, the then director of the AAIP made a similar argument for why mainstreaming was the program of the future by pointing out that America's 'minority' population was growing far faster than its 'white' population. The upshot of both arguments was that if Colonial Williamsburg wanted to keep market-share it should produce the new history.

Needless to say, such arguments are made in the museum world constantly, and they are often countered with similar audience-based arguments. Audience-based arguments allow factions internal to the institution to fight ideological battles through safely silent proxies, thus obviating the need to face up to deep schisms and differences of opinion (see Perin, 1992; Ames, 1992).

6 This became the guiding theme of *Teaching History* (Colonial Williamsburg Foundation 1985), the official policy-statement and historiographical outline for Williamsburg's historiographical mission after 1981.

7 In conversations with us, and in conversations with the public (eg, Carson, 1994), the new social historians tended to downplay any internal resistance to their agenda. They argued that they were totally free to design and implement historiographical policy without interference from either the 'business side' or chief administrators. Yet, evidence that this way of portraying pedagogic freedom may have been a form of impression management occasionally was revealed in official pronouncements. For example, in a 1981 'Annual Report' ('Communicating the Past to the Present') President Longsworth cautions: 'It would be easy and perhaps popular to embrace social history with passionate abandon and forsake the patriots, retaining their memory as symbolic of an outworn and naive view of America's past. But I know of no one who advocates this course. One needs to retain always a cautious view of any claim of exclusive access to the true history. I believe one must accept the puzzlement, confusion, ambiguity, and uncertainty that characterizes scholarship – the

search for truth.' Longsworth borrows from the rhetoric of the new social history by recognizing that the 'reasonable and dispassionate interpretation of evidence' is fogged by 'some ideological base.' But asserts that because history cannot escape ideology, Colonial Williamsburg should 'maintain an ideological blend rather than develop a pure strain.' Ultimately this ideological blend of 'the dramatic, inspiring story that never loses its significance' and the new social history is good for Colonial Williamsburg is the strategy that guarantees survival, for it is blends that the public wants because historically that is what Colonial Williamsburg has gotten them used to: 'An organization such as this has by its longevity and its success created certain expectations. They may not be blunted summarily by a generation of scholars or administrators who have discovered the new historiography.'

8 All quotations of frontline employees are taken from transcripts of tape-recordings made by the researchers. In quoting these transcripts, I follow conventions among cultural anthropologists. Names and dates are not given to protect the identities of the employees.

9 For a more complete and nuanced account of what motivated AAIP interpreters at Colonial Williamsburg, see Lawson, 1995.

10 If the guide dis-identifies with miscegenation, he also, perhaps, over-identifies with the white protagonist in the story. He is careful to protect Wythe's reputation. Wythe is more than a symbol. He is a person, and perhaps he is the personification of Colonial Williamsburg as an institution. Ultimately, and perhaps most significantly, certain elements of the past (of the 'documented') seem to have a greater claim to being intrinsically or self-evidently true, than other elements.

11 The Wythe house is an 'original' building. The decor, however, is not. This is entirely a recreation based on educated guesses motivated by an agenda. At the time of our research this agenda encompassed mainstreaming. Once the curators and historians had decided that Wythe should be portrayed as an exemplar of 'enlightenment culture' they filled it with certain furnishings, all meant to signal enlightenment taste. Once they decided to 'mainstream' the history of the 'other half' they let Wythe define, in a sense the characters of the other members of the house. Beside a slave's pallet upstairs in a trunk room is a necklace of African beads, lest we forget that 'African culture' (like enlightenment culture?) survived the Middle Passage. On top of the cook's, Lydia Broadnax's, bed is a book left open – as if in mid-sentence, while she went about her chores – to remind us that slaves at the top of the hierarchy appropriated, as their own, and for their own uses, the master's culture. Although trainees were told that all of these artifacts represented the best current scholarship of the social historians, they were also taught to 'discover' these artifacts as if they were the traces of the past itself (see Gable and Handler, 1994).

12 As Richard Handler and I have argued elsewhere (Gable and Handler, 1994), guides were also given double messages about the 'authority of documents'. In training sessions they received a binder of primary sources, secondary sources, memos on crowd control, memos on comportment and so on. Some of these 'documents' were to be read as commands, and, inevitably, the 'documented' as an ensemble took on the authority of management's outline of a job description. Trainees were not taught to read historical documents critically; they were taught to use them as resources from which to make public presentations.

Bibliography

Ames, Michael, (1992), *Cannibal Tours and Glass Boxes: The Anthropology of Museums*. Vancouver: University of British Columbia Press.

Blatti, Jo, (1987), 'Past Meets Present: Fieldnotes on Historical Sites, Programs, Professionalism, and Visitors.' In *Past Meets Present: Essays about Historic Interpretation and Public Audiences*. Jo Blatti (ed.), Washington D.C.: Smithsonian Institution Press.

Bordewich, Fergus M., (1988), 'Revising Colonial America', *The Atlantic Monthly*, December: 26–32.

Carson, Cary, (1981), 'Living Museums in Everyman's History', *Harvard Magazine*, 83: 22–3.

Carson, Cary, (1991), 'Front and Center: Local History Comes of Age', in *Local History, National Heritage: Reflections on the History of AASLH*. Federick L. Rath Jr. et al., Nashville.

Carson, Cary, (1994), 'Lost in the Funhouse: A Commentary on Anthropologists' First Contact with History Museums'. *Journal of American History*, 81(10):137–50.

Chappell, Edward A., (1989), *Social Responsibility and the American History Museum*, Winterthur Portfolio, 24.

Colonial Williamsburg Foundation, (1985), *Teaching History at Colonial Williamsburg*.

Cotter, John, (1970), 'Exhibit Review: Colonial Williamsburg,' *Technology and Culture*, 11:417–27.

Ettema, Michael, (1987), 'History Museums and the Culture of Materialism,' in *Past Meets Present: Essays about Historic Interpretation and Public Audiences*, Jo Blatti (ed.), Washington, D.C.: Smithsonian Institution Press.

Friedman, Lawrence, (1970), *The White Savage: Racial Fantasies in the Postbellum South*, Englewood Cliffs: Prentice Hall Inc.

Gable, Eric, (forthcoming), 'Commemorative Site/Contested Terrain: The View from Monticello,' in *Commemoration, Resistance and Revitalization: Reflections on the Columbian Quincentenary and Other Commemorative Events*, Pauline Turner Strong (ed.), Duke University Press.

Gable, Eric and Handler, Richard, (1993), 'Deep Dirt: Messing up the Past at Colonial Williamsburg'. *Social Analysis: Journal of Social and Cultural Practice*. 34:3–16.

Gable, Eric and Handler, Richard, (1994), 'The Authority of Documents at Some American History Museums'. *The Journal of American History*, 81(1):119–36.

Gable, Eric, Handler, Richard and Lawson, Anna, (1992), 'On the Uses of Relativism: Fact, Conjecture, and Black and White Histories at Colonial Williamsburg', *American Ethnologist*, 19(4):791–805.

Handsman, Russell G. and Leone, Mark P., (1989), 'Living History and Critical Archeology in the Reconstruction of the Past', in *Critical Traditions in Contemporary Archeology: Essays in the Philosophy, History, and Socio-Politics of Archeology*. Valerie Pinsky and Alison Wylie (eds), Cambridge: Cambridge University Press.

Handler, Richard, (forthcoming), ' "Imagine Being the Millionth Anything": Commemoration, Business and Culture at Colonial Williamsburg', in *Commemoration, Resistance and Revitalization: Reflections on the Columbian*

Quincentenary and Other Commemorative Events, Pauline Turner Strong (ed.), Duke University Press.

Haizlip, Shirlee Taylor, (1994), *The Sweeter the Juice*, New York: Simon and Schuster.

Hernton, Calvin, (1965), *Sex and Racism in America*, New York: Grove Press.

Horton, James Oliver, and Crew, Spencer R., (1989), 'Afro–Americans and Museums: Towards a Policy of Inclusion', in *History Museums in the United States: A Critical Assessment*. Warren Leon and Roy Rosenzweig (eds), pp. 215–36. Urbana and Chicago: University of Illinois Press.

Hustable, Ada Louise, (1963), 'Dissent at Colonial Williamsburg', *New York Times*, 22 September.

Hustable, Ada Louise, (1992), 'Inventing American Reality', *New York Review of Books*, 39(20):24–9.

Jordan, Winthrop, (1974), *The White Man's Burden: Historical Origins of Racism in the United States*.

Lawson, Anna Logan, (1995), *The 'Other Half': Making African–American History at Colonial Williamsburg*. PhD. Dissertation, Department of Anthropology, University of Virginia, May 1995.

Leon, Warren and Piatt, Margaret, (1989), 'Living-History Museums', in *History Museums in the United States: A Critical Assessment*, Warren Leon and Roy Rosenzweig (eds), pp. 64–97. Urbana and Chicago: University of Illinois Press.

Leone, Mark, (1981), 'Archaeology's Relationship to the Present and the Past', in *Modern Material Culture*, R.A. Gould and M.B. Schiffler (eds), pp. 5–14. New York: Academic Press.

Perin, Constance, (1992), 'The Communicative Circle: Museums as Communities', in *Museums and Communities: The Politics of Public Culture*, Ivan Karp, Christine Muller Kraemer and Steven D. Lavine (eds), Washington, D.C.: Smithsonian Institution Press.

Stember, Charles, (1976), *Sexual Racism: The Emotional Barrier to an Integrated Society*, New York: Elsevier.

Van West, Carroll, and Hoffschwelle, Mary, (1984), 'Slumbering on its Old Foundations': Interpretation at Colonial Williamsburg, *South Atlantic Quarterly* 83(2): 157–75.

Wallace, Michael, (1986a), 'Visiting the Past: History Museums in the United States', in *Presenting the Past: Essays on History and the Public*, S.P. Benson, S. Brier, and R. Rosensweig (eds), pp. 137–61. Philadelphia: Temple University Press.

Wallace, Michael, (1986b), 'Reflections on the History of Historic Preservation', in Benson et al. (eds), pp. 165–99.

Wallace, Michael, (1987), 'The Politics of Public History', in *Past Meets Present: Essays about Historic Interpretation and Public Audiences*, Jo Blatti (ed.), Washington D.C.: Smithsonian Institution Press.

Washington, Joseph R. Jr. (1970), *Marriage in Black and White*, Boston: Beacon.

Wells, Camille, (1993), 'Interior Designs: Room Furnishings and Historical Interpretations at Colonial Williamsburg', *Southern Quarterly* 31: 89–111.

Williamson, Joel, (1980), *New People: Miscegenation and Mulattoes in the United States*, New York: Free Press.

A Trojan Horse at the Tate: theorizing the museum as agency and structure

Gordon Fyfe

Abstract

It is argued that sociology lacks an adequate conceptualization of the museum/society relationship. It is further argued (1) that the museum is an agency of classification; (2) that it is a relationship of cultural interdependence and (3) that museums have an internal relationship to modernization. The institution of the museum is shown to arise out of the indeterminacies of modernization. A dispute in the early history of London's Tate Gallery is explored as it illuminates that institution's organization of the contradictions of modernization. *Pace* Bourdieu and Elias, a key contradiction is seen to arise from a differentiation of the field of power and the cultural field. It is argued, against essentialist accounts of museums, that the Tate produced its point of view through the medium of this contradiction.

Introduction

Flowing from Bourdieu's synthetic alternative to the either/or of structure and agency is his thesis that museum visiting is implicated in the reproduction of the social order. An art museum visit may be testing for working class visitors who fearing that they will fail the test, silently devalue their own taste in a misrecognition of power as Culture (Bourdieu and Darbel, 1991:51). Bourdieu's argument is that museums conceal the arbitrariness of taste and sanction élite taste as culture; they institutionalize the cultural arbitrary. In this way museums are sites of symbolic violence, *viz.* 'a violence which is exercised upon a social agent with his or her complicity' (Bourdieu, 1992:167–8). The claims of the art museum to disseminate the message of universal genius to all are, it transpires, interwoven with cultural inequalities which the museum implicitly endorses.

Bourdieu's is a formidable account of how class is accomplished through the medium of culture, of how taste is interwoven with inequality, of how élite culture practices contribute to social reproduction. However, his *oeuvre* has attracted a sustained, often sympathetic, but critical response that it amounts to a covert determinism (Alexander, 1995; Connell, 1983; Jenkins, 1992; Layder, 1994; Thompson, 1984). Three points are important for this chapter.

First, Bourdieu trades on unfounded assumptions concerning integration; the concept of misrecognition requires finessing so that it accommodates more complex and differentiated relationships of culture and power in which subordinate groups may partially penetrate the cultural arbitrary. Further, in stressing the misrecognition that is collusion with power Bourdieu diverts attention from fragmentation as a basis for a subjectless ordering of social relations: social reproduction may occur through 'a proliferation of divisions' rather than through incorporation (Thompson, 1984). Second, it has been argued that social reproduction is a misnomer for the uncertain outcomes of human action and that, in the final analysis, Bourdieu portrays structure as unfolding into individuals. Third, as Jenkins points out, institutions and organizations are absent from his account of social reproduction.

How is the museum located in a world marked by normative divisions and divisions of interest? How might this institution or any other be interwoven with the external order of people and things? In these connections Bourdieu's critics have not made it clear why the neglect of institutions matters. After all there are good reasons, adduced by Bourdieu, for being wary of arguments that assign authorship of difference to, say, the state (Bourdieu, 1990). On the other hand there is Bourdieu's laconic observation that the process of state formation has been, in part, a monopolization of the means of symbolic violence (Bourdieu, 1992). Now if Bourdieu and Darbel (1991) show us that the national art museum is one such monopoly, Duncan and Wallach (1980) show that it is also an institution at which identities of nation and genius are made palpable.

Bourdieu implies that museums are not univocal; minor works (eg furniture, ceramics) are more accessible to working-class visitors whilst 'sometimes, several museums really co-exist in the same building' (Bourdieu and Darbel, 1991:56, 72, 85). If museum meanings are differentiated then it is plausible that symbolic violence is, in part, internal to museums and that its exercise may be an aspect of museum dynamics. If symbolic violence is a process of disempowerment in which taste is separated from the sensibilities of the disprivileged, separation may be seen as an historical process that is organizationally sanctioned by the museum.

What is a museum?

Recent research had advanced our understanding of the role of museums in defining art and fixing identities (eg Crimp, 1993; Duncan and Wallach, 1980; Sherman, 1987; Zolberg, 1981). These authors explore the museum's role in producing the multiple authorships of art (eg those of artists, crafts people, collectors, donors, patrons and nations) rather than simply communicating their effects. However, whilst they share a broadly deconstructionist perspective there are significant differences of emphasis between these scholars.

Where Duncan and Wallach provide a grand narrative of the national art museum's (especially that of the Louvre) evolving service to capitalism, Sherman plots the eventful, plural and provincial process through which (French) local bourgeoisies produced themselves at the museum from the 1840s. Where Duncan and Wallach see the museum's discourse of nation and genius as being fixed by the interests of a dominant patron class, others have stressed the shifting, unstable and contingent character of museum identities. The point, as Crimp has made clear, is to recover the history of the making of the museum from the essentialisms of founding myths, eg evolutionary first origins and the psychology of collecting. Thus Sherman (1987) takes Duncan and Wallach to task for an emphasis on the systemic that ignores the museum's complexity and contingency. Where Duncan and Wallach see the museum as a space at which the dominant class's interests are represented, Sherman considers the way in which museums are invented as the bourgeoisie goes along: '. . . both the institution and the ideology are constructed . . . neither the transformation nor the construction ever stops' (Sherman, 1987:54).

The Duncan-Wallach thesis is that whilst museums enclose impersonal and transparent spaces they possess a discursive weight. However, whilst museum discourses are acknowledged to be objects of struggle (Duncan, 1991) such facts are largely unspecified, unstudied and untheorized by Duncan and Wallach who are less sensitive to museums as places of conflict than they are to their role in meeting the functional requirements of capitalism. They present an over-integrated account of the state-museum-class configuration whilst their portrait of capitalism fails to capture the complexities of the class/museum relationship.

This said, Sherman's analysis is vitiated by elements it shares with that of Duncan and Wallach. Both emphasize class power over museums. In Sherman, despite references to the agency of museums, they remain creatures of a dominant class, albeit the latter is a local bourgeoisie that is uncertainly making itself as a class by revising museum culture. Little is said about the internal dynamics of the museum as they might be interwoven with the structuration of a dominant class. Does the museum merely execute the class aesthetic intentions of the bourgeoise? It would appear so, that the museum is a reflex of local bourgeoisie dignataries and those cultural institutions that the latter dominate. Thirdly, whilst Sherman concludes that the meaning of museums results from the interplay between system and contingency it is not clear, theoretically, how these might be related to the action of museum building.

In this respect Zolberg's is a vital contribution to museum theory. Her study of the evolution of the Art Institute of Chicago exposes the museum's internal tensions and cleavages and provides an insight into how museums produce themselves through the medium of their exchanges with the external world. She explores the dynamics of submerging and surfacing of museum identities. The museum as a contested arena, in which different organizational actors (trustees, professionals and marketeers) vie for control of the levers of power, is Zolberg's subject. Her account of the shifting balances of power between different constituencies within the museum alerts us to the endogamy and exogamy of museum worlds and to the plural possibilities implied by the question: on behalf of whom does the museum speak?

However, what remains unclear in Zolberg's account is how the macro and the micro are to be theorized as they intersect at the museum. As an organization the museum is not, *a priori*, a micro organism in a macro-world. Some museum curators, particularly those who curate world class national museums, are beneficiaries of processes of state formation that have made their institutions into concentrations of cultural power. They are, as Mouzelis (1991:106–9) has it, macro actors: that is, their decisions stretch across time and space to affect the sensibilities of millions.

An illustration: in the twentieth century generations of British school children learnt their history as they gazed upon textbook pictures of historical events. These depictions were frequently derived from the National Gallery of British Art, ie the Tate Gallery. Their selection often began, as we shall see, with a small group of male artists who controlled acquisitions at the Gallery. Their decisions rippled through the social structure, through the decisions of publishers and purchasing officers, through the medium of mass education and the mass production of illustrated histories to be appropriated by elementary school children. Children might literally colour-in the course of British history (Figures 8 and 9).

Museums, modernization and the cultural field

Sherman's and Zolberg's work converges with recent work on organizations (see Clegg, 1989 and others but also Brown, 1977). A theoretical renaissance has purged organizational analysis of inner principles such as functional necessity, exploitation or rationality (Brown, 1977:196–200; Clegg, 1989:197, Cooper and Burrell 1988). Analysis of museums has sometimes responded to the essentialism of art by replacing it with the essentialism of class. Recent developments in organization theory offer the prospect of theorizing museums as acts of interpretation that are constantly produced through the medium of unstable relations of power. Following Clegg museums may be theorized as institutions founded on the divisions of modernization.

There is an internal relationship between museums and modernization. The former are agencies of cultural classification; they are sites for interpreting and regulating the uncertainties that flow from the divisions of modernization. One uncertainty flowed from the differentiation of what Bourdieu calls the cultural field from the field of power. A field is a relatively autonomous social space whose structure 'is a *state* of the power relations among the agents or institutions engaged in the struggle [to define and monopolize authority]' (Bourdieu, 1993:73). A field is in flux, it has the energy of those more or less competent individuals who

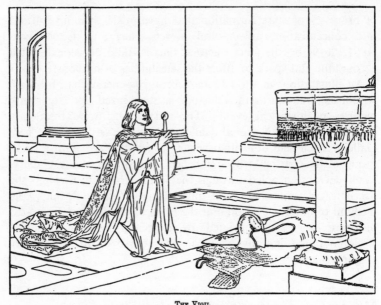

THE VIGIL.

After the picture by John Pettie, R.A., in the National Gallery, British Art, London.

SUGGESTIONS FOR COLOURING LIKE THE ORIGINAL PICTURE.

Knight's robe, slightly shaded with **pale greenish-yellow—White**.

Knight's cloak—**Maroon**.

Upper part of altar ; the part of floor where knight is kneeling—**Very pale yellowish-white**.

Altar pillar, also fringe ; knight's shield ; pillar nearest altar ; knight's hair, hands, and face—**Light greenish-brown**.

Floor below altar and patches on floor ; the other two pillars and wall space near them ; a lighter tone for armour in front of altar—**Dark blackish-brown**.

Knight's sword, sleeves, stockings, and girdle—**Black**.

The last two spaces between pillars and the door in the distance ; the rest of floor ; a darker tone for **space behind the altar and space beyond first pillar—Dull bluish-green**.

3   17

Figure 8 *'The Vigil': line reproduction with colouring instructions from an elementary history book illustration, circa 1925. The original oil painting by John Pettie RA was acquired for the nation through the Chantrey Bequest for £1,000 in 1884.*

play the game but to whose individual characteristics the game cannot be reduced.

The field of cultural production is the space of social relations and positions in which artists, critics and other cultural agents determine legitimate art. Bourdieu asks how the point of view of

© The Editorial Board of The Sociological Review 1996

NAPOLEON ON BOARD THE "BELLEROPHON."
*(From the picture by W. Q. Orchardson, R.A., in the National Gallery of British Art.
By permission of the Berlin Photographic Co.)*

Figure 9 *Black and white reproduction of 'Napoleon on Board the Bellerophon' by W. Q. Orchardson RA illustrating a school history book circa 1910. The original painting was acquired for the nation in 1880, under the terms of the Chantrey Bequest and for the sum of £2.000.*

an artist or (one might add) a museum director, is constituted through the medium of an historically produced space understood as a field of struggles for the monopoly of the power to define art. What 'carries works of art along' (Bourdieu, 1993:183) is the struggle among different kinds of artists and interpreters with different positions and dispositions.

It is necessary, Bourdieu argues, to grasp the logic of the cultural field as irreducible to the field of power which is structured according to the hierarchies of the dominant economic and political classes. The artistic field has a relative autonomy so that it refracts the power of dominant classes' influences (Bourdieu, 1993:45–6). Bourdieu is partly concerned with its autonomization – a process whose origins predate the 1800s but which accelerated in the second half of the last century.

I propose to theorize the museum both structurally and historically in terms of the differentiation of the cultural field and the field of power; the internal organization of the museum is interwoven with but not determined by the differentiation of economic and cultural monopolies. Implicit in Sherman's analysis are the museum's cultural codings of class power in a world where economic success is not matched by the certainty of cultural success but where the cultural field is still relatively undifferentiated: where as councillors, mayors and arts society dignitaries the new economic and political bourgeoisie has its hands directly on the levers of local cultural power.

Museums move through social space interpreting, fusing and fissioning as they are caught in the cross cutting pressures of fields. The centre of gravity of a museum may be close to the pole of the field of power (so that the residues of patrimonial power are evident in the management, say, of the National Gallery in London by aristocratic trustees). The museum may bear the signature of patronage by élite collectors as trustees and donors; perhaps the building was once a palace, perhaps the patron retains control over access and interpretation (Zolberg, 1995). Justification for expenditure on museums, perhaps proposed by arts and museum professionals, may be in the need to preserve national art, to instruct the masses in civilization, to inculcate the principles of industrial design or some other project through which the artistic interests of a dominant class are constructed.

Modes of regulation of museums (eg by government departments, by trustees) along with funding and tax policies speak for the creativity of those who manage the museum together through the medium of these tensions. As Zolberg shows, museums accommodate agents with conflicting visions of what a museum should be (trustees, professional curators, accountants and marketeers) who are continuously putting the museum together as a more or less coherent project. The histories of museums are punctuated by spurts of political and economic change which entail a rapid differentiation perhaps through re-organization or revolution. Acceleration of the cultural field's autonomy may yield tensions with the field of power which irrupt into the museum.

The field of cultural production is not disconnected from other fields: 'the struggles within the field of power are never entirely independent of the struggle between the dominated classes and the dominant class' (Bourdieu, 1993:44). In this respect the concepts of homology and habitus are crucial; they allow us to conceptualize social reproduction through the articulation of fields (eg economic, cultural, scientific, sporting) without assigning priority to any one of these. Players in different fields may pursue conscious and unconscious strategies according to an underlying grammar or habitus which more or less corresponds to the logic of the field. The habitus consists of (embodied) structuring dispositions through which actors appropriate the world in particular ways – making distinctions in, for example, the domain of art. As a structuring structure which provides an enduring orientation to the world, the habitus is acquired through the labour of socialization that is rooted in class experiences of the world.

According to Bourdieu the autonomization of the cultural field yields a visual habitus, a grammar of looking which eschews the popular – *viz.* a Kantian or pure aesthetic. The pure and the popular refer not to the intrinsic attributes of artefacts but to different modes of appropriating them which are grounded in class situations. They are antagonistic, asymmetric and interdependent modes of ordering the world. The pure aesthetic is apparently disinterested and universal yet it is a refusal of the art of subordinate classes; it promotes the formalism of, say, a post-impressionist painting against the content of, say, a Victorian narrative or subject painting. Bourdieu's analysis seems to have an Eliasian aspect; refusal of the popular implies a self-disciplining of the body so that the eye does not give itself up to an evident subject or sentimental anecdote. Rather it looks beyond these immediate satisfactions for an aesthetic of style and form which celebrates the purely visual properties of the world.

The museum's spatial ordering of this struggle has, as Bourdieu hints and Duncan and Wallach (1980) demonstrate, been a dimension of the politics of symbolic violence. That is, the pure gaze is physically sanctioned by the museum as meriting public cultivation. Yet, as Bourdieu states and as Elias argues, classification may entail a process of confiscation in which dominant groups finesse distinction and raise the stakes of civilization by attaching it to new accomplishments. An outcome of such struggles (which according to Bourdieu have been going on since the seventeenth century) has been a process of classification and reclassification which has continuously transformed the museum canon – sometimes with revolutionary effects. The agency of the museum arises in connection with its organizing some identities whilst disorganizing others. In interpreting their collections, in accommodating and evicting artefacts, art museums have been and continue to be enmeshed in struggles for distinction which have centred on the cultivation of the eye.

Museum curators ride the juggernaut of modernization's contradictions (Giddens, 1990). In policing the boundary between popular culture and high art, in mediating the multiple discourses of art, in producing the universal but cultural story of the artist-as-creator in face of divisions of age, gender, ethnicity and class, museums more or less stabilize a process of modernization which always threatens to disrupt them. The museum is a multipolar institution with complex local, national and global associations and there are of course different kinds of museums which express the priority of particular interdependencies – art museums, industrial museums, science museums, folk museums, museums of childhood etc.

Here one may speak of a process of museumification which, since the early eighteenth century, has been a dimension in the ordering of groups (of various kinds and at local, national and global levels). As an agency of classification the museum sanctions discourses of art and collecting. Such discourses or rules of classification are not the reflection of preconstituted interests. Rather the identities of classes (and other groups) are produced partly through the medium of museums which interpret class relations. In this, museumification has been a medium of class formation.

Art classification is, therefore, not something which one group or agency (such as the state) does to another, but of cultural interdependencies between two or more groups which compete for the advantages of symbolic power and difference. Such interdependencies may take the form, not of a single relationship between two groups, but of a chain of interdependent classes or groups (eg the business class, professions, fractions of the middle class and working class). A feature of cultural interdependency is the struggle of dominant groups to stabilize signs, to freeze classification whilst disrupting the classification of subordinate groups. Stabilization can be fragile – the flux that is the multi-polarity of classification may offer the potential of hybridizations and of realignments between groups which transform the rules of classification and admit new artefacts to the canon. This is why any attempt to assign the museum to a class or class fraction, to make it the creature of a class or the state, is unproductive.

Inscribed in museum histories, in their politics and modes of regulation, are the tensions and conflicts of interdependency. To give this a formulation closer to Elias than to Bourdieu, modernization entailed the autonomization of economic power from symbolic power (Elias, 1983). The development of art museums was a containment of the conspicuous consumption of traditional élites as state expenditure was subjected to bourgeois modes of economic calculation (Fyfe, 1995). Museums ordered the interests of super-ordinate classes, proposing artistic and aesthetic services which apparently earned their keep such as industrial design, educating the masses or representing national artistic powers.

Bourdieu is both penetrating and partial when he refers to the 'properly historical event which is born at the crossroads of relatively autonomous histories' (Bourdieu, 1988). For Abrams by contrast an event is 'a moment of becoming at which action and structure meet' (1982:192). Becoming might refer to the institution of an academy, the building of a museum, a celebrated exhibition or a scandalous curatorial decision. Abrams enjoins us to attend to the action that is the taking of opportunity, sometimes the opportunism, that is born in the medium of structure.

We are in the domain of what Layder (1994), following Goffman, calls the interaction order – that is face-to-face exchanges which are the day-to-day production of social life such as the professional lives of museum officials and artists. Layder's point is that external structural forces do not unfold into the domain of the interaction order. The interaction order, in our case that of the museum, is a medium through which external processes are interpreted and through which cultural agents produce a sense of purpose. Our understanding of the museum as a site of inequality requires attention to the interweaving strategies of classification through which actors, as it were, fix homologies.

This chapter explores the organizational dynamics of a museum as it interprets homology through the events of its history. It explores officialdom's incorporation of modern paintings, eg the Impressionists and post-Impressionists, into the canon. In early twentieth century England the Tate Gallery (the National Gallery of British Art) became a fragile coalition of academicians who controlled acquisitions and curators who were forced to accept purchases made by the academy. This unusual situation became a crisis that was a transformation of the cultural field as academicians were displaced from the museum's story of art. Luke Fildes, the celebrated late Victorian and Edwardian painter, found it difficult to accept the removal of his celebrated *The Doctor* from the walls of London's Tate Gallery in the 1920s. Casting her mind back to the 1920s, from the 1960s, Mary Clive of the Pakenham and Anglo–Irish landowning family recalled a privileged Edwardian childhood and a culture that had lost official recognition – anecdotal paintings such as *And When did you Last See Your Father?* and *The Day of Reckoning* had been relegated to museum stores, school rooms and boarding houses (Clive, 1965). I take up this story as a means of developing the thesis that a museum is a relationship of cultural interdependence and not a creature of class power.

The Tate Gallery and the Chantrey Bequest

Founded in 1897 as the National Gallery of British Art, that is with a British remit as opposed to the European Old Master concerns of the National Gallery at Trafalgar Square, the Tate was intimately associated with the Royal Academy of Arts (RA). The RA, founded in 1768, represented the most successful British artists; its influence ran deep into fine arts officialdom. The RA's Exhibition publicly displayed the artistic achievements of Academicians and of those outsiders the RA judged worthy of the privilege. The Exhibition and the Academy dinner were fashionable annual events, strands in the fabric of the Season, through which the aristocratic ethos of the upper class was secured against the class vagaries of capitalist development. The RA was a visible source of cultural power; its Exhibition illuminated the presence of a Good Society that was centred on the monarchy which had been an instrument of its foundation. Under arrangements determined by the Treasury, the Tate's purchasing fund was the Chantrey Bequest which had been donated by the fashionable sculptor Sir Francis Chantrey (1781–1841) but which was not activated until the late 1870s.

Chantrey instructed that his Bequest be devoted to the encouragement of British Fine Art only and that the fund be administered by the RA.[1] The object was partly to draw the state into legislating the distinction between two kinds of art practiced by academicians – high art and popular art. The gift was a response to the widely appreciated problem that the received academic tradition gave precedence to an art form for which there was little demand by private patrons or by officialdom – *viz.* history painting in the grand manner – and was most probably inspired by the failure of such works to sell at the RA Exhibition.

Whatever Chantrey's intentions, as applied by the RA, the Bequest became a collection dominated by academicians who specialized in so-called subject paintings. By 1903, 110 Chantrey works had been acquired of which 105 had been purchased at the RA's annual Exhibition (*Chantrey and his Bequest* 27–31). The collection was always more heterogeneous than the stereotypes of its critics but it contained a large number of anecdotal, literary and popular historical subjects of a didactic kind that were heavily reproduced for school rooms and elementary history books. The reputations and fortunes of Chantrey artists were partly grounded in a market for reproductions which was hegemonized by the RA. Of about £60,000 expended up to 1903, 'over £30,000 was paid to members of the Academy, between £17,000 and £18,000 to those who shortly after became members, between £12,000 and £13,000 to other exhibitors' (MacColl, 1904:4–5).

Henry Tate, whose philanthropy paid for the erection of the Tate, was in the tradition of nineteenth century entrepreneur patrons such as Robert Vernon (1774–1849) and John Sheepshanks (1787–1863). They had forged a non-aristocratic patronage of anecdotal and moralizing art by academy artists thought of as a British School to be measured against European standards. In becoming the home of the Chantrey Bequest and in acquiring the collection of Henry Tate, the Gallery was the centre of a broadly middle-class art grounded in a popular aesthetic. Furthermore, the Bequest became an arrangement which permitted the RA (as Chantrey trustee) to determine the contents of the National Gallery of British Art. To the officers of the Tate it may have seemed that the Treasury had smuggled in a Trojan horse out of which emerged a steady trickle of academicians who occupied their walls.

In the early years three developments turned the collection into a scandal. First, it was the subject of a campaigning journalism which stigmatized it as inferior art, unrepresentative of British art, and accused the RA of maladministration. One issue was the failure to admit modern art, eg Impressionism and post-impressionism to the canon. Impressionist paintings were first exhibited in Britain in 1870. At two London exhibitions of modern French painting (1910 and 1912) Roger Fry the artist, critic and curator, famously staged an English reception for modern artists whilst rubbishing Victorian academy art. At stake was the museum status of these new kinds of producers (some of whom had forged their own independent institutions) and for whom a creative life outside the academy seemed possible. These moderns were promoted by dealers and by critics, amongst the latter the so-called New Critics (D.S. MacColl, R.A. Stevenson and George Moore). They introduced the middle class to the discourse of the pure gaze, marginalized the subject painting as art and called for the recognition of a new ontology – the quality of the medium, the formal properties of style (Flint, 1984). Their vocabulary was at odds with the narrative and literary aesthetic associated with the RA and which was so heavily represented by Chantrey acquisitions in the early Tate Gallery.

Second, from the early 1900s RA/Tate relations entered a period of conflict punctuated by episodes of uncertain co-operation. The quarrel was a British dimension of the symbolic revolution of modern art which overturned the authority of the academy (White & White, 1965; Bourdieu, 1993). Broadly speaking, until the 1870s, the RA had contained conflicts between different kinds of producers, between popular and élite artists. Now, the Chantrey conflict dramatized a process with parallels in other countries – the separation of academicians from the determination of art museums. The conflict spluttered on for two generations, occasionally publicized through exhibition and newspaper exchanges, until, in the 1950s and early '60s, the Tate's autonomy and mutual co-operation were firmly established.

Third, a sequence of public inquiries consolidated an official view that the collection was bad art.[2] The Bequest was the sole topic of one (the Crewe Inquiry of 1904) and one of two topics addressed by another (the Curzon Inquiry of 1911). The reports sanctioned a radically individuated discourse of creativity which, in stigmatizing academy art, uncoupled cultural authority from Good Society. They recognized the difference between presently successful RA artists and unknown artists whose professional reputations would be converted to renown but who were currently unrecognized, ie excluded from the Exhibition. They called for reforms that would empower the Tate at the expense of the RA. The Curzon Report proposed expropriation of the Bequest from the RA whilst both reports endorsed the critical campaign which had stigmatized the Chantrey collection as bad and popular art. The Massey Inquiry and a PEP report, both of 1946, took Chantrey inferiority for granted.

The Tate, although without an alternative purchasing fund, did acquire works independently of the Bequest. Its Keepers presided over the Tate's colonization by modern and foreign art by means of gifts and this development was officially sanctioned by a Treasury Minute of 1917. In the '20s the Tate's post-war renaissance was announced with a transfer of British masters from Trafalgar Square and the admission of 'the most advanced types of painting' (Galerien, 1921:187). In 1924 the essayist E.V. Lucas noted the presence of 'old Royal Academy favourites' *and* the works of foreign artists – Boudin, Degas, Gauguin and Rousseau. In 1934 the *Birmingham Post* observed the promotion of a 'peaceful revolution' and the elimination of 'a certain incongruous mixture of Victorianism with contemporary work' (Buckman, 1973:38).

In 1906 the appointment of a Chantrey critic, D.S. MacColl, was a strengthening of the anti-Academy lobby in official circles. MacColl claimed (before the Curzon Inquiry) that he had been encouraged by the Treasury to create deadlock with the RA by refusing to accept Chantrey pictures. By the late 1930s the balance of power within the state had shifted, allowing the Tate's officers to exploit *de facto* control of a gallery space and to challenge (though not overturn) the RA's legal rights in the Bequest. At the end of the 1930s the Tate was asserting its position, refusing to hang Chantrey works (Rothenstein, 1966:207–17). In 1939 the director of the Tate admitted there was justification for a Major Cardew's charge that 'the work of all painters prominent in England from 1850–1900 [including many Chantrey works] is practically excluded' from exhibition (Tate Gallery Chantrey Files[3]: Cardew to Lutyens, June 8, 1939; Rothenstein to Lamb, June 14, 1939). There were rumours that the worst Chantrey examples were displayed by the Tate 'as a standing reproach' to the Academy. To the Tate the standard of the collection was 'deplorable': 'Alpine valleys, puppies in baskets, ladies in eighteenth century dress standing on chairs, affrighted by mice, and the like' – all exhibited as the 'climax' of the Tate's collection (Rothenstein, 1966:4).

In 1949 the collection (now in excess of 400 works) was exhibited as a whole. The proposal for exhibition had come from the Tate and was understood (by the President of the RA) to be a challenge by the Tate to the RA. It attracted a large winter audience: over 99,000. Much of the middle-class press was hostile: 'the equivalent of the best seller in fiction' (*The Times*, 8 Jan. 1949); a 'freak show, a bland, unashamed affirmation of a collective taste informed by little more than ostentatious materialism and its concomitant sentimentality' (*The Guardian*, 8 Jan. 1949); '. . . a skeleton which the Academy has long kept in the Tate Gallery's cupboard' (*The News Chronicle*, 8 Jan. 1949).

The RA remained a force within the cultural state as the voice of the midcult taste of the middle and lower middle classes: '[w]hat the British public wants is pictures of dogs and babies, of 'Granny's chairs' and Mother's darlings, of moving tales by flood and field'. In the 1930s one academician opined that it was 'mainly concerned with the unsophisticated visitor who hopes to apprehend readily what he sees . . . ' (Lambert, 1938). In describing its mission the RA presented itself pragmatically 'as a steadying influence on the haste or extravagance of innovators' (Lamb, 1951:115).

In the 1840s an academician-donor sought to preserve the integrity of the RA as the fount of a universal art which was the mark of distinction. Though he failed, though the Bequest yielded a collection that was stigmatized, the RA survived as a major art institution. By the 1940s, after fifty years of conflict, the RA had moved through the social space of the cultural field to become the officially suspect English voice of a popular aesthetic. Charged with the stewardship of popular British Art, the Tate had a modernist trajectory that gave it an élitist foreign connotation.

The Tate, the state and the development of the cultural field

The early Tate was a contested space and shaped by a disintegrating coalition which had been imposed by the Treasury. It was caught in the crossfire between (i) commercially successful RAs who were widely thought of as the British School, who had been patronized by a new fraction of the capitalist upper class and who were oriented towards a broad middle class conception of art and nation and (ii) those artists who had emerged from the modernist revolution and who were oriented towards the field of restricted production (Bourdieu, 1993). The Tate was stretched across the fields of power and culture; in Bourdieu's terms the Chantrey crisis reproduced tensions within the cultural field (between the domains of heteronomous, commercial production and restricted production). The Tate was pulled towards a popular national art which equated merit with RA Exhibition success and towards an élitism which did not expect validation from a contemporary art public.

Late nineteenth century class and state formation (an acceleration decline of the landed aristocracy, fusion of the capitalist class, expansion of the state sponsored professional class) shifted the balance of power within the cultural state (Savage et al., 1992; Scott, 1991). Attacks on the RA's Chantrey prerogatives were aspects of this transformation. The consequence was a conflict over art classification which centred on the Tate. On the one hand the class politics of British democracy deepened the state's commitment to delivering a national pictorial culture to subordinate classes. On the other the process of state formation spawned a stratum of professionals whose reproduction as a class depended on the struggle for distinction from economically superordinate and culturally subordinate groups. The outcome was an aesthetic partnership between the state, the professional class and a declining aristocracy. This manifested itself as an affinity between the Tate's officers and a reformed Treasury's officers who shared a habitus of distinction (Fyfe, 1995).

In Bourdieu's terms there is a triple homology. There was (i) the conflict between different kinds of producers (academicians oriented towards large-scale production and moderns oriented towards restricted production), (ii) the tensions between (plutocratic) economic capital and the professions and (iii) the latter's strategy of social closure and distinction from the expanding lower middle class. The reproduction of the professional class placed it at odds with Chantrey pictures for two reasons. Their accessibility via the codes of school history, literature and Victorian morality gave these works irredeemable provincial and lower middle class associations. Second, their passage through the Exhibition tarred them with the brushes of interest and of a conspicuous consumption that lacked the ease of distinction.

The RA and the Tate were not passive effects of conjunctural forces. The conflict was one in which the protagonists made themselves up and were made up – there was no essential Tate, no essential RA. The key players – the RA, the Tate and the Treasury – formed a configuration of shifting institutional power caught up in cross-cutting ties of cultural interdependence which extended into the wider society. The Tate and the RA put conjuncture together through the routine intercourse of their members' institutional lives. The Tate produced itself through an active but uncertain making of homology. Its history might be partly written as the private and public voicing of questions for which there were no immediately certain answers. Will there be a national gallery of British Art? What was Sir Francis Chantrey's intention? What is British art? Will the Tate have an independent Board? What will the Treasury do? Will the RA have representatives on this Board? Will the Chantrey Bequest be expropriated . . .?

In the following illustrations I explore the Tate as a site of structure and agency at which people struggled to fix the meaning of its mission. The first concerns the donor's intentions. Given Treasury arrangements were not Chantrey's intentions the bedrock on which the meaning of the Tate was to be determined? His intentions were something that the Chantrey inquiries sought to establish. The second concerns British art. Had not Chantrey intended his gift to fund the creation of a collection of works by British artists? On that interpretation the Tate was founded as a gallery which would realize his intentions. He had expressed the hope that the government would do just this. But what did British mean? The third is a dispute about Board membership of the Tate Gallery when it seemed that the RA might enhance its power at the Tate.

Chantrey's Will

Chantrey's instructions (those assigning a central role to the RA) emanated from a world which took as natural the association between central academies and consecrated art. The nineteenth-century RA was a visible source of cultural power so that Society and the academy shared centres. The turning of the Chantrey Bequest into a problem was an assault on that mode of authorizing creativity. The residues of academic power were sustained and challenged at the Crewe and Curzon inquiries as RAs and their enemies tried to pin down the Will's terms and defend their definitions of art. For RAs it was difficult to accept that the best pictures did not come to their Exhibition. For art officialdom and those art critics arraigned against the RA it was evident that important art might be discovered elsewhere if only the RAs would go out and look for it.

The Crewe and Curzon Inquiries are windows of opportunity for viewing the relationship between the state and museum classification. They projected the wishes of a donor who had died in 1841 onto the early twentieth-century art world; they interpreted his instructions by reference to early nineteenth-century fine art practices. Thus, some questions were resolved by reference to the orthodoxies of early nineteenth-century high art or history painting, the kind of art upon which the academic tradition was based. What did early nineteenth-century high art connote in the early 1900s? Chantrey was projected into the twentieth century by MacColl, as someone who would have professed support for artists such as Degas, Monet, Pissarro and Rodin: 'You must suppose the testator to be a continuing being. If he has to pronounce a judgement on the art of our day you must not have him cut off dead in his grave and put to him things which had not come about in his time' (Crewe: 593).

MacColl's whimsy sheds light on the museum; it reflects the need to justify practices by reference to an enduring inner principle – in this case the intentions of the testator. That is what classification does, it freezes the process that is modernity. Yet, such inner principles (whether of art or donors' intentions) are fabrications; they are evidence of the process that is the making of the museum. MacColl tears Chantrey from his context and converts him into a disembodied capacity to recognize genius.

A National Gallery of British Art?

The Tate promised something which seemed, until 1897, to lack coherent museum representation – British art. Through the Bequest it was armed with a fund that allowed it to receive British art. What was British art and how did Chantrey define it? Problems emerged which suggest that the Tate was not a response to the priority of Chantrey's real intentions. Rather than being a medium through which the intrinsic Britishness of its collection was disclosed, the Tate was a contested site at which the significance of nation and the meaning of British art were determined.

The Chantrey Inquiries revealed anomalies arising from attempts to map the history of British art onto historic periods which had lacked a concept of the British artist. When and where were British artists? Chantrey instructed that works purchased might be executed by artists of any nation provided that they were entirely executed within the *shores of Great Britain*. Such an instruction cannot have been at odds with the heterogeneous national composition of the early RA. However the Will, as interpreted by RA purchases, proposed a more narrowly national definition of British art. A question raised at the Chantrey Inquiries concerned the meaning in Chantrey's Will of 'British Fine Art'? Did it mean art produced in Britain and perhaps by foreign artists or did it mean art produced by British nationals?

Before Curzon, Sir William Armstrong of the National Gallery of Ireland declared that: 'art, to be interesting must be national' (Curzon:64). However, confronted with the ambiguous story of nation building, the Inquiries' classification of British art ran into the sands of anachronicity. How many of the early Academicians were foreign (Crewe:521–1)? Was van Dyck, as an artist who had painted in England, to be assigned to the National at Trafalgar Square 'as a foreigner or to the Tate as an Englishman'? (Curzon:406). If the Chantrey Bequest was a national gallery of British art why were no selections made from Scottish exhibitions? (Crewe:562–3) What was British art? Was modern art really foreign art?

These were years in which citizenship was defined legislatively (in 1905 and 1914). As others have shown, the museum was one of a panoply of institutions which registered a British imperial identity in which class divisions were supposedly to be dissolved (Coombes, 1991). Some of the witnesses called before the Chantrey Inquiries of 1904 and 1911 felt compelled to point up the contrast between British and foreign art – frequently defending the former's integrity from the dangers of contemporary French influences.

In Europe the dominance of Paris established French painters and painting, both positively and negatively, as a measure of developing local venaculars. As an international centre of training and exposition Paris provided alternatives to the RA with consequences which gave academic versus modern a national connotation. The Impressionist and post-Impressionist exhibitions of 1905, 1910 and 1912 provoked outraged accusations that modern art was degenerate (Bullen 1988). The coding of bourgeois taste as national academic style made the artistic controversies of this period potent and acrimonious; in its challenge to academic classification post-impressionist discourse threatened the concept of a national school. Where the years 1892–1905 had marked a period of 'retrenchment' in which British roots for Impressionism were discovered (Gruetzner, 1979; McConkey, 1989), the post-impressionist shows were expositions of works which were assimilated by supporters of the RA as symptoms of national degeneracy and mental illness.

Board membership of the Tate

The Tate was founded as a department of the National Gallery in Trafalgar Square and correspondingly did not have its own board. In 1917 the Treasury endorsed proposals that the Tate should have its own Board of Trustees (Tate Gallery Chantrey Files, hereafter *cf*: Treasury Minute March 24 1917). Proposals emerged for artist-members of the Board. The Treasury appears to have thought it appropriate to include the President of the RA (PRA), Aston Webb, as an *ex officio* member.

It seemed that the RA's influence would be enhanced. Keeper Charles Aitken threatened resignation. Concern was voiced that the RA 'failing to get a favourable reception at the Treasury' had agreed 'nominally to a policy of friendly discussion'. On this account the aim of the RA was to 'limit concession to polite words and meanwhile secure as many Trusteeships as possible with a view to learning the policy of the Board if not dominating it . . .' (*cf*: Statement by the Director in Regard to the Four Chantrey Conferences and the Attitude of the Board towards the Treasury in Respect of the Chantrey Bequest). Significantly, however, the portion of the statement referring to RA policy is marked 'omitted' in the archive document.

Challenged by the National Gallery Board, the Treasury accepted the need to avoid official representation for the RA, reporting that the PRA also accepted this. Aitken was not reassured despite Treasury protestations that he had not 'been "given away" '. The Treasury, by now exasperated with Aitken, pleaded for co-operation rather than resignation:

> I have not been expressing any views of my own on the points that you [Aitken] mention. I have merely explained to you and others (with whom I have been in semi-official communication . . .) the official effect of perfectly definite undertakings and decisions arrived at by the Heads of the Treasury from time to time . . .' (*cf*: Davies to Aitken, May 18 1920, Davies to Aitken June 23 1920).

The moment passed though Aitken remained vigilant. In 1926, the RA having *lost* its copy of the relevant Treasury correspondence, Aitken reminded it of the terms of Webb's appointment whilst explaining that his Board would greet appointment of Sir Frank Dicksee (PRA) as an infringement of Treasury rules (*cf*: Aitken to RA 19 Nov. 1926).

A key to these skirmishes is the autonomization of the cultural field. However, autonomy was a contested process which cut across institutions and people. Lost correspondence, amended records, misunderstandings, hopes, a sense of betrayal, official decisions whose outcomes are not fully appreciated – these are tokens of the routine messiness of official lives which yield episodes of co-operation, institutional deadlock, unexpected outcomes and structured inequalities. These are events which do not reflect structural contradictions; they are evidence of institutional actors struggling to put homology on the road, to think what they might or might not have in common.

Conclusion

This chapter has drawn on sources which reside on the margins of art history and which may alert us to the untidiness of institutional worlds that do not fit well with a theory that museums are reflexes of the demands of class and social reproduction. However, worldly untidiness is amenable to a theoretical approach purged of untidiness. The focus has been on the museum's project of classifying modernity. The argument has been that museums are of the modern world and that they emerged neither as passive effects of conjuncture nor as the outward manifestations of inner essences such as the truth of art. It is in the nature of museums that they express the coincidences of an interweaving of power relations for they are relations of cultural interdependence.

Recently much has been said concerning museums as sites of competing museological discourses. However, there has been little if any systematic attempt to map the interdependencies which are sources both of discursive conflict at museums and of museum building itself. The thesis of this chapter is that the museum (with or without walls) is simultaneously an agency of classification and a relationship of cultural interdependence between groups. As Elias notes, marked asymmetries between groups may yield stigmatizing strategies through which a dominant group secures its 'superiority' and a subordinate group experiences inferiority (Elias, 1992). Viewed in the long term, museums have a polyphonous character as places in which conflict over the meaning and value of artefacts breaks out to disrupt the canon and problematize the museum as a cultural project.

Today, shifts in the balance of power between western and non-western states have altered the meaning of the museum and perhaps accelerated its diffusion as a mode of ordering the world (Clifford, 1988). I have argued that modernization, associated with the institutionalization of modern art, was a re-ordering which separated academicians from the control over museums. That separation characterized the development of the cultural field elsewhere (Mainardi, 1993; White and White, 1965). The early Tate was a local variation of this widespread structural change in cultural authority. A key to understanding the Tate's evolution as a museum of modern art is its location within a particular, shifting balance of class power at the turn of the century.

The production of nineteenth century professional power was a transformation that tended to separate economic power from cultural power. One site of this separation was in the field of art, where the Chantrey dispute dramatized and exposed struggles which attended the autonomization of the cultural field and produced (partly through official discourse) a language of distinction. The Tate produced itself as a gallery of modern art through the medium of this separation but in doing so, and in concert with others, it submerged a generation of popular academy artists who were stigmatized by art officialdom.

The dynamics of cultural institutions (of schools, academies and museums) include their treatments of their Crocker Harrises, those producers such as Terence Rattigan's fictional Latin teacher who find themselves separated from dignity by ineluctable progress. Resistance, protests, submission and eviction are aspects of the amnesic modernization of cultural institutions in which such actors emerge as oddballs or eccentrics. Humiliation is an aspect of the internal dynamics of cultural institutions as they engage with external constituencies to erase the old order and to reconfigure themselves as new hierarchies.

Analysis of submerging and surfacing identities within museums is crucial to understanding their dynamics as classifying agencies. The episode discussed suggests the need to consider the power of museums to classify the world as that power is constituted by social processes which are enabling and constraining for different constituencies within the museum. Neither the essence of art nor the needs of capitalism were the points of origin of the Tate; rather the early Tate produced its point of view as a museum of modern art through the contradictions of the cultural forces in which it was enmeshed.

Notes

1 Chantrey's Will was published as an appendix to the Royal Commission inquiring into the affairs of the RA: United Kingdom Parliamentary Papers, 1863,

3205; also in Chantrey and his Bequest (1904) 15–22 (extract); MacColl, D.S. (1904).

2 The Chantrey Bequest was sole subject of the Crewe Inquiry, one of two subjects covered by the Curzon Inquiry and one of several covered by the Massey Inquiry and also a PEP (1946). Chantrey Trust: Report, Proceedings and Minutes of Evidence, Select Committee House of Lords, UK Parliamentary Papers (1904), 357, v, 493 (Crewe Inquiry). National Gallery, Committee of Trustees, UK Parliamentary Papers, 1914–16 Cd. 7878, 1914–16 Cd. 7879 (Curzon Inquiry). The Report of the Committee on the Functions of National Gallery and Tate Gallery and, in respect of paintings, of the Victoria and Albert Museum together with a Memorandum thereon by the Standing Commission on Museums and Galleries, UK, Parliamentary Papers, Cmnd. 6827, May 1946, 4 (Massey Inquiry).

3 I am grateful to the Tate Gallery for access to the Chantrey Files.

References

Abrams, P., (1982), *Historical Sociology*, London: Open Books.

Alexander, J.C., (1995), *Fin de Siecle Social Theory: Relativism, Reduction, and the Problem of Reason*, London: Verso Press.

Bernstein, Basil, (1971), *Class, Codes and Control*, Volume 1, London: Routledge & Kegan Paul.

Bourdieu, P., (1984), *Distinction: A Social Critique of the Judgement of Taste*, London: Routledge and Kegan Paul.

Bourdieu, P., (1988), *Homo Academicus*, Oxford: Polity Press.

Bourdieu, P., (1990), *In Other Words: Essays Towards a Reflexive Sociology*, Oxford: Policy Press.

Bourdieu, P. and Darbel, A., (1991), *The Love of Art: European Art Museums and their Public*, Oxford: Polity Press.

Bourdieu, P. and Wacquant, L.J.D., (1992), *An Invitation to Reflexive Sociology*, Oxford: Polity Press.

Bourdieu, P., (1993), *The Field of Cultural Production*, Oxford: Polity Press.

Brown, R., (1977), 'The Growth of Industrial Bureaucracy – chance, choice or necessity' in Gleichmann, P., Goudsblom, J. and Korte, H. (eds), *Human Figurations: Essays for Norbert Elias*, Stichting Amsterdams Sociologisch Tijdschrift, Amsterdam, 191–210.

Buckmann, D., (1973), *James Bolivar Manson 1879–1975*, London: Maltzahn Gallery.

Bullen, J.B., (ed.), (1988), *Post-Impressionists in Britain: The Critical Reception*, London: Routledge.

Chantrey and his Bequest: a complete illustrated record of the purchases of the Trustees, with a biographical note, text of the will etc. (1904), London: Cassell.

Clegg, Stewart R., (1989), *Frameworks of Power*, London: Sage.

Clifford, J., (1988), *The Predicament of Culture*, Cambridge, Mass.: Harvard University Press.

Clive, M., (1964), *The Day of Reckoning*, London: Macmillan.

Cooper, R. and Burrell, G., (1988), 'Modernism, Postmodernism & Organisational Analysis: an Introduction' in *Organisation Studies*, vol. 9, no. 1, 91–112.

Connell, R.W., (1983), *Which Way is Up? Essays on Class, Sex and Culture*, North Sydney: George Allen and Unwin.

Coombes, A.E., (1991), 'Ethnography and the Formation of National Identities', 189–214 in Hiller, S. (ed.), *The Myth of Primitivism*, London: Routledge.

Corrigan, P. and Sayer, D., (1985), *The Great Arch: English State Formation as Cultural Revolution*, Oxford: Basil Blackwell.

Crimp, D., (1993), *On the Museum's Ruins*, Cambridge, Mass.: MIT Press.

Davidoff, L., (1976), *The Best Circles*, London: Croom Helm.

Duncan, C. and Wallach, A., (1980), 'The Universal Survey Museum', *Art History*, vol. 3, no. 4, 448–69.

Duncan, C., (1991), 'Art Museums and the Ritual of Citizenship', 88–103 in Ivan Karp and S.D. Lavine (eds), *Exhibiting Cultures: The Poetics of Politics of Museum Display*, Washington and London: The Smithsonian Institute.

Elias, N. and Scotson, J., (1965), *The Established and the Outsiders*, London: Frank Cass.

Elias, N. and Scotson, J., (1994), *The Established and the Outsiders* (2nd edition with new introduction by Norbert Elias), London: Sage.

Elias, N., (1978), *The Civilizing Process*; Vol. 1 'The History of Manners', Oxford: Basil Blackwell.

Elias, N., (1982), *The Civilizing Process*; Vol. 2 'State Formation and Civilization', Oxford: Basil Blackwell.

Elias, N., (1983), *The Court Society*, Oxford: Basil Blackwell.

Fisher, P., (1991), *Making and Effacing Art*, New York/Oxford: Oxford University Press.

Flint, K., (ed.), (1984), *Impressionists in England: The Critical Reception*, London: Routledge & Kegan Paul.

Fyfe, G.J., (1995), 'The Chantrey Episode: Art Classification, Museums and the State, c.1870–1920', in S. Pearce (ed.), *Art in Museums: New Research in Museum Studies*, Vol. 5, 5–41, London: Athlone Press.

Galerien, T., (1921), 'The Renaissance of the Tate Gallery', *The Studio*, Vol. 82, no. 344, 187–97.

Giddens, A., (1990), *The Consequences of Modernity*, Oxford: Polity Press.

Gruetzner, A., (1979), 'Two Reactions to French Painting in Britain', in *Post Impressionism: Cross-currents in European painting*, London: Royal Academy of Arts/Weidenfeld & Nicolson, 178–82.

Hall, S., (1984), 'The Rise of the Representative/Interventionist State', 7–49 in G. Maclennan, D. Held & S. Hall, (eds), *State and Society in Contemporary Britain*, Oxford: Polity Press.

Hamlyn, R., (1991), 'Tate Gallery' in Waterfield, G. (ed.), *Palaces of Art: Art Galleries in Britain 1790–1990*, London: Dulwich Picture Gallery, 113–16.

High Roads of History (nd) Book VII, 'High Roads of British History', London: Thomas Nelson & Sons.

Hutchison, S.C., (1968), *The History of the Royal Academy*, London: Chapman and Hall.

Jenkins, R., (1992), *Pierre Bourdieu*, London: Routledge.

Jones, T., (1960), *Henry Tate 1819–1899: A Biographical Sketch*, London: Tate & Lyle Ltd.

Lamb, W.R.M., (1951), *The Royal Academy*, London: G. Bell & Sons.

Lambert, R.S., (ed.), (1938), *Art in London*, Harmondsworth: Penguin.

Layder, D., (1994), *Understanding Social Theory*, London: Sage.

Lucas, E.V., (1924), *A Wanderer among Pictures: A Companion to the Galleries of Europe*, London: Methuen.

MacColl, D.S., (1904), *The Administration of the Chantrey Bequest: Articles reprinted from 'The Saturday Review', with additional matter, including the text of Chantrey's Will and a list of purchases*. London: Grant Richards.

MacConkey, K., (1989), *British Impressionism*, London: Phaidon Press.

Macleod, D.S., (1987), 'Art Collecting and Victorian Middle Class Taste', *Art History*, vol. 10, no. 3, 328–50.

Nightingale, A., (nd) *Visual History: A Practical Method of Teaching Introductory History*, London: A. & C. Black Ltd.

PEP (1946), *The Visual Arts*, A Report Sponsored by the Dartington Hall Trustees, London: Oxford University Press.

Rattigan, T., (1953), 'The Browning Version' in *The Collected Plays of Terence Rattigan*, Vol. 2, 1–48, London: Hamish Hamilton.

Rothenstein, John, (1962), *The Tate Gallery*, London: Thames & Hudson.

Rothenstein, John, (1966), *Brave Day Hideous Night*, London: Hamish Hamilton.

Rothenstein, William, (1932), *Men and Memories: recollections of William Rothenstein 1900–1922*, London: Faber & Faber.

Rothenstein, William, (1939), *Men and Memories; recollections of William Rothenstein 1922–1938*, London: Faber & Faber.

Savage, M., Barlow, J., Dickens, P. and Fielding, T., (1992), *Property, Bureaucracy and Culture: Middle-Class Formation in Contemporary Britain*, London: Routledge.

Scott, John, (1991), *Who Rules Britain?* Oxford: Polity Press.

Sherman, D., (1987), 'The Bourgeoisie, Cultural Appropriation, and the Art Museum in Nineteenth Century France', in *Radical History Review*, vol. 38, 38–58.

Thompson, J.B., (1984), *Studies in the Theory of Ideology*, Oxford: Polity Press.

Tillyard, S.K., (1988), *The Impact of Modernism*, London: Routledge.

White, H.C. and White, C.A., (1965), *Canvases and Careers*, New York: John Wiley & Sons.

Zolberg, V., (1981), 'Conflicting Visions in American Art Museums' in *Theory & Society*, 10, 81–102.

Zolberg, V., (1995), 'The Collection Despite Barnes: From Private Preserve to Blockbuster' in S. Pearce (ed.) *Art in Museums*, New Research in Museum Studies, Vol. 5, 94–108, London: Athlone Press.

Notes on contributors

Gordon Fyfe is Lecturer in Sociology, Keele University. He has published articles on the historical sociology of art with particular reference to art markets, the mass production of fine art, and the development of museums of art. Current research interests include contemporary patterns of museum visiting. He is co-editor (with John Law) of *Picturing Power* (Routledge 1988) and was, for many years, reviews editor of *The Sociological Review*.

Eric Gable received his PhD in anthropology from the University of Virginia. He has done fieldwork in Guinea-Bissau and in Sulawesi (Indonesia) on religious change in the postcolonial context, and more recently has been studying the production and consumption of public history at American heritage sites. He currently teaches anthropology at Virginia Commonwealth University.

Kevin Hetherington is Lecturer in Sociology at Keele University and holds a PhD in sociology from Lancaster University. He is currently undertaking research into 'technologies of place,' looking at the materiality of place and its social ordering effects, with special reference to Wedgwood's factory at Etruria in the 1770s. He is reviews editor of *The Sociological Review* and currently writing two books: *The Badlands of Modernity* (Routledge, 1996) and *Expressions of Identity* (Sage, 1997).

Sharon Macdonald received a DPhil in social anthropology from Oxford University. Her research is particularly concerned with the interrelationship between national, regional and local identities; and she has carried out fieldwork in the Scottish

Hebrides and in the Science Museum, London. Her publications include *Inside European Identities* (ed., Berg, 1993) and *Science on Display* (ed., special issue of *Science as Culture*, 1995). Between 1990 and 1995 she was Lecturer in Social Anthropology at Keele University, and is now Lecturer in Social Anthropology and Sociology at the University of Sheffield.

Gaby Porter has worked in museums for over twenty years, formerly as a curator and now as a manager at the Manchester Museum of Science and Industry. She was recently awarded a doctorate in Museum Studies from the University of Leicester. A founder-member of Women, Heritage and Museums, she has also contributed to a national equal opportunities strategy for the Museums Association.

Martin Prösler is a freelance consultant of the Linden Museum in Stuttgart and the Haus das Dokumentarfilms, Stuttgart. He studied cultural anthropology and sociology at the University of Tübingen and has carried out anthropological research in Sri Lanka since 1985. He has also been involved in a collaborative museum project there since 1987, and in setting up a semi-professional video studio and training a group of local people in the making of documentaries.

Henriette Riegel holds postgraduate degrees in anthropology and in museum studies from York University, Canada. She has carried out museum research in Stuttgart and is currently conducting research on the concept of 'Heimat' in German museums.

Max Ross graduated in Sociology and English from Keele University in 1992 and is currently completing a PhD thesis on museums, consumption and identity in the Potteries. He has published several articles on aspects of museums.

John Urry is Professor of Sociology at Lancaster University. He is author of *The Tourist Gaze* (Sage, 1990), *Economies of Signs and Spaces* (with Scott Lash; Polity, 1994) and *Consuming Places* (Routledge, 1995).

Vera Zolberg is author of *Constructuring a Sociology of the Arts* (Cambridge University press, 1990) and has published extensively on museums, art and cultural policy. Her PhD thesis (University of Chicago) dealt with the emergence and transformations of American art museums. She has held the Boekman

Foundation Chair in the Sociology of Art at the University of Amsterdam and currently teaches sociology at the New School of Social Research, New York. At present, she is collaborating on a book that deals with the phenomenon of outsider art.

Index

Index

de-traditionalization, 58–9
distance, 84–8, 94, 96
Douglas, Mary, 134–5
Doxtator, D., 95
Duncan, C., 204, 205–6, 211
Durkheim, E., 71

earth mysteries tradition, 167, 171
Edensor, T., 56
Elias, N., 134, 211, 212, 224
elites, 212–13
    culture of, 203, 204
    heritage of, 57–8
empiricism, 108, 109, 113
English Heritage, 165, 167
Enola Gay controversy, 10–11, 72–4,
    77, 80
Europe
    early museums in, 25, 28–9
    nationalist movements and museums
        in, 33–5
exhibitions, 7, 12–13, 14, 34, 89, 114
    feminist, 118–25
    sexual identity and narratives of,
        110–11
    visitors to, 86–7

Fabian, Johannes, 88
feminism, and museums, 106–25
Fildes, Luke, 213
Fisher, M. M. J., 91, 100
Foucault, Michel, 79, 158–60
    Order of Things, 29–30
France, national collection in, 32
free festivals, 164–5, 168
Fry, Roger, 215

gaze, 131–3, 147, 210
Geffrye, Museum, Putting on the Style,
    118–19
Geoffrey of Monmouth, 163
German Museum Association, 35
Germany, national museum in, 33
Glenbow Museum, 95, 101
globalization, 21–40
Gregory, Sir William, 25
Grimm, Jacob, 33
guides, at Colonial Williamsburg, 178,
    179, 180, 198, 200
    and miscegenation, 184–95

habitus, 144
    class and, 132–3, 134–5
    culture and, 210–11
Haizlip, S., 199
Halbwachs, Maurice, 71, 79

Handler, Richard, 7, 98
Hanley City Museum, 136, 139, 140
Harwit, M. O., 74
Heidegger, M., 48
heritage, memory and, 51–61
heritage sites, 62
    readings of, 53–4
Hermitage, St Petersburg, 32
heterotopia, 157, 158–60
    Stonehenge and, 163, 172
Heyman, I. M., 74
history, 62, 145–6
    commodification of, 52–3
    representation of, 69–70, 76–7
Hobsbawm, E., 33
Holocaust Memorial Museum, 1
homology, 210, 213, 219
Hooper-Greenhill, E., 130, 131
Hudson, K., 24
Hungary, 33, 34
Hutcheon, Linda, 93, 98
Huyssen, A., 63

identity, 9–10, 22, 36, 78, 205
    community and, 144–5
    museum visiting and, 98, 142, 143
interdependency, 212, 218, 224
International Council of Museums, 22,
    36
International Museums Office, 36
Internet, 2, 21
Ireland, Museum of Famine, 1
irony, 84, 89–100
Italy, 34
    museums in, 32, 33
    private collections in, 29

Japanese, 72, 77, 79–80
    and American commemorative
        stamps, 74–5
    and Enola Gay exhibition, 73
    in USA, 78
Jones, Inigo, 165–6

Karp, I., 23, 89
Kershaw, B., 54–5
Kirshenblatt-Gimblett, B., 86
knowledge, 4, 27–31, 111

Lacan, Jacques, 111
Lash, S., 146
Latin America, museums in, 24, 25
Lavine, S. D., 23, 89
Layder, D., 213
Lewis, G. D., 23
Liverpool Museum, 34

234

Index